HIGH PRAISE FOR JOHN C. TUCKER'S
MAY GOD HAVE MERCY

"A POWERFUL AND ABSORBING BOOK THAT WILL CHALLENGE THE WAY YOU THINK ABOUT THE JUSTICE SYSTEM."—Vincent Bugliosi, author of *Outrage* and *Helter Skelter*

"On one level, this book is a gripping murder mystery . . . but, on a deeper level, [it] is a fierce indictment of a callous system."—Sister Helen Prejean, CSJ, author of *Dead Man Walking*

"RIVETING . . . The most compelling description yet written of how a man—who was probably innocent—can be executed in America today . . . beautifully written . . . [a] rare combination of controlled outrage and painstaking honesty."—Stuart Taylor, Jr., *The American Lawyer*

"EXTRAORDINARILY WELL-WRITTEN . . . a gripping story of flesh and blood, of lives and deaths . . . the book propels the reader on an emotional roller coaster from the awful night of the crime to the equally awful night of the execution . . . vividly detailed images of every step of the process flow from the pages."—*The Champion*

"THIS GRIPPING BOOK . . . demonstrates all that is wrong with capital punishment while proving that a good and well-told account of a real case is far more intriguing than any mystery novel."—*The Baltimore Sun*

May God Have Mercy

A True Story of Crime and Punishment

John C. Tucker

Delta
Trade Paperbacks

A Delta Book
Published by
Dell Publishing
a division of
Bantam Doubleday Dell Publishing Group, Inc.
1540 Broadway
New York, New York 10036

ISBN: 0-385-33294-7

Reprinted by arrangement with
W. W. Norton & Company, Inc.

Manufactured in the United States of America
Published simultaneously in Canada

September 1998

10   9   8   7   6   5   4   3   2   1

BVG

For Jayne, who made everything possible

Contents

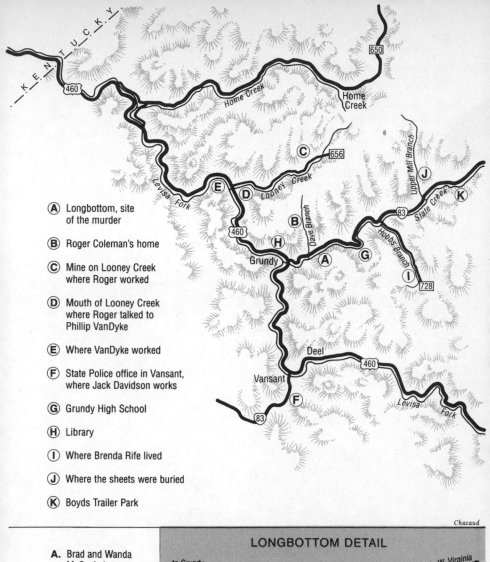

- **A** Longbottom, site of the murder
- **B** Roger Coleman's home
- **C** Mine on Looney Creek where Roger worked
- **D** Mouth of Looney Creek where Roger talked to Phillip VanDyke
- **E** Where VanDyke worked
- **F** State Police office in Vansant, where Jack Davidson works
- **G** Grundy High School
- **H** Library
- **I** Where Brenda Rife lived
- **J** Where the sheets were buried
- **K** Boyds Trailer Park

Chazaud

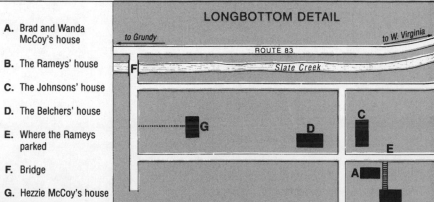

LONGBOTTOM DETAIL

- **A.** Brad and Wanda McCoy's house
- **B.** The Rameys' house
- **C.** The Johnsons' house
- **D.** The Belchers' house
- **E.** Where the Rameys parked
- **F.** Bridge
- **G.** Hezzie McCoy's house

to Grundy — ROUTE 83 — to W. Virginia

Slate Creek

Book I

—

Murder

Chapter 1

Buchanan County, Virginia

The town of Grundy doesn't fit the usual gracious public image of Virginia. Grundy is the county seat of Buchanan County, in the heart of Appalachia. It is farther south than most of Kentucky, and farther west than all but a sliver of West Virginia. It is so far west that the mixture of mud, water and coal dust that flows through town in the Levisa Fork River runs west to the Mississippi instead of east to the Atlantic Ocean.

It's nearly a seven-hour drive from Grundy to Virginia's capital in Richmond, but only thirteen miles to West Virginia—due east. You can't buy a drink of liquor in Grundy, so some of its less reputable citizens make the short trip to the Acapulco Club, just over the state line. Others drink the moonshine made in Buchanan County's mountain hollows. It's a toss-up whether you're more likely to go blind from drinking the moonshine or getting slashed by a broken beer bottle at the Acapulco.

If you head west from Grundy, it's sixteen miles to Pike County, Kentucky—site of the feud between the Hatfields and the McCoys, and some celebrated battles between revenuers and moonshiners. During Prohibition, the revenue men rarely ventured into Virginia—it was too dangerous, and besides, Virginia politicians didn't care any more for federal intervention in whiskey-making than they did forty years later when the issue was segregation. In 1935 Sherwood Anderson wrote about a moonshining case tried in federal court in Roanoke. The defendants included the sheriff of Franklin County and the county prosecutor, Carter Lee, Robert E.'s grandnephew. From the evidence, Anderson wrote, it seemed as if Franklin County, Virginia, was "the wettest spot in the United States." Up the road in Buchanan County, some of the residents smiled.

Today, the only significant business in Buchanan County is mining coal. Unless you have a private airplane, you're most likely to approach Grundy by driving northwest on U.S. Route 460. Once you cross the height of land, the headwaters of Levisa Fork appear and the highway follows its valley. Soon road and river are joined by the tracks of the Norfolk & Western Railroad, built to carry the rich coal deposits of Buchanan County to market.

In 1931, shortly before the railroad announced a plan to extend its tracks in Buchanan County, a few prominent citizens began purchasing mineral rights from the families who had settled the area a century earlier. The Depression was on and life was even harder than usual for families trying to scratch a living from Buchanan's steep slopes and thin soil. For a man who owned a couple of hundred acres of mostly untillable mountainside, the dollar an acre he was offered for whatever was underneath was found money—money he was too poor to turn down even if he suspected that the buyer knew something he didn't. Thus, in early 1931 thousands of acres of Buchanan County mineral rights changed hands for next to nothing. A few years later, while most of its citizens remained dirt poor, Buchanan County boasted some of the wealthiest families in Virginia—and still does. Among them today are the McGlothlins and the Streets, founders and owners of United Coal Company, one of the largest privately owned coal companies in America. Organized in 1970 by a group of local lawyers and businessmen who decided to invest in some then-depressed coal properties, United grew rapidly, just in time for the 1973 Arab oil boycott to multiply the price of coal and the value of United's holdings. Two decades later, Jim McGlothlin, United's CEO and largest shareholder, is one of the richest men in America.

Coal is mined three ways in Buchanan County—strip mining, drift mining and deep shaft mining. The strip mines use giant earth movers to chew off the tops of mountains and ridges. Drift mines tunnel straight into the side of a mountain, removing the narrow bands of coal that followed its contours when the mountain was raised up by the massive force of colliding tectonic plates. The deep shaft mines burrow straight down to where the largest seams of coal were formed, far beneath the surface.

As you approach Grundy, large industrial compounds appear along the roadside, each with its own rail spur and a windowless, square-sided tower sheathed in corrugated metal. These are the shaft mines where miners work far below the surface, raised and lowered in cages attached to a cable. The mine on your left in Vansant, just east of Grundy, is Consolidated Coal Company's Pocahontas Mine No. 3. Its shaft descends some fifteen hundred feet straight down to the Pocahontas seam, which runs beneath much of Buchanan County. Once the seam is reached, tunnels spread out in many directions, following the rich deposits of coal. Some tunnels run for miles, with a maze of side tunnels as well. The mountain whose insides are now being devoured by Pocahontas No. 3 is not even visible from the mine entrance in Vansant.

The shaft mines of Buchanan County are among the deepest and most dangerous coal mines in America. Because they release so much deadly and explosive methane gas, they require exceptionally strong air circulation, so that working in them is like working in a wind tunnel. In a place that is always damp and cold, a wind blowing at a steady twenty-five miles an hour may keep the mine from exploding, but after an eight-hour shift some miners think favorably of the fiery cremation chosen by Sam McGee in the Robert Service poem.

Even so, the miners who work the deep shafts have two advantages over those who work the drift mines that tunnel into the mountainsides of nearly every hollow in Buchanan County. One is that the deep shaft mines are unionized, while United Coal and most companies that own drift mines are not. The other is that a shaft miner can usually stand up while he works. The Pocahontas seam is nearly five feet thick, and the tunnels that work it are at least as high as the seam, but the drift-mine seams and the tunnels that follow them are typically thirty-six inches high or less. A drift miner works on his hands and knees. For a miner who avoids being crippled, burned or buried alive, the usual question is which will give out first—his lungs, his back or his knees.

As U.S. 460 enters Grundy from the east, it becomes the main street of the business district. Although Grundy's population is less than two thousand, it is the only incorporated town in Buchanan County and the main commercial center for the surrounding area. The left side of the road is lined with a variety of businesses. In the center of town, on the right, is the Buchanan County Courthouse, an ugly eighty-eight-year-old structure of gray stone. After World War II a new wing was added, with an entrance of concrete blocks molded to imitate the stone. At the corner of the building, where a short side street runs off to the right, a striking bronze sculpture of a coal miner stands on a black marble base. He is dressed in work boots and coveralls, his pant legs taped over his boot tops to keep out the coal dust. His miner's helmet and headlamp are tilted back at a jaunty angle, revealing longish hair that is surely blond in real life. He stands erect, holding a miner's pick waist-high, and seems to gaze off to a distant horizon— a pose suggesting either that the sculptor had never been in a coal mine or that the mine owners who contributed to his commission were disinclined to show their workers crawling on hands and knees in a tunnel barely three feet high.

Beyond the courthouse, Slate Creek approaches the highway from the right, passes beneath it and empties into Levisa Fork, which there makes a sharp bend to the west, leaving the highway to fetch up against a sheer cliff of gray stone. On the face of the stone, members of the latest graduating class of Grundy Senior High School paint their class numerals and a pictorial tribute to the incongruous school mascot, a golden wave.

To avoid the cliff, Route 460 pauses at a stoplight and turns 90 degrees left to follow the river to Kentucky, while another road heads off to the right, following Slate Creek upstream to West Virginia.

For many years, Tuffy's barbershop occupied the building on the corner where the highway turns. In the basement of the shop was a shower room where, for a small fee, coal miners coming from work could remove their work clothes and wash some of the black coal dust off their skin and out of their hair before returning home. The barbershop and bathhouse are closed now, so unless he works at one of the big mines with its own shower room, a miner takes his coating of coal dust home.

For the most part, Grundy's citizens are hard-working, God-fearing people. There are, however, some notable exceptions, and while the coal miner's statue next to the courthouse pays tribute to the economic heartbeat of Buchanan County, the courthouse itself plays a central role in one of the region's principal recreational activities—violence, especially murder, rape and wife beating, with an occasional dose of labor strife thrown in.

While Grundy can't boast a strike as bloody as the one that brought nearby Harlan, Kentucky, the nickname Bloody Harlan, a few years ago the most violent coal strike in decades was centered next door in Dickenson County. Before it was over hundreds of miners had been jailed, and a judge named McGlothlin had fined the United Mine Workers millions of dollars. In the next election, Buchanan County's incumbent state representative, also a McGlothlin, lost his seat to the president of the Mineworkers local.

As for casual violence, Grundy's recent generation of young layabouts and drug dealers can hold their own in any league. In February 1981, under the headline MURDER NO LONGER SAFE IN BUCHANAN, Grundy's newspaper, *The Virginia Mountaineer*, profiled a young lawyer who was the county's Commonwealth's Attorney, or prosecutor—Jim McGlothlin's younger brother Michael. The article reported that since taking office a year earlier, Mickey McGlothlin had successfully prosecuted seven murder cases. It didn't mention that the seven murders reported in Buchanan County in 1980 gave the community a murder rate more than twice that of the state as a whole.

A month after the article praising Mickey McGlothlin appeared in the *Mountaineer*, Grundy's young Commonwealth's Attorney had another murder to prosecute.

Chapter 2

Brad and Wanda

Wanda Fay Thompson was born on November 5, 1961, the second youngest of sixteen children—eight girls and eight boys. Wanda's father is a retired coal miner. The Thompsons raised their sixteen children in a frame house on Home Creek, a small tributary of Levisa Fork about twelve miles northwest of Grundy, a stone's throw from Kentucky.

The family has always been close. All the sons are in some kind of coal-mining job, and two of them, Pal and Danny Ray, have built their own houses on the hill just above the house where they were raised and their mother and father still live. Most of the other Thompson children live close by. All the girls are pretty, and Wanda Fay, with her strawberry-blond hair and ready smile, was no exception. Although she enjoyed the outdoor games her brothers and sisters played together whenever chores and good weather permitted, Wanda's favorite pastime was making clothes and crafts. In high school she was an average student, quiet and obedient. With strangers, she was almost painfully shy. No one can recall her ever doing anything mean or hurtful. Her sister Peggy says, "I guess you'd have to say she was just about perfect."

Brad McCoy is Max "Hezzie" McCoy's youngest son. Hezzie works for United Coal and drives a white stretch limousine that he rents out and chauffeurs himself for weddings and other occasions. He is a proud member of the McCoy clan. Brad is slight of build and as soft-spoken and gentle as his legendary forebears were crude and ill-tempered.

Brad McCoy and Wanda Fay Thompson were high school sweethearts at Grundy Senior High School. Brad was a member of the class of 1978; Wanda was two years behind him. They met through Wanda's older sister Lydia, who worked with Brad at the Piggly Wiggly. Brad had a crush on Lydia, but she passed him off to her younger sister.

The pass was complete. In July, a few weeks after Brad graduated, Brad McCoy and Wanda Fay Thompson were married at the Grundy Baptist Church. Wanda's family attended a church on Home Creek, but Brad had become close to Rev. Jack Mutter, the minister at Grundy Baptist, whose son, a close friend of Brad's, had been killed in a car accident not long before. It was typical of Brad that he would think it might give Mutter some comfort to celebrate the wedding of his son's friend, and Wanda and her parents agreed to his suggestion that the ceremony be held at Grundy Baptist. Bill Pierce, a friend, stood up for Brad. Wanda was attended by her younger sister Patricia. Both sets of parents thought the marriage was a perfect match, and for as long as it lasted it seemed they were right.

On June 16, three days after Brad graduated from high school, he went to work at United Coal. Perhaps because of his temperament and slight build, or perhaps because he seemed a little smarter than the average Grundy High School graduate, Brad was employed aboveground, as a parts clerk in one of the company repair shops.

If you turn left at the Grundy stoplight and follow Route 460 toward Kentucky, in about two miles you come to United Coal Shop No. 1, where Brad McCoy was assigned. If you turn right at the light and follow the road toward West Virginia, the narrow valley formed by Slate Creek widens a bit about three quarters of a mile east of town. There a bridge spans the creek and leads into a small subdivision called Longbottom. The first two rows back from the creek are well-kept brick and frame ranch homes whose middle-class owners are likely to be teachers, shop owners or coal company supervisors. Farther back a few older frame houses are more typical of the area's working-class population. In 1980, Hezzie and Betty McCoy lived in one of those houses, and after they were married, Brad and Wanda were able to rent another one, less than two blocks from Brad's mother and father.

When they were married, Wanda thought she might return to high school in the fall, but she soon found she enjoyed the life of a housewife. Brad's salary was enough to sustain their simple needs, and Wanda decided to drop out of school. Working, keeping house, visiting friends and family, Brad and Wanda settled into the rented house in Longbottom and remained there until the night Wanda Fay McCoy was murdered.

Chapter 3

March 10, 1981

March 10, 1981, was a Tuesday, and Brad had to work. Wanda disliked being alone at night, but Brad was assigned to the swing shift, three to eleven P.M. At least his work was safe and clean. At least he didn't work underground.

In March the weather in Grundy is unpredictable. Farther south in the valley between the Appalachians and the Blue Ridge you can count on some nice spring days, with the forsythia blooming and dogwood starting to bud, but up in the mountains it's likely to be raw and cold, with a possibility of snow and the creeks muddy and swollen with water cascading off the upper slopes. The previous Thursday it had rained almost an inch, swelling Slate Creek even more than usual, but by Tuesday the creek was almost back to normal. That morning Brad and Wanda stayed home. Wanda sewed and watched television. Brad read the newspaper and puttered around the house. Mid-forties is a common high for early March in Grundy, and it was 42 degrees when Brad left the house about 2:15 P.M. to run some errands and go to work.

The next day was garbage-collection day in Longbottom, and Brad may have taken the garbage out to the curb when he left, though he's not sure. It was years later before it occurred to anyone that who took out the garbage that day, and when, could be important.

Brad's shift at work that night was routine. United Coal Company's Shop No. 1 supplies parts and repairs machinery and equipment for coal mines in the Grundy area. Brad's job mostly involved waiting around for someone to come in for spare parts for one of the mines, or to deliver parts from a supplier. The job became hectic only if there was a major breakdown, which required locating crucial replacement parts or equipment and getting them delivered as quickly as possible. A mine shutdown because of an accident or equipment failure could cost the company thousands of dollars a day. Breakdowns were not infrequent, but none occurred on March 10, and Brad was able to take his regular dinner break to eat the food Wanda had fixed and packed in his lunch bucket. At nine o'clock he had a coffee break, and, as he did whenever possible, Brad called Wanda to make sure she was all right—and to break up the loneliness of her evening.

Wanda answered the phone and they talked for almost fifteen minutes—about how the day was going, how they would spend a tax-refund check they were expecting to receive and what Wanda was watching on television—*BJ and the Bear*. When she hung up, Wanda returned to her TV program, sitting on the sofa in the parlor, protected from the chill draft by a handmade afghan. She drank a Coke, and left the empty bottle on the coffee table. The television set was still on when her husband arrived home.

Brad's shift at work ended at eleven. When he left the shop he drove straight home. At that hour there was no traffic. Once he crossed the bridge over Slate Creek and drove the block up to Oak Street, Brad would have seen anyone coming out his front door, the only door in the house.

Built on a hillside with a half-basement and a single story of living space, Brad and Wanda's house had a living room and kitchen area in front, with two small bedrooms divided by a bath in back. The front door opens into the living room from a small front stoop about ten steps above street level. When Brad reached home he checked around the outside of the house to make sure that everything was all right, and that dogs hadn't gotten into the garbage. He noticed that the porch light was off. Wanda usually left it on for him, and Brad wondered if the bulb needed changing.

He climbed the steps to the porch and knocked on the door, but no one came. Peeking through a peephole he had scratched in the paint that covered the glass door pane, Brad saw his wife's afghan lying on the couch, but he could not see Wanda. He wondered if she was hiding from him to play a trick. He opened the door with his key, entered the parlor and lifted the afghan, thinking Wanda might be hiding under it. She was not. He saw that the coffee table in front of the couch had been shoved out of line, and that an empty Coke bottle was lying on the floor, as if it had fallen off when the table was moved.

Brad McCoy began to sense something was wrong. He put his lunch bucket down on the floor. A light was on in the spare bedroom. Perhaps Wanda was doing something in there, he thought, and walked a few steps to the bedroom door.

Wanda McCoy was lying on her back on the floor, naked from her chest down except for her blue striped socks. Her sweater and bra were pushed up around her neck, revealing her breasts. A pair of blue jeans lay on the bed, and dark blue satin panties were hooked around her left ankle.

A large pool of blood surrounded Wanda McCoy's head, and Brad could see that she had been stabbed twice in the chest. Blood still oozed onto the floor from somewhere under her sweater.

Brad McCoy knew his wife was dead, and he knew she hadn't been dead for long. The pool of blood around her head, still growing, told him both things. He did not try to feel Wanda's pulse or touch her in any way. Instead, he quickly looked around the small house to see if the killers were still there, and then called his father from the phone in the parlor. "Daddy, come over, come quick," he stammered. "Wanda's been raped or killed."

Still fearful that a killer was hiding in the house, Brad turned on the porch light and went outside to wait for his father. Growing more and more frightened and agitated, after a few minutes he could not stay on the porch any longer and took off down the hill toward his father's house. As Brad reached the house, Hezzie was pulling his car out of the garage. Brad was crying. He sobbed over and over, "Why would anyone do this? Why would they do this to me?" Hezzie decided to go back inside for a gun, and, when he realized that Brad had not done so, he called the sheriff. Hezzie later estimated that ten minutes had elapsed between Brad's call to him and his call to the sheriff. Hezzie's call to the sheriff was logged in at 11:21 P.M.

The two men got into Hezzie's car and drove back up the hill to

Brad and Wanda's. When they reached the house and went inside, Hezzie McCoy took one look at Wanda and told his son she was dead. Brad and Hezzie went back onto the front porch just as Deputy Sheriffs Steve Coleman and Mike Shell arrived at the house. It was 11:25 P.M.

When Steve Coleman entered the house he went immediately to the bedroom where Wanda lay on the floor. Her heavy sweater was still pulled up around her neck. Coleman knelt beside her, lifted a fold of the sweater, and reached beneath it to feel for a pulse. His fingers, searching for the artery in her neck, found a gaping hole. A knife had slashed her throat so deeply that Wanda McCoy's head was nearly severed from her body.

Coleman stood up. Trying to keep from vomiting, he walked outside, where several more deputy sheriffs and town police were now arriving, among them Grundy's police chief Randall Jackson. Randy Jackson had been chief of police for two years. He was twenty-eight years old.

Coleman told the new arrivals that a woman was dead in the bedroom, and instructed Brad and Hezzie McCoy to go back to Hezzie's house and wait. As Randy Jackson entered the house the television was still on. Passing through the living room, he heard Ed McMahon say: "Heeeere's Johnny!" It was 11:31.

When Jackson reached the bedroom where Wanda McCoy's body lay, he could see fresh blood still emerging from under her sweater. He thought the crime had been committed so recently that, like Brad, he wondered if a killer might still be in the house. After feeling briefly for a pulse on Wanda's left wrist and finding none, Jackson instructed the men who were with him to secure the house and let no one in. Two men were dispatched to search the basement, and Jackson himself searched the living area again.

Finding no one, Jackson sent patrolman Owens to pick up Dr. Thomas McDonald, a family physician and licensed medical examiner who lived a few blocks away. Next he called the home of special agent Jack Davidson of the Virginia State Police, the investigator assigned to provide assistance to local police departments in major cases. Davidson agreed to come at once from his home in Vansant.

A few minutes later patrolman Owens returned with Dr. McDonald. Jackson told Owens to go down to Hezzie McCoy's house and stay there with Hezzie and Brad, and to ask some questions. As in any murder case, Wanda's husband was a suspect.

Jackson entered the house again, this time with Dr. McDonald, and McDonald quickly declared Wanda dead. It was between 11:40 and 11:45 P.M. Dr. McDonald told Randy Jackson that Wanda McCoy had not been dead long—"about a half hour." Dr. McDonald returned home. Jackson and the others secured the house and went outside to await the arrival of Jack Davidson. Randy Jackson hoped to pass responsibility for the investigation over to Davidson. Jack Davidson fully intended to take it.

Inside the house Wanda finally stopped bleeding, and her body began to stiffen. Wanda Fay McCoy was nineteen years old.

—

Book II

Roger

Chapter 4

Roger and Trish:
Flash Floods and
Mountain Hollows

Even before Hezzie McCoy left his son's house he called his wife to tell her what he had seen, and as soon as he and Brad arrived home he called Wanda's father, Sam Thompson, with the tragic news. Word spread quickly within the Thompson family, and Wanda's sister Peggy took it upon herself to deliver the news in person to their youngest sister, Trish.

Patricia Thompson Coleman was sixteen when Wanda was killed. She and her husband, Roger Keith Coleman, were frequent visitors to Brad and Wanda's house, and Trish was Wanda's closest friend and favorite sister. The night Wanda was killed, Roger and Trish were living with Roger's grandmother in a house on the mountainside above Dave's Branch, the creek that forms a hollow just west of Longbottom. By road it was less than two miles from Trish and Roger's house to the house where Wanda was murdered.

Roger Keith Coleman was born on November 1, 1958, to William and Mary Coleman in the base hospital at Fort Gordon, Georgia. William Coleman was a career serviceman, and eight months after Roger was born he transferred to Germany. Roger and his mother moved back to Grundy to live with William's parents, George and Garnett Coleman. After four months Mary moved out, leaving Roger with his grandparents.

A few months later, Mary moved to Michigan, where she obtained a divorce. Ultimately she sent for Roger, who lived with her in Michigan for three years, but when he was six she returned him to his grandparents in Grundy, where he grew up. Roger's father remarried, but he too had no apparent interest in raising his son, and in 1972 George and Garnett Coleman formally adopted him. That same year, at age thirteen, Roger and a friend got caught making dirty phone calls to some girls they knew. Roger had never previously been in any trouble at home or at school, and was a good student. He said he had made the calls because he was lonely. A social worker recommended that he receive psychiatric counseling, which he did.

The intermittently dry bed of Dave's Branch winds down a steep slope, passes through the grounds of Mountain Mission School, a religious school founded for orphaned or abandoned children, and enters Slate Creek. To reach the house where Roger was raised it is necessary to drive through the school grounds and emerge on a narrow road that winds up the hollow. After about a mile, a steep dirt drive appears on the left, entering the road at an angle far too sharp to turn in. Go past the driveway and back into it and up the steep hill for several hundred feet, taking care not to slip off the downhill side and tumble back into the creek. Back up as far as you can, just beyond where the drive switches sharply back to the right. Now you can go forward up the next leg to the house, a hundred feet or so of elevation above the creek bed.

When your heart rate returns to normal, the view of the surrounding hills and valleys is lovely, and you will soon notice that a house trailer shares the hillside with the Coleman house. Roger's uncle, Roger Lee Coleman, lives in the trailer with his wife, Geneva. When Roger Keith was young, Roger Lee, who was sixteen years older, had been his best friend, a combination older brother and surrogate father.

George Coleman died in 1979, and Garnett followed about three years later, so the white frame house where Roger was raised is now occupied by Roger Lee's son, the son's girlfriend and their young daughter. Roger Lee had rheumatic fever as a child, and the doctor said it was too far for him to walk out of the hollow to where a school bus would pick him up at the main road. There was no other way to get there, so he had to quit school after the fourth grade. When Roger Lee Coleman turned eighteen he went to work in the drift mines. After twenty-three years of working bent over or crawling on his hands and knees in the low tunnels, his back and knees gave out so he could no longer work, thus saving him from some but not all the effects of black lung. At forty-one, Roger Lee Coleman could walk only with a cane and a severe limp, and his only regular income since 1983 has been from workmen's compensation and Social Security.

Roger Keith loved Roger Lee, and saw what working in the drift mines was doing to him. Roger Keith Coleman vowed he would never work in a coal mine. In high school Roger was an above-average student, although his grades were not as high as his IQ predicted. He loved athletics, and there his tenacity allowed him to succeed beyond his natural ability, making the basketball team despite standing only five feet nine. He worked after school and weekends for pocket money and to help pay for food and clothes. When he wasn't working or going to school, Roger loved nothing better than to wander the mountains and valleys of Buchanan County, fishing, hunting and just exploring the countryside. When he was not outside he was an avid reader of books of all kinds.

Roger Keith Coleman believed he had the ability to avoid the coal mines and escape the dead-end life of blue-collar Buchanan County. He knew he had the desire. He wanted to go to college, but, like so many Americans from similar backgrounds, he could see only one way that would be possible—by first serving in the military. By the spring of 1977 Roger had already been accepted for enlistment in the army after graduation from high school in June. Then came the flood.

People who live in hill country sometimes refer to the rest of us as flatlanders. The term suggests differences of life experience that extend beyond the mere absence of contour lines on a topographical map. One difference between hill people and flatlanders is the matter of floods. To a flatlander, a flood is usually something that happens over a period of days, to a drumbeat of weather reports and predictions of when, where and how high the flood will crest. In the flatlands, a flash flood is a rare event, having to do with a creek suddenly overflowing in a heavy rainstorm, perhaps washing across a road, occasionally even pulling away a human being or car caught in its path. In the mountains, however, with steep valleys quickly funneling all the water from vast mountainsides into a narrow bowl, most floods are flash floods, and when they occur they can wash away cars, bridges and whole buildings in a matter of minutes.

In some buildings in Florence, Italy, there are photographs or marks on the wall commemorating the great flood of 1966, when, in a few short hours, the Arno rose far above its banks, threatening to destroy the Ponte Vecchio, lapping up the walls of the Ufizzi Gallery and knocking on the carved bronze doors of the Baptistery. There are no Botticelli paintings or Michelangelo sculptures in Grundy, but the photographs and high-water marks in the Buchanan County Courthouse and other Main Street buildings memorializing the flood of April 1977 are eerily similar to those in Florence.

The people of Grundy are no strangers to flash floods, but no one had seen anything to compare with the flood of April 4, 1977. It began raining hard on the third, and continued through the night. The next morning the ground was saturated, and by noon the continuing downpour had created raging water several feet deep in mountain creeks that had held no more than a few inches the day before. As those torrents tore down the narrow hollows into Slate Creek and Levisa Fork, they brought with them rocks and trees and old appliances, and then boulders and trailers and whole houses that smashed everything in their way, inundating first the narrow roads which ran up the hollows, and then the larger roads which crossed their paths, and finally roaring down the main street of Grundy. Bridges were wiped out, and as terrified spectators watched from the top floor of the United Coal Company offices, the Central Auto Parts building on Main Street was ripped from its foundation. The building was quickly carried down Levisa Fork and destroyed. A few minutes later, a brick building that housed a TV and appliance store suddenly crumbled and disappeared under the flood waters. According to the weather service, fifteen inches of rain had fallen, and Levisa Fork was thirty feet above its banks.

Like most flash floods, the water departed almost as fast as it had come, but the wreckage it left behind was another story. Route 83, the road to West Virginia along Slate Creek, was closed by mud and boulders for three days, and Route 460 through Grundy was closed to all but special traffic for several more.

The flood also closed Grundy Senior High School, east of town on Slate Creek, about a mile beyond Longbottom. On April 7, the first day a car could travel to the school from town, the school's superintendent, Frank Spraker, and his daughter Cynthia went to see what damage it had suffered from the flood. As Spraker recalls, it was about 10:00 or 10:15 A.M. when they arrived at the school. Sometime later he and his daughter were standing in the parking lot when Roger Coleman appeared. Roger and the Sprakers knew each other, and they talked together about the flood and the condition of the high school for a half hour or so. Roger left sometime between 10:30 and 11:00, crossing the bridge over Slate Creek on foot.

About two miles east of the high school, near the head of another hollow, called Hobbs Branch, Preston and Brenda Rife lived with their six-year-old daughter, Megan, in a newly constructed A-frame house. Preston and Brenda were both schoolteachers, and Preston operated a used-car lot after school and on weekends.

At about 9:30 on the morning Roger Coleman and the Sprakers met at Grundy Senior High School, Preston Rife left home to see if the road through Grundy had been cleared enough to get through to his used-car lot in Vansant. He wanted to see how much damage his business had incurred in the flood. With school still closed, Brenda and Megan remained home. According to Brenda, after Preston left she had begun washing the breakfast dishes when there was a knock on the front door. She thinks it was about 10:15. Brenda told her daughter to look through the front window to see who was there, and Megan reported that a boy was at the door.

When Brenda Rife opened her front door she saw a young man about eighteen years old wearing a Grundy High School letter jacket and a white sailor hat. He said he was working with a crew of volunteers cleaning up the flood damage, and asked for a glass of water. Although the Rifes were still without electricity, their water supply was gravity-fed and Brenda was able to comply. The boy drank the water while they engaged in small talk about the flood, but when he finished he did not leave. Brenda offered him another glass of water, which he accepted. As she returned from her kitchen with the water, Brenda Rife saw the boy remove a pistol from the pocket of his jacket.

As Brenda described them to the police, the events that followed were frightening, and fantastic. Pointing the pistol at her, the boy ordered Brenda to have her daughter sit in a chair, and to tape her hands and legs together with a roll of adhesive tape, which he produced from a pocket. At gunpoint he then took Brenda on a tour of the downstairs of her house, and from there to the upstairs and into her bedroom. He ordered her to remove her clothes, and when she refused he put the gun down on a table in the hall just outside the bedroom door, ripped open her bathrobe and threw her onto the bed. He pinned her down, holding her hands above her head, and tried to kiss her. She resisted, moving her head back and forth, and when he let go of her hands to try to hold her head still she scratched him hard on the neck.

The boy raised himself up. "Now you've made me mad," he said. "Let me get my gun." He took a few steps to the bedroom door. Brenda jumped up and ran past him. Before he could react, she was down the stairs, through the living room and out the sliding door, calling Megan to follow her, but Megan couldn't move, so Brenda ran back into the living room, grabbed her daughter and just made it back out the door when the boy reached her. He grabbed Brenda's arm and tried to pull her back into the house, but she had stepped into a hole in the unfinished floor of the porch, and her leg was stuck.

As the boy tried to pull her into the house, Brenda somehow got hold of his gun and threw it through the hole and under the porch. The boy let go of her and went to retrieve the gun. Brenda, her leg still stuck, was screaming for help, and as the boy came back onto the porch, she could hear two neighbors coming up the hill toward the house. Suddenly the boy realized his hat was missing. He ran into the house, looking for it, and as the neighbors approached, Brenda Rife saw him run out the side door of the house, up the road and into the woods.

Because her attacker had been wearing a Grundy High letter jacket, after she recovered her composure Brenda decided to look through the last few years of high school yearbooks. Within a few minutes she found a picture of a boy she thought was the one. It was Roger Coleman.

Brenda was afraid to stay in her house, so one of her neighbors drove her into Grundy to her father's house, and someone else went to fetch her husband. Once Preston heard his wife's story he quickly determined where Roger lived, and that he was not at home but at a friend's house on Newhouse Branch, just east of town. Everyone connected with the Grundy police and the Buchanan County sheriff was occupied with the flood, but Preston Rife and John Fleenor, Brenda's father, devised a plan. Preston took the delivery van from his father-in-law's florist shop and headed for Roger's friend's house. When he arrived and found Roger, he said Roger's grandfather had sent him—they needed someone to work cleaning up after the flood at the florist shop, and he had been told Roger was a good worker. The pay would be good, and if Roger was interested, they would go pick up Mr. Fleenor and start working at once. Roger was willing. Preston drove him to the Fleenor house, went in and got Brenda and her father, and when Brenda came out and said, "Yes, that's the boy," Preston Rife and John Fleenor drove Roger directly to the sheriff's office in the Buchanan County Jail. There he was promptly charged with attempted rape. Brenda's father was Grundy's mayor, and the police agreed there was no need for her to come down to the jail.

Later that night Roger Lee Coleman was informed of the arrest and Roger was bailed out in his custody. According to Roger Lee, there was no sign that Roger had been scratched on the neck, and no police photograph showing such a scratch was ever presented. Roger Coleman vehemently denied having anything to do with the attack on Brenda Rife, but despite his denials and the testimony of the Sprakers, three months later a jury found him guilty and sentenced him to three years in prison.

Roger's lawyer, Robert Williams, was a respected former prosecutor trying one of his first cases as a defense lawyer. Today, he is Buchanan County's circuit judge. At the time of the trial, Williams says, he was convinced that Coleman was innocent, the victim of a mistaken identification. When the jury returned its verdict he was devastated. It was the worst moment of his professional life, at least up to that time.

Despite the pending charges, Roger Coleman graduated from high school on June 17, 1977. He was sentenced to prison on July 29. As soon as the army learned of his conviction, his enlistment was canceled and his dream of joining the service and escaping the coal mines was over. Coleman spent twenty months and one day in prison. He was released on March 30, 1979, and a few weeks later began work in a drift mine a few miles from Grundy.

That summer Roger met Patricia Thompson. She was fifteen years old and entranced by the older boy, especially by his reputation as a tough ex-convict who at the same time seemed thoughtful, articulate and intelligent. Roger, in turn, was attracted to the beautiful and vivacious young redhead. Soon they began dating, and then talking marriage. Trish's parents made known that they were less than enthusiastic about her choice of an ex-convict for a husband, and that in any event she should finish high school, but Trish would not be deterred. Ultimately the Thompsons consented to the marriage, which was celebrated on August 8, 1980.

The Thompsons are a close and loving family, and soon their opposition to the marriage was forgotten and Roger was welcomed into the family. Because Trish and Wanda were close, Roger and Brad became friends as well.

At first, Roger and Trish lived in a rented trailer, but it was hard to stretch Roger's wages to cover expenses, and in February 1981 the young couple moved back into the house on Dave's Branch with Roger's grandmother.

It was just after midnight on March 11 when Peggy Thompson Stiltner maneuvered her car up the steep driveway to the Coleman house and woke its sleeping occupants to give them the news of Wanda's murder. Trish and Roger dressed quickly and drove to the Thompson family home, where the children were gathering to support and comfort Wanda's parents and each other, and to ponder the questions of who and why. One brother, Danny Ray Thompson, had friends on the police force and decided to drive up to the McCoy house to see what he could find out.

Chapter 5

The Investigation

Just over six feet tall, slim, athletic, with a neat mustache and a short military haircut, Senior Special Agent Jack Davidson looks the role he has played in real life since 1974—criminal investigator for the Virginia State Police.

Davidson was born in Lee County, Virginia, the far western tip of the state. After high school he joined the army and spent two years in the military police, primarily in Germany. When he got out in 1968, he applied for a position with the Virginia State Police, was accepted, and after a period of training became a uniformed trooper in Buchanan County. In 1971 he began a two-year stint as an under-cover investigator of drug cases, then spent another year in uniform, and in 1974 was promoted to investigator, a position now called special agent. Over the years he obtained a bachelor's degree in criminal justice, was promoted again, this time to senior special agent, read law with a local law firm, and in 1994 took and passed the Virginia Bar exam. His wife, Linda, is a nurse practitioner with a master's degree in public health and nursing science; his daughter, Charlayne, is in law school; and his son, Jason, is an electrical engineer. In Buchanan County, Davidson's reputation is summed up by the comment of a younger state trooper: "If Jack Davidson was after me, I'd just lie down and give up. I'd turn myself in, 'cause I know he'd get me."

In 1981, Davidson was thirty-three years old. He lived only a few minutes from his office in Vansant, just east of Grundy. When Randy Jackson called at about 11:35 P.M. on the night of March 10, Davidson had just gone to bed. He dressed and left immediately for Longbottom, reporting his mission to state police headquarters as he drove. The road was dry, with little traffic, and Davidson reached the McCoy house on Slate Creek before midnight.

Randy Jackson met Davidson as he arrived, and after a short briefing the two men entered the house so Davidson could see the scene for himself. Using a phone in Brad and Wanda's living room, Davidson called a dispatcher to send an evidence van and a forensic investigator and then ordered the house sealed until they arrived. That would take two hours or more—the nearest evidence van was a hundred mountain miles away in Wytheville. In the meantime, Jack Davidson would begin where the investigation of such a murder always begins—with the victim's husband, Brad McCoy.

Given the percentage of married murder victims whose killer turns out to be their spouse, and especially given Dr. McDonald's estimate of the time of death, which was consistent with Brad killing his wife upon arriving home from work, Davidson would not have been surprised to find his solution waiting two blocks away at Hezzie McCoy's house, where Brad had been sent a half hour earlier.

As Davidson and Randy Jackson walked down the hill to interview Brad, they knew that if he was the killer it should not be hard to tell. A husband mad enough at his wife to kill her, especially the way Wanda McCoy was killed, is not often very good at lying about it, and besides, whoever severed Wanda McCoy's jugular was likely to have blood on him that would be difficult to conceal in the short time that had elapsed between the commission of the crime and the arrival of the police. Moreover, Davidson and Jackson had noticed that Wanda McCoy's fingernails were jagged and broken and that furniture in the living room was out of place, suggesting a struggle. Wanda had tried to fight off her attacker, and it seemed likely he would bear her marks on his hands and face.

When Jackson and Davidson reached Hezzie McCoy's house they first spoke to Teddy Owens, the town policeman Jackson had sent to stay with Brad. Owens reported that Brad seemed deeply distressed by his wife's death, cursing and weeping copiously. Owens also said that Brad was wearing the same clothes he had on when the police arrived at his house, and that he had seen no sign of blood on his clothes or fresh scratches on his hands or face. Brad had seemed so distraught that Owens had decided not to question him until receiving further instructions from Jackson.

Inside the house, Brad McCoy had regained some of his composure, and Davidson began to question him, establishing at once that he would take charge of the case. As Brad talked, Davidson made notes, beginning with a description of his clothes, and the observation that he had a cut on his left thumb. The cut, however, did not appear to be fresh.

According to Davidson's notes, after describing the discovery of his wife's body, Brad revealed that the last person to visit the house had been Wanda's sister, Trish Coleman; that some months earlier Wanda had received obscene phone calls; that the last person who came to the house other than Patricia had been Brad's friend and co-worker Junior Stevenson; and that they had had problems with a neighbor, whom Brad McCoy named. With a different, bolder pen, Jack Davidson added to his handwritten notes, above the mention of Patricia Coleman, the name of her husband, Roger Coleman.

Eight days later, on March 19, Jack Davidson dictated the notes of his interview, which were transcribed by a state police secretary on March 23 and became the official interview report. In the typewritten report Davidson added some information not reflected in his interview notes, including the assertion that Wanda was afraid to stay alone at night, always kept the door locked and bolted and would never let a stranger into the house. Although Davidson's notes make no mention of it, the typed statement also quotes Brad as saying that only Junior Stevenson, Danny Ray Stiltner (an ex-brother-in-law) and Roger Keith Coleman would have been admitted to the house by Wanda.

In retrospect, the inclusion of Danny Ray Stiltner in the list of people who might have been admitted to the house seems strange, since Danny Ray and Wanda's sister Peggy were divorced, and the Thompson family believed he was the person who had made the obscene phone calls to Wanda. Wanda believed she had recognized his voice.

Even stranger was Davidson's omission of any reference to the troublesome neighbor in his official report.

That Davidson took the time to go back and add Coleman's name to the handwritten notes of his interview with Brad, however, was not so strange. When Brad said that Wanda McCoy's sister was married to Roger Coleman, the name was not unknown to Jack Davidson and Randy Jackson. They knew that Roger Coleman was an ex-convict, and that his conviction had been for attempted rape.

By the time Jack Davidson was ready to leave Hezzie McCoy's house he felt quite sure Brad was not the killer, although given the frequency of wife killing, Brad still had to be considered a suspect. Davidson asked Brad to take a lie-detector test, and while no report was apparently made, Davidson says he also went to the United shop and checked to find out when Brad clocked out, and to make sure he had not left work anytime earlier on the night of the murder.

Later that night Brad McCoy became agitated again. His parents took him to the hospital, where he was sedated and then sent home. About two weeks later Brad took and passed the polygraph test Davidson had requested.

If the interview with Brad had failed to provide a solution to the murder, in the investigators' minds it had produced a good suspect. As Randy Jackson would put it years later, when we heard Coleman's name, if "the lightbulb didn't light up, the switch was about to come on."

Given his prior record, unless Roger Coleman had an airtight alibi, he was certain to be a focus of the investigation, especially since the police had told Davidson they had seen no evidence of forcible entry to the murder house, and Coleman was supposedly one of the few people Wanda would have admitted voluntarily. While Davidson was waiting for the evidence van to arrive, Wanda's brother Danny Ray Thompson had come to the house. Jack Davidson talked to him, and his notes of the conversation suggest that it involved a single topic: Where had Roger Coleman been that evening, and where was he now? Danny Ray told Davidson that Roger normally would have been at work when Wanda McCoy was killed, but that night he had been unexpectedly laid off.

In March 1981 special agent Kelly Andrews had been with the state police for twenty years, specializing in the collection of forensic evidence at crime scenes. Shortly after midnight on the night of the murder, Andrews was reached by the police dispatcher at his home not far from Wytheville, Virginia, where the police maintained a vehicle equipped with the tools used in a modern crime-scene investigation. By the time Andrews dressed, retrieved the van and made the long drive to the McCoy house, it was after 3 A.M. By then Roger Owens, another state police investigator, had also arrived at the scene.

Starting from the outside of the house, Andrews, Davidson and Owens began searching for evidence. On the outside screen door, Andrews was able to detect and lift a latent fingerprint. On the front-door molding, three feet two inches above the floor, a pressure mark was found, which, according to Jack Davidson's report, "appeared to be a pry mark."

Moving into the house, the three investigators began searching for and photographing additional evidence. There was a small bloodstain on the floor of the living room, and it appeared that something had been dragged through it. Another small bloodstain was found on the living-room wall, and a few drops of blood appeared on the white shade of a lamp standing on a table at the entrance to the hall that led to the bedrooms. These small bloodstains in the living room were photographed, and samples of the blood were collected for later analysis. To Davidson's eye, the blood in the living room came from the defensive wounds on Wanda's hands. The spatters on the wall and lampshade were apparently thrown off her hands as she fell backward, and the floor stain suggested that she had been dragged, unconscious, from the living room into the bedroom.

Photographs were also taken of the coffee table, which sat in front of the living-room sofa, and the Coke bottle, which had apparently fallen to the floor when the coffee table was moved. While the table itself was no longer in alignment with the couch, a framed photograph and three china figures on the table remained upright, suggesting that the movement of the table had not been very abrupt or violent.

If the scene in the McCoys' living room was relatively benign, it changed dramatically when the investigators moved to the bedroom. Wanda McCoy lay on her back just as her husband had found her, her head surrounded by a huge pool of blood. In the satin panties hooked over her left ankle they noticed a safety pin, suggesting, as her husband later confirmed, that she had been menstruating. Next to her panties on the floor was a yellow toilet tissue or Kleenex, which may have served as a substitute for a sanitary napkin.

It was clear from the large puddle of blood in the bedroom and the small amount in the living room that Wanda's throat had been cut where she lay, and the fact that her arms were splayed out above her head in the direction of the bedroom door indicated to Davidson that she had been dragged into the bedroom feet first, and never regained consciousness. If she had, he reasoned, her hands would have been back down around her throat as she tried to fight off the fatal wound.

The two stab wounds in Wanda's abdomen and chest were visible, but her slashed throat was covered by the heavy sweater pulled above her breasts. Her hands were cut and bloody and coated with a dark black substance, which Davidson felt sure was coal dust from the clothes of her killer. What appeared to be the same black substance that covered her hands also covered her upper thighs and the sleeves of her sweater, and there was a red blood smear on her right upper leg. Her fingernails were jagged and broken.

Special agent Kelly Andrews photographed the scene and procured samples of the various bloodstains and the black substance. Owens drew a diagram of the house, showing the location of the objects he observed, including furniture, bloodstains and Wanda's body. He prepared a separate page of the diagram that "laid down" the vertical walls of the house onto the flat plane of his paper in order to show the location of the bloodstain on the living-room wall and the pry mark on the door frame. The floors and furniture were vacuumed and the contents of the vacuum bags retained and labeled for further analysis, as were Wanda's clothes and other relevant physical items. Finally, after Dr. McDonald returned to examine the body further, taking measurements and rolling the body over on the floor to make sure there were no wounds on her back, paper bags were placed over Wanda McCoy's hands to protect the substances on them from loss or contamination, and she was placed in a body bag to be taken to Roanoke for autopsy. It was 9:30 A.M.

Kelly Andrews drove the evidence van back to Wytheville to begin processing the items he had gathered while Randy Jackson and several town policemen and deputy sheriffs interviewed the neighbors about anything they had seen or heard the night before. They were warned to keep an eye out for anyone with fresh scratches on his face or hands.

Jack Davidson had a different assignment in mind for himself. He wanted to talk to Wanda McCoy's family—especially Trish and Roger Coleman. Danny Thompson had said that Roger, Trish and the rest of the family were gathered at Wanda's parents' house on Home Creek. Davidson and Roger Owens set out for the Thompsons', but by the time they arrived, Roger and Trish had returned to their home at Dave's Branch. Although Wanda's mother, Marie, was in a state of near shock, she agreed to talk briefly to the police.

According to Jack Davidson's notes, Mrs. Thompson said that she didn't know who would want to kill Wanda, that the only person she "thought of" was someone named Wayne Stiltner, that there was no trouble between Wanda and Brad and that the only problem Wanda had had was the obscene phone calls she had received about a year earlier. She also reported that she had seen Wanda yesterday afternoon and she had seemed fine. In response to Davidson's questions, she confirmed that Roger Coleman had not worked the night before, but said that in her opinion Roger would not harm Wanda.

A couple of hours after talking to Mrs. Thompson, Davidson and Owens also interviewed Peggy Thompson Stiltner. According to Davidson's report, Peggy mentioned the family's belief that Wanda's obscene phone calls had come from her former husband, Danny Ray, and that Brad had accused him of being the caller. She also suggested they check on Junior Stevenson, who, she said, had had a falling out with Brad a month earlier. (In fact, Davidson may have been confused about what he was told. Peggy has no recollection of saying there was any falling out between Brad and Stevenson, and Brad says there was none.) In any event, when Davidson prepared the official report of his earlier interview with Brad McCoy, two of the three people he claimed Brad had named as the only men his wife would let into the house were men Peggy had named as possible suspects. The third was Davidson's own suspect, Roger Coleman.

Despite Mrs. Thompson's endorsement and the other names the family had supplied, Davidson and Owens headed back to Grundy to find Roger Coleman. Later Davidson would say his focus that day on Coleman rather than on the suspects named by Wanda's family was because, of the people he wanted to talk to, Coleman was the closest. In fact, Davidson had driven more than fifteen miles from the murder scene to the Thompsons' house primarily to find Coleman, and then drove all the way back to the other side of Grundy to interview him before any of the other suspects mentioned by Brad or the Thompsons. The evidence suggests that Jack Davidson decided Roger Coleman was his prime suspect from the moment he learned that Wanda's brother-in-law was an ex-convict, and that he had not worked the night of the murder.

It was shortly after noon when the two state policemen climbed the steep dirt driveway to the small white house Roger and Trish Coleman shared with Roger's grandmother. Garnett Coleman answered the door, and Roger appeared behind her. As he had planned, Davidson asked Roger to come out to his car to talk, while Owens remained in the house to question Trish and Roger's grandmother. There was a concealed tape recorder in the police car, which Davidson would use to record whatever Coleman said.

To Davidson's disappointment, Roger Coleman, like Brad McCoy, had no fresh scratches on his face or hands, and when he complied with a request that he remove his shirt, there were none on his torso, either. Still, Wanda could well have broken her fingernails on a heavily clad killer's shirt or jacket without inflicting noticeable damage.

Davidson began his interview by asking Coleman to recite how he had learned about his sister-in-law's death, and what he had been doing since. He then moved quickly to the subject of Coleman's whereabouts the previous evening.

Like Davidson, Coleman had been awake for more than twenty-four hours, much of it stressful. Nevertheless, he was able to give a detailed and surprisingly accurate account of the times, places and people he had encountered from the time he left home for work the previous evening at about 8:00 or 8:30 until arriving back home some-time after 11:00.

Coleman had been working the night shift in a drift mine above Looney Creek, which runs into Levisa Fork about three miles north of Grundy. There was a good road from the mouth of the creek to where the mine road cut off up the mountainside about three miles up the hollow, but from there the road was narrow and rough, so the mining company had one of its employees provide a man trip—a van that picked up the men in a parking area at the mouth of the creek and drove them to the mine site.

The man trip for Roger's shift usually left the parking lot at about

8:45. On Tuesday, March 10, Roger stopped off at Chuck Crabtree's store on his way to work, and by the time he got to the mouth of the creek the man trip had left, so Roger began driving up to the mine in his own truck. He noticed that none of the other men's vehicles were parked at the mouth of the creek, and wondered why. When he reached Breedings grocery store a few miles up the road he saw the man-trip van parked by the store. There Johnny Stiltner,* the driver, told him his shift had been laid off without notice. Stiltner confirmed that the reason probably had to do with a conflict between the mine superintendent and the third-shift boss. After talking to Stiltner for a while, Roger started back home, but when he reached Grundy he remembered he had left his coveralls and knee pads at the mine. He planned to start looking for another job the next day, so he turned around and drove back to the mine, arriving at about 9:45 or 9:50.

After retrieving his equipment and talking briefly to the second-shift foreman and a couple of other workers, Coleman left the mine site at about 10:00 P.M. As he drove back down the Looney Creek road he saw a friend, Philip VanDyke. The two men spoke briefly and then drove in their own vehicles back to the parking area at the mouth of the creek, where they sat and talked until VanDyke had to leave for work. He worked at the Black Watch Coal Company, only a few hundred yards from where he and Roger had been talking. Roger told Davidson it was about 10:30 P.M. when he and Philip VanDyke parted.

According to Coleman, from Looney Creek he drove back to Grundy and out the Slate Creek road to Boyd's Trailer Park, about three and a half miles beyond Longbottom. There he intended to visit another friend, Tom Keller, who had worked with him. He knew Keller was also out of work, and thought the two of them might go job-hunting together the next day. When he arrived at the trailer park and drove to Keller's trailer, he saw that all the lights were out, so he did not go up to the door. Roger thought it was about 10:45.

Roger had apparently forgotten, or left out, one thing. Across the

---

* In Buchanan County a few family names cover a lot of the population. Johnny Stiltner was not closely related to Wanda's brother-in-law Danny Ray. Nor is either of them closely related to Scott Stiltner, who will appear shortly. The same is true with other people of the same name who appear in this book, unless otherwise stated.

street from Keller's trailer he had seen that the television was on in a trailer occupied by Scott and Sandra Stiltner. Four days earlier Coleman had left an eight-track music tape there while talking to Sandra and some of her neighbors, and he decided to retrieve it. Scott Stiltner answered the door, Coleman explained his mission, obtained his tape and left.

According to Coleman, after leaving Boyd's Trailer Park he returned to Grundy and went to the miner's bathhouse in Tuffy's barbershop. He was wearing the same work clothes he had worn in the mine the preceding two days. They were coated with coal dust, and even though he had not worked in the mine that day the clothes had made him dirty. Following his usual routine, at the bathhouse Coleman removed his work clothes, took a shower and changed into the clean clothes he always took with him to work. Putting his work clothes back in a plastic bag, Roger Coleman went home, arriving, he said, at about 11:05. His grandmother let him in, and after asking her to wake him in the morning so he could start looking for work, he joined his wife, who was reading in bed.

When Coleman finished his recitation Davidson asked what clothes he had on the evening before, and whether he would turn them over for examination. Coleman readily agreed, and fetched Davidson the plastic bag of clothes he had described. Before leaving, Davidson examined the bag of clothes, which contained long underwear, a flannel shirt, blue jeans, socks, a black cap and the coveralls Roger had retrieved from the mine. In addition, there was a wet washcloth and a damp towel. Davidson noticed that the legs of the blue jeans also were wet. Coleman said they probably got wet at the mine.

Roger Coleman's story, if corroborated by the people he said had seen him the night of the murder, presented grave problems for Jack Davidson's belief that Coleman was his most promising suspect. Since Dr. Thompson had placed Wanda's time of death at about 11:00 P.M. or even a few minutes later, it seemed impossible that Roger could have returned home, in clean unbloodied clothes anytime close to when he said he did, and while Davidson knew he could probably push McDonald back some on the time of death, the observations of Randy Jackson and other policemen that Wanda's wound was still oozing fresh blood when they reached the scene at about 11:30 meant it couldn't reasonably be pushed back very far. Moreover, if Coleman really was at the mouth of Looney Creek until 10:30 or so, and then went to Boyd's Trailer Park, there was no time for him to return to Longbottom, gain entrance to Wanda's house, commit the violent crime Davidson had observed and escape through the front and only door of the house before Brad arrived shortly after 11:00. Of course, from what he said, Roger did not have a witness to his trip to Boyd's, so if no one saw him there, that part of his story could be challenged.

When Davidson finished his interview he retrieved Owens from the house, and the two men compared notes as they drove away. According to Owens, Garnett Coleman said her grandson had returned home just as the news was ending, which would make it 11:30, not 11:05. Owens's report not only made it possible that Coleman had committed the murder between 10:30 and 11:00, at least if the trip to Boyd's could be eliminated or pushed back earlier in time; it also suggested to Davidson that Roger Coleman had lied about when he got home. Of course, either he or his grandmother could simply be mistaken about the time, but Davidson thought the first hypothesis was more likely, and he could think of only one reason for Coleman to lie.

Back in Longbottom, the town police were continuing their interviews of Brad and Wanda's neighbors. The two houses closest to the McCoy house were occupied by the Johnson and Ramey families. Patton Johnson and his wife, Geneva, lived directly across the street and below the McCoys. The living room of the McCoy house, where Wanda was first attacked, and the bedroom where she was killed are about ten feet above the level of the Johnson house and perhaps fifty feet away. The Ramey house sits on the hill above and behind the McCoy house. Steps lead from the Rameys' down the hill to the street that separates the McCoys' and the Johnsons' houses, passing within a few feet of the back wall of the McCoys' bedroom. The street is wide enough to provide a place for the Rameys to park two or three vehicles across from the bottom of the stairs.

Pat Johnson had been interviewed by Jack Davidson at about 9:00 A.M. on the eleventh, just after the crime-scene investigation ended. Johnson said he had left home for work at 9:40 P.M. the night before. When he left, he saw three vehicles parked below the Rameys' stairs— a Ford car and a pickup truck that he recognized as belonging to the Rameys, and a third vehicle that he didn't recognize. The third vehicle had its parking lights on. Mr. Johnson wasn't sure if it was a car or a pickup truck, but he thought it had round taillights. There was no one visible inside it. Mr. Johnson also noticed that the McCoys' porch light was not on when he left.

Pat Johnson's wife, Geneva, was also interviewed, and she confirmed that her husband had gone to work at about 9:30 P.M. She said that at about 11:05 she heard one or two cars pull up and park, and thereafter she heard conversation that she could not understand. She then fell asleep until a policeman knocked on her door and reported what had happened. Mrs. Johnson confirmed Brad McCoy's assertion that Wanda was shy and almost always kept her door locked.

At about the same time Jack Davidson talked to Pat Johnson, several town policemen climbed the stairs behind the McCoys' house to the dilapidated frame house occupied by Helen and Bobby Ramey, one of their daughters, Portia, and two of their sons, Michael and Donnie. Davidson and Randy Jackson may have gone to the house as well.

According to what Helen Ramey said later, when the police arrived her husband, Bobby, had already left for work, and Michael, then sixteen, had gone to school. Although the street below their house and the McCoys' driveway were filled with police cars, an ambulance and the state police evidence van, apparently neither of them had stopped to find out what was going on, or gone back to inform Mrs. Ramey of the scene below her house. When she answered the door to the police, she professed ignorance of the murder and any information about the prior night's events. Donnie Ramey was asleep in a bedroom, and when he emerged he too denied hearing or seeing anything of interest the night before. According to Donnie's later statements, the police looked him over for scratches but found none.

Several hours later Randy Jackson and some other policeman apparently went to the high school and interviewed Michael Ramey. According to Michael he too was unscratched, and unable to provide assistance.

One other neighbor who was interviewed on March 11 had information that seemed relevant. Mary Smith lived directly across from the front of the McCoy house and had taken out her garbage at about 10:30 P.M. the night before. She said she thought the McCoys' porch light was on at that time. According to Mrs. Smith, Wanda always turned on the light at dark and left it on until Brad came home. Mrs. Smith also said she heard Brad come home about 11:15 P.M., and within a few minutes heard him crying and shouting. When she looked out her window she saw Brad and his father on the porch. She knew something was wrong.

Several days later another neighbor said he had returned home shortly after 10:00 on the night of the murder and watched television in his house until 10:45 P.M. At about 10:15, he heard a vehicle go by traveling very fast. He jumped up to look out the window but could see only taillights disappearing, going east. He could not tell if it was a car or a pickup truck.

When Jack Davidson finished interviewing Roger Coleman on March 11, he returned to Longbottom to see how the town-police investigation was going. Randy Jackson reported the relatively meager results of the neighborhood canvass. Apparently no one had heard any screams or sounds of a struggle, nor had they seen anyone in the area who seemed suspicious. The one thing Jackson could say for sure was that as news of the murder had spread, everyone in Grundy was shocked and scared.

Jack Davidson filled Jackson in on his interviews with Roger Coleman and the Thompson family, and suggested that Jackson's men ask the people they interviewed whether they had seen a truck like Coleman's in Longbottom on the night of the murder. Afterward, Davidson says, he checked at the United Shop to confirm Brad's story, then went to examine the shower room at Tuffy's. It was possible, he figured, that Coleman was telling the truth about going to Tuffy's, but lying about the murder. Certainly the damp towel and washcloth in Coleman's clothes bag tended to support his story about taking a shower. Maybe Davidson could find traces of blood or some other evidence. Apparently he didn't, although no report of his visit to the shower room has been found in any of the available records.*

It was late, but Davidson decided to see if he could find Philip VanDyke before quitting for the day. VanDyke was the last person Coleman said he had seen on the night of the murder. If he failed to

---

* These include the complete file maintained by the Buchanan County Commonwealth's Attorney, which appears to include almost all the reports compiled by the state police during the investigation.

corroborate Coleman's story that they met and talked at the mouth of Looney Creek until about 10:30, Coleman's alibi was essentially destroyed. Davidson had learned that VanDyke lived with his mother in Royal City, an area along Route 460 between Grundy and Vansant. He and Roger Owens drove the short distance to Royal City, turned up a steep hillside and located the VanDykes' among a small cluster of houses that clung to a hillside overlooking the highway and the valley formed by the Levisa River. Philip was at home.

Yes, he said, he knew about the murder. He and his fiancée knew Brad and Wanda and were friends with Wanda's sister Trish and her husband, Roger. They had called and told him about the murder. Roger had said the police would probably be contacting Philip, since they had already talked to Roger and he had told them about seeing Philip the night before. Well, Davidson asked, *had* he seen Coleman? And if so, when?

Without hesitation or apparent nervousness VanDyke said that he and Roger had talked at the mouth of Looney Creek until about 10:30 P.M. His explanation of how he gauged the time was logical—and provable. When he left Roger, VanDyke explained, he went straight to work at the Black Watch Coal Company, only a quarter of a mile away. There he put on his boots and clocked in. The whole thing couldn't have taken more than five or ten minutes, VanDyke explained, so if you find out when I clocked in, you can tell when I left Roger within a few minutes one way or the other.

Jack Davidson had to be worried that Philip VanDyke had just eliminated his best suspect. If the time card substantiated VanDyke's estimate, it was hard to believe Roger Coleman had time to commit the crime even if he went straight to Wanda's house from Looney Creek. If he went first to Boyd's Trailer Park, it would have been impossible. From Looney Creek to Boyd's the drive alone would take about fifteen minutes, and then Coleman would have to retrace his route to Longbottom, gain entrance to the house, struggle with Wanda, remove her clothes, almost certainly rape her (although that was not yet confirmed), kill her and leave before Brad arrived shortly after 11:00. There simply wasn't time.

Jack Davidson had not been to bed for more than forty hours. It was time to go home and sleep on it.

At 8:30 A.M. on Thursday, March 12, Dr. David Oxley began his autopsy of the body of Wanda Fay McCoy. According to his report, Wanda's death was caused by the wound to her throat, which Oxley described as a slash wound that completely severed her jugular vein, carotid artery and larynx. The wound ran from Wanda's right to left, and downward. It was made with a single stroke by a sharp instrument.

Wanda had also been stabbed twice, once in the chest near the inside of her left breast and once just below the breastbone. The first wound penetrated Wanda's left lung and heart, the second penetrated her liver. Neither wound resulted in any significant bleeding, and Oxley concluded they were inflicted when Wanda was already dead or near death from the throat wound. Both stab wounds were four inches deep, and only one sixteenth of an inch wide. According to the autopsy report, these three wounds were Wanda's only observable injuries.

During the autopsy Dr. Oxley preserved a number of items for further analysis. He took swabs from the vagina and rectum to test for sperm, and observed no traumatic injury to either area. He found two hairs in Wanda's pubic area that appeared different from her own pubic hair, and preserved them for examination. Samples of Wanda's blood, a swab of the black substance that covered her hands and the clothes from her body were also preserved. Dr. Oxley saw that Wanda's fingernails were broken and her hands covered with blood, but reported that there was "no appreciable quantity of material beneath the nails," and made no effort to preserve whatever was there for analysis. Neither did he attempt to determine whether any of the blood on her hands had come from the killer rather than her own wounds. His report made no mention of any defensive wounds on Wanda's hands, nor of what seems to be a large bruise or abrasion on her upper right arm that appears in an autopsy photograph.

Later that day the evidence gathered by Dr. Oxley was transferred to the Virginia Division of Forensic Science. The swabs of black material from Wanda's hands were transferred to Elmer Miller, an expert in the identification of soils and minerals who had joined the State Crime Lab after retiring from the FBI as chief of the FBI Mineralogy Unit. The remaining evidence was assigned to Elmer Gist, a blood and hair analyst in the Bureau's Roanoke office.

At about the time Dr. Oxley began his autopsy, Jack Davidson finished his breakfast after a good night's sleep and resumed his investigation of Wanda McCoy's murder.

It is not clear exactly when he checked on VanDyke's time card—VanDyke had the feeling he had already done so the first time they talked; Davidson doesn't recall. In any event, Davidson visited the offices of the Black Watch Coal Company, crossing the company's private bridge across the Levisa River just beyond the mouth of Looney Creek. Yes, he was told, Philip VanDyke worked there; yes, he had worked Tuesday night; and yes, he would have clocked in and his time card was available.

The card showed that VanDyke had clocked in to work the night of March 10 at 10:41 P.M. The time was consistent with VanDyke's usual time of arrival, and Davidson could develop no evidence to support a theory that the time card was inaccurate or had somehow been altered. Of course, VanDyke could have been lying about going directly to work after talking to Roger, or about seeing him at all, but for Roger to make up the story on the spur of the moment the morning after the murder without knowing whether he could get VanDyke to support it seemed too farfetched. Besides, why would VanDyke lie? He was a friend of Roger's, but not so close that one could reasonably believe he would commit perjury and cover up a murder.

Troublesome as VanDyke's statement and supporting time card were, Jack Davidson was not about to give up on Roger Coleman. Coleman had said he had gone from Looney Creek to Boyd's, but he hadn't claimed that anyone saw him there. Davidson would see for himself. He knew Boyd's Trailer Park, and he knew that if someone had pulled in to the park at 10:45 P.M. on a weeknight in a truck like Coleman's, there was a good chance someone had seen him. If they did, and they agreed it was about 10:45 P.M., fine. But if not, if no one had seen him, Roger Coleman was going to remain at or near the top of Davidson's suspect list. It was close, but if Coleman had gone straight to Longbottom from Looney Creek, VanDyke could be right about the time and Coleman could still be the killer.

With the company's permission, Davidson took VanDyke's time card with him and headed for Boyd's. Passing Longbottom and continuing east toward West Virginia, it was shortly after 11:00 A.M. when he turned right on the narrow concrete bridge that spans Slate Creek and leads into the trailer park.

Davidson began by locating Tom Keller's trailer, where Roger said he had pulled up the night of the murder. There was no one home. Davidson cannot recall whether he next talked to someone who suggested he visit the trailer across the road from Keller's or just noticed that someone was home there and decided to ask if they had seen Roger's truck the night before. In any event, Davidson's notes say it was 11:33 A.M. when he began interviewing the man who lived there, Gary Scott Stiltner.

In response to Davidson's questions, Scott Stiltner said that he not only knew Roger Coleman, he had seen him when he came by the trailer on Tuesday night. You mean you saw him across the street, Davidson asked. No, Stiltner said, he came to my house and knocked on the door. Said he'd left a tape with my wife. He had, too. She pulled it out of the stereo and gave it to him. I didn't know nothin' about it, but I guess he left it when he was around here last week.

If Jack Davidson's heart sunk at Stiltner's words, he was soon revived. Stiltner said the time of Coleman's visit was between 10:15 and 10:30, which he knew because he and his wife were watching *Hart to Hart*, a television program that started at 10:00, and it had "just gotten interesting." It was, he said, right at the time of a commercial. Stiltner went on to explain that normally he would have been at work, but that day, for no particular reason, he had decided to stay home.

When Jack Davidson finished interviewing Scott Stiltner, he turned to Sandy Stiltner, who had returned home while Davidson was talking to her husband. Sandy described the events of the previous Friday, when she saw Roger Coleman and her neighbors Tom and David Keller and Gary Owens visiting outside her trailer. Later the same day, Coleman, along with Gary Owens and Denise Skeens, another neighbor, came to the Stiltner trailer. According to Sandy, Coleman said he knew her husband. They began talking about music, and Coleman mentioned having a tape of Supertramp that Owens wanted to hear. Roger retrieved the tape from his truck and they played it on Sandy Stiltner's stereo. After Gary Owens left, Roger offered Sandy a drink of liquor from a bottle in his truck, but she declined. When Coleman left he forgot to take his tape.

Although Jack Davidson undoubtedly asked Sandy Stiltner about what happened on the night of the murder, and in particular what time she thought Coleman had come to her trailer that night, no notes or written report of her answers are in the prosecutor's file or other available records. Sandy Stiltner recalls that Davidson came back and talked to her again on several occasions, but there apparently is no report of those conversations either. In a memo prepared by Davidson seven months later, he reported that Sandy, like Scott, would testify that Roger had arrived at their house between 10:00 and 10:30 P.M.

Davidson must have left Boyd's Trailer Park with mixed emotions. On the one hand, the Stiltners had confirmed Roger's claim that he went to Boyd's after leaving Looney Creek. On the other hand, their story created a mystery, and an inconsistency in Roger's story of the day before. For whatever reason, Roger apparently had not mentioned his stop at the Stiltners', although under the circumstances he could easily have simply forgotten it when Davidson questioned him the day after the murder. More important, if their estimate of the time he was there was correct, Coleman and VanDyke were wrong. If Roger Coleman left Boyd's sometime before 10:30 P.M., rather than about 10:45, he was arguably a viable suspect again. And that, Davidson thought, was the most likely reason Coleman had failed to mention his visit to Stiltners'.

While Jack Davidson was pursuing his investigation at Boyd's Trailer Park, he had enlisted the help of B. I. Sparks, another state policeman in the Vansant office, to check out Coleman's story with the men at the TMJ mine, where Roger had worked before he was laid off. After Davidson left Boyd's he met Sparks to obtain his report. According to Sparks, the men at the mine had basically supported Coleman's story, including the approximate time of their conversations, which in turn fit Philip VanDyke's estimate that he first saw Roger coming down the Looney Creek road a little after 10:00 P.M. Sparks did obtain one piece of useful information at the mine, however. Ronald Perkins, the second-shift foreman, said that as far as he recalled, Roger Coleman's pants had not been wet when he left the mine. Sparks may have also reported that there were boards across parts of the mine site that were wet or muddy.

It was hardly an inconsistency from Coleman's statement that his pants "probably" got wet at the mine, but Davidson thought it might be useful. It is a classic technique of criminal investigation to confront a suspect with a small inconsistency in his story in the hope that it will lead him to make up a new, unlikely or disprovable explanation. An accumulation of false or unlikely statements, even on inconsequential subjects, may lead a suspect to feel trapped and confess, or at least provide ammunition for challenging his credibility at trial. Moreover, Davidson was developing a theory that might make the issue far from inconsequential. The theory was that Roger Coleman had waded Slate Creek on his way to or from the murder of Wanda McCoy.

After talking to Sparks, Davidson decided to confront Coleman at once with the "news" that he did not get his pants wet at the mine. Although all Davidson knew was that Perkins had not noticed water on Coleman's pants, Davidson told Coleman he had been up to the mine site and found that it was dry and that Coleman's pants could not have gotten wet there. Rather than argue, Coleman said that in that case they must have gotten wet when he took them off and laid them on the floor of the shower room at Tuffy's.

In Longbottom, the town-police canvass of the neighborhood was taking longer than expected. Approaching doors that were typically unlocked and readily answered, the officers discovered that ringing a doorbell would often bring only the surreptitious movement of a closed curtain as someone tried to see who was there. Unless he was recognized by the resident or wearing a uniform, the door would remain unanswered, and if someone did appear, the conversations were usually short and nervous, consisting mostly of anxious questions about whether there was any progress in finding the killer. Randy Jackson spent much of the day assuring citizens and city officials that everything possible was being done.

Ending the day at his office in Vansant, Jack Davidson spoke briefly to Jackson and obtained a report on Dr. Oxley's autopsy. Vaginal, anal and oral swabs had been sent to the forensic lab, and by Monday they would know if they contained sperm. If so, and if whoever produced the sperm was one of the 85 percent of men whose blood type can be determined from their sperm, it would be possible to compare those characteristics with the blood of a suspect and at least see if they were the same. In addition, the hairs Oxley had collected from Wanda's pubis could be compared with a suspect's pubic hair, to see if they were consistent. These tests, however, would take time—and samples from a suspect.

Reviewing what he knew, Jack Davidson was as inclined as ever to believe that his hunch about Roger Coleman was correct. Most murders are committed by someone who knows the victim, and Roger was such a person. This murder in particular seemed to have been committed by someone the victim would have admitted to her house, and that included Coleman. Of course, there was the pry mark on the door, but, asked about it years later, Davidson would insist that in his opinion it could not have been the means of gaining entry to the house.

Coleman's alibi was not bad, but there were discrepancies, and in Davidson's mind the discrepancies were beginning to look almost worse than no alibi at all. Coleman claimed he got home at about 11:05, and for now his wife was supporting his estimate, but his grandmother, questioned separately, had said it was when the news was going off. VanDyke's insistence that Coleman was still at the mouth of Looney Creek at 10:30 P.M. was exculpatory and troublesome, but Scott and Sandy Stiltner's story disputed it. VanDyke was a friend. Davidson believed the Stiltners. Then there was the wet pants, and Coleman's changing story about how they got wet. And finally, of course, there was the reason why Davidson had started down this path in the first place—Roger Coleman's prior conviction for attempted rape. To Davidson, it was not only a similar offense because sexual assault was involved; there was a similar modus operandi. According to Brenda Rife, Coleman had gained entrance to her home by subterfuge—pretending to want a glass of water. Davidson figured Roger had gained entrance to Wanda's home by a similar artifice—probably some tale about his wife or another family member.

Jack Davidson denies that from March 12 onward the entire focus of his investigation was to develop evidence against Roger Coleman. It is true that he went ahead with Brad McCoy's lie-detector test and finally paid a visit to Danny Ray Stiltner, the family's prime suspect, two weeks after the murder. But as a practical matter Brad had been eliminated as an active participant on the night of the murder, and the delay in interviewing Stiltner certainly suggests that Davidson had other priorities.

Davidson decided that on the next day, Friday, March 13, he would try to obtain blood and hair samples from Coleman and send them down to Roanoke so the forensic lab would have them as soon as possible. Randy Jackson agreed—now he could report to the mayor and town council that a suspect had been identified.

There probably wasn't enough evidence to obtain an order compelling Roger Coleman to provide blood and hair samples, but Jack Davidson was confident he could persuade Coleman to provide the samples voluntarily. The entire Thompson family, including Roger and Trish, were spending almost all their time at the Thompson home on Home Creek, supporting Wanda's parents and each other and preparing for the funeral on Saturday. At least one of the Thompson brothers had been following the investigation and knew Roger was a suspect. Davidson doubted that Roger Coleman was in any position to refuse to cooperate with the police. As they had hoped, on Friday Davidson and Jackson found Roger with his wife's family at the Thompson home. He readily agreed to sign a consent form and accompany them to Grundy Hospital, where his blood was drawn and hairs were pulled from his head and pubic region. No one else would be asked to submit to such procedures, not even Brad or Danny Ray Stiltner. The samples obtained from Coleman were sent to Roanoke that same day, and received by Elmer Gist on Monday.

On Saturday afternoon, March 14, Wanda Fay McCoy's funeral was held at the Big Rock Freewill Baptist Church. Sam and Marie Thompson had been regular worshipers there for most of their lives, and all sixteen Thompson children had attended Sunday school in the plain cinder-block building. Jack Mutter, who had married Brad and Wanda, joined two ministers from the church in conducting the ceremony. Among the pallbearers were the husbands of four of Wanda's seven sisters, including Roger Coleman. Following the church service Wanda was buried at Mountain Valley Memorial Park in Big Rock. Nearly everyone in the congregation attended the funeral, and so did a lot of people who did not belong to the church and had no personal connection with the departed.

Wanda McCoy's murder had stunned the residents of Grundy and its surrounding communities. Violence and murder were hardly strangers to the area, but most of them were what Randy Jackson called "smokin' barrel murders." You get to the scene, and "the guy that done it's standing there too," holding the murder weapon. These crimes usually involved family or "business" disputes between members of the sizable population of moonshiners, drug dealers and unemployed ne'er-do-wells of the region, not hard-working, God-fearing people like the Thompsons. The murder of a beautiful young woman from a good family, in her own home, by someone who was not yet known but apparently was not her husband or boyfriend—that was another story. It drew a lot of people to the funeral, some out of curiosity, some to show community solidarity against the crime.

Back in Grundy, Jack Davidson could only wait impatiently for Elmer Gist and Elmer Miller to report the results of their scientific tests. In the meantime, he began to check out some other men who might become suspects in the event the tests cleared Roger Coleman.

On the day of the funeral, B. I. Sparks was sent to interview Junior Stevenson, whom Wanda's sister Peggy had supposedly named as a possible suspect because of a fight he had with Brad McCoy, and whom Brad had named as one of the people Wanda might have admitted to the house. Stevenson said he had come home from work on the afternoon of the murder so tired his wife had to help him out of his truck, and had fallen asleep on a couch and slept until he had to get ready to go to work the next morning. His wife, Belinda, confirmed the story.

Over the next several days a few more of the McCoy neighbors were located and interviewed, and while each was asked about Roger Coleman, and whether anyone had seen a blue truck (like Coleman's) in the neighborhood on the night of the murder, no one had any useful information. Meanwhile, Davidson and Jackson worked on Philip VanDyke, looking for holes in his story about when he had seen Roger. Jackson recalls that on one occasion he and Davidson met VanDyke at the Black Watch tipple where he worked and had him walk through his activities on the night of the murder, trying to show that he could have left Roger before 10:25 or 10:30 and still not clocked in at work until 10:41. They failed. VanDyke insisted that it could not have taken more than about ten minutes for him to reach the tipple and clock in, even if he changed his clothes before punching the clock. The walkthrough showed he was right, unless he had stopped to do something else, which he adamantly denied.

On another occasion they questioned VanDyke at the apartment where his fiancée (now his wife), Sonya, lived, just down the hill from his mother's house. To Philip, it seemed as if Davidson was suggesting he was lying, and it made him angry. The questioning got so hostile that Sonya thought Davidson was inferring that Philip was involved in the murder, and she took Jackson aside and asked him indignantly if that were the case. Jackson said no—but Davidson's accusatory tone continued.

Under the circumstances, many witnesses would have given Davidson all he really needed—an admission that it *could* have been earlier when Roger left—but VanDyke stuck to his guns. Today, in addition to his regular job, VanDyke is assistant chief of the Grundy Volunteer Fire Department. Over the years, he has worked with Davidson from time to time and admires him. He no longer thinks Davidson was accusing him of lying—he was just trying to be sure of the facts. But, he adds, the facts haven't changed. He left Roger Coleman at the mouth of Looney Creek at about 10:30 P.M.

The man Wanda's family seemed to think was the most likely suspect was Danny Ray Stiltner. Stiltner had moved from Grundy to Betsy Layne, Kentucky, to avoid warrants Peggy had obtained for nonsupport of their child, and although Betsy Layne was on Route 460 not far across the state line from the Thompsons' house, it was March 24 before Jack Davidson interviewed him. Stiltner denied making obscene phone calls to Wanda, and denied involvement in the murder. He said that when he was married to Peggy, Roger Coleman was always bringing liquor to his house, that in his opinion Coleman was responsible for the breakup of his marriage, and that he thought Coleman was crazy and probably guilty of the murder. As for himself, Stiltner claimed he had been with his mother and father on the night of the murder.

It wasn't much of an alibi, but according to Stiltner, Davidson never followed up on his suggestion that Danny Ray take a lie-detector test.

At about the time Davidson interviewed Stiltner, he received preliminary results of the tests done by Elmer Gist. On Monday, March 16, Davidson learned that microscopic examination had revealed sperm on both the vaginal and anal swabs Dr. Oxley had taken during his autopsy. When Elmer Gist set out to see if he could determine the blood type of the person or persons whose sperm was on those swabs, the information he could hope to obtain was less extensive and specific than it is now. Today, a variety of tests involving DNA comparisons can provide an enormously high degree of individual identification, which most scientists agree is on the order of one in several million. In 1981, however, none of the DNA identification techniques were available. From the sperm of a secretor, the Virginia Bureau of

Forensic Science in 1981 had the ability to determine the donor's blood type (A, B, AB and O), and certain enzyme factors known as phosphoglucomutase (PGM).

From the saliva and blood samples provided by Roger Coleman, Gist could make the same determinations. Testing those samples, Gist determined that Coleman *was* a secretor, and that his blood type was B, a type that occurs in about 13 percent of the population in the southeastern United States.

Determining blood type from sperm is a little more complicated than determining it directly from blood, although a competent analyst should be able to do it without difficulty. For some reason, however, when Gist first tested the sperm on the vaginal swab, the "signal" he got was "weak," and he decided to perform a second test. This time, he says, the signal was clear enough to report a result. The person who produced the vaginal sperm was a secretor, with blood type B. Gist also tested the sperm on the anal swab, but reported that the result was "inconclusive."

The PGM enzyme test identifies three additional blood characteristics, and could have either eliminated Roger Coleman as the source of the sperm or included him in a greatly reduced number of possible donors. Gist, however, did not perform the PGM test. Years later he would claim that by doing the ABO test twice he was left with insufficient material to do more testing.

Gist was also able to detect the presence of two or three small patches of blood on the right leg of the blue jeans Coleman turned over to Jack Davidson the morning after the murder, and an even smaller speck on the left leg. He cut tiny patches out of the material where the blood appeared and reported that he had identified it as type O, the same type as Wanda McCoy (and about 45 percent of the population). With blood, not only the PGM test but three other enzyme tests were commonly done in 1981, which, in combination, would have either eliminated Wanda McCoy as the source of the blood on Coleman's jeans or made it nearly certain that it was indeed her blood. Again, for whatever reason, no additional tests were conducted.

Gist also tested two knives Coleman had voluntarily turned over to the police. He reported that one of them, a pocketknife with a three-inch blade, showed a trace of blood so small he could not even tell if it were human or animal.

If Gist's report of his blood testing did little more than fail to elimi-nate Roger Coleman as Wanda McCoy's murderer, to Jack Davidson they were confirmation of his already strong suspicion that Coleman was guilty. And a third aspect of Gist's report was even more gratify-ing. According to Gist, he had microscopically compared the pubic hair found on Wanda McCoy with those removed from Roger Coleman on March 13, and they were "consistent."

Most experts agree that if a sufficient number of samples are avail-able, a comparison of hairs may serve to eliminate someone as the donor, but that a finding of consistency in the absence of some unusu-al characteristic of the hair does little more than avoid elimination. Unlike fingerprints, hairs are not positive identifiers, and unlike blood types, there is no scientifically accepted figure for the number or per-centage of people whose hair is "consistent" with one another. A find-ing of consistency is highly subjective, and experts may and often do disagree about such a finding. But as Jack Davidson and Mickey McGlothlin knew, or would soon find out, Elmer Gist had often testi-fied, and would surely testify again, that it is "possible, but unlikely" that consistent hairs could come from different people. When com-bined with the other circumstantial evidence Jack Davidson had gath-ered, that testimony might eliminate the reasonable doubt a juror would otherwise entertain about Roger Coleman's guilt.

The Gist report was everything Jack Davidson could ask for, but the report from Elmer Miller was an unexpected blow. Like any coal miner, the blue jeans and coveralls Coleman worked in and turned over to the police were saturated with coal dust, and Davidson had felt certain that the black smudges that covered Wanda McCoy's hands, arms, sweater and upper thighs were also coal dust. It would be one more piece of circumstantial evidence that could be said to point to Coleman as the killer, although in Buchanan County it would be hard to find a laborer whose work clothes were not infused with coal dust. But to Davidson's surprise and chagrin, Elmer Miller report-ed that the swab he had been supplied from Wanda McCoy's hands contained no coal dust, but rather a small amount of organic soil and plant material. The quantity was insufficient for further identification.

If it occurred to Jack Davidson that Miller's report had greater implications than the loss of a fairly unimportant piece of the circum-stantial case he was building against Roger Coleman, there is no indication of it in his conduct at the time. Whatever the dark substance was, no sign of it had been found anywhere in the house except on Wanda McCoy's clothes and body. It had to be related to the murder, and probably came from the killer's clothes or from the area where Wanda was first attacked. Either way, it was important evidence. Wanda McCoy had been buried, but her sweater, which was also covered with the substance, was in the police evidence room.

Perhaps Davidson concluded that the odds were too strong that further efforts to solve the mystery of the soil would hurt rather than help the case against Roger Coleman, or perhaps, as he says now, he just didn't believe further tests would provide any useful new information. In any event, no further effort was made to identify or trace the black substance that covered Wanda McCoy. When Jack Davidson received the report from Elmer Gist he declared the murder of Wanda McCoy solved, and reported his findings to the Commonwealth's Attorney.

Chapter 6

———

Indictment

If you drive through downtown Grundy and turn right from Main Street onto Walnut, just past the Buchanan County Courthouse, you will come to the storefront office where Michael G. "Mickey" McGlothlin now practices law. It is across from the courthouse on the left side of the street; the best-looking storefront in Grundy. Its broad windows and entrance door are shaded by a green awning on which, in gold letters, appears the name of the firm—MCGLOTHLIN AND WIFE. "Wife" is Sandra Keen McGlothlin, daughter of another prominent Buchanan County family. Keen Mountain and the village of Keen, Virginia, are testaments to the family's historical antecedents in the area.

When Mickey McGlothlin followed his older brother Jim in becoming a lawyer, most people figured he would practice with the firm where his brother had been a partner before taking over management of the coal company. The firm, now known as Street, Street, Street, Scott and Bowman, is the largest in Grundy, with the richest clientele. It would have provided a comfortable sinecure for Mickey McGlothlin, who, in truth, hardly needed the money.

To Mickey McGlothlin, however, that kind of practice didn't seem very interesting, and so in 1979, when the incumbent Commonwealth's

Attorney decided not to run for reelection, McGlothlin ran to replace him. He was only two years out of law school, but no one thought it was feasible to oppose him. Thus, in late March 1981, it was Mickey McGlothlin who had to decide whether the evidence gathered by Jack Davidson was strong enough to justify charging Roger Coleman with murder, and, if so, whether the state should seek the death penalty.

Although the evidence was wholly circumstantial, McGlothlin now says the decision to indict was easy. While he may not have attached quite as much significance to Roger Coleman's prior record as Jack Davidson had, McGlothlin believed the combination of that record with the family connection, the apparent lack of forced entry to the house and the blood and hair evidence were too much to be coincidental. Indeed, in McGlothlin's mind, once Davidson put it all together for him, the evidence of guilt seemed quite strong.

If the decision to indict was easy, the decision to seek the death penalty was harder. It was not a multiple murder, nor was it the kind of open-and-shut case that is usually needed to persuade a jury to impose the ultimate penalty. However, given the brutality of the murder, the evidence of rape and sodomy and Coleman's prior record, McGlothlin concluded that he would at least start out asking for death. Later, he might consider a lesser sentence in return for a plea. On March 31, 1981, McGlothlin informed Jack Davidson that he would seek an indictment for capital murder from the April 1981 Buchanan County grand jury. Grand juries almost never refuse a prosecutor's request.

Coleman could have been arrested at once and charged with murder, but McGlothlin and Davidson agreed it was best to wait for a grand jury indictment. If Coleman was arrested now, he would be entitled to a preliminary hearing before a judge, in which the state would have to produce much of their evidence in order to show probable cause. McGlothlin wanted to avoid revealing the details of his case before trial. Besides, Davidson was hoping to gather more evidence, perhaps even obtain a confession, before Coleman obtained a lawyer.

When Randy Jackson told the police committee of the town council about McGlothlin's decision, they were less than thrilled with the idea of Coleman remaining free for another two weeks, and at their request Jackson placed Coleman under twenty-four-hour-a-day surveillance.

The council agreed to appropriate money to pay for the necessary overtime.

One of the surveillance officers recalls that one day as he was following Coleman, he somehow lost track of him. As he frantically tried to find Coleman, the officer drove around the back of town by the river and found Coleman's truck parked by the side of the road. Roger was sitting on the river bank, fishing.

Over the next two weeks Davidson tried hard to strengthen his case. On April 2, he asked Coleman to consent to having his medical, employment and financial records turned over to the police. Coleman agreed. And according to Roger Lee Coleman, Davidson came up to the house on Dave's Branch almost every day to confront Coleman and try to obtain a confession. All the usual devices were employed—claims that the state had an indisputable case based on the scientific tests; claims that the state had other evidence and witnesses who would testify against him; and, of course, the assertion that if Roger would only tell the truth and confess, he would be better off, he would feel better about himself, they would help him and be lenient, whereas if he refused he would surely be charged, convicted and executed.

Coleman continued to deny any participation in the crime, and his wife, Trish, continued to support him, telling Sonya VanDyke and others that she *knew* he had arrived home at 11:05 P.M. the night of the murder because she was in bed reading, and when she heard him come home early, she looked at her watch.

Despite Davidson's efforts, neither the questioning nor the surveillance resulted in any new evidence, and on April 13, 1981, Mickey McGlothlin obtained an indictment for rape and capital murder. Although Coleman had cooperated with Davidson at every turn, and appeared voluntarily for questioning whenever asked, that evening Davidson and Randy Jackson took a group of armed men up to the mine where Coleman was working for the Snow Ball Coal Company, had him called out of the mine and at gunpoint placed him in shackles and handcuffs. When he was searched, a pocketknife was found in his pocket and sent to the crime lab for analysis, but no blood was found. With no better choice, McGlothlin and Davidson decided to declare that the three-inch pocketknife with the unidentifiable trace of blood was the probable murder weapon.

Roger Coleman was twenty-two years old when he was charged

with the capital murder of Wanda McCoy and jailed without bond. If he was convicted there were only two possible sentences: life in prison, or death in the electric chair.

In addition to capital murder and rape, Coleman was also charged with indecent exposure. On January 12, two months before Wanda McCoy was murdered, someone had entered the Buchanan County Public Library just before closing time and exposed himself in front of Pat Hatfield and Jean Gilbert, two female librarians. According to the librarians, the man was also masturbating, and sprayed semen across their checkout desk before turning and running out the door.

At first, the police suspected a well-known town drunk and troublemaker who had run naked through downtown Grundy a week or so earlier. Sometime prior to April 13, however, the two librarians identified a picture of Roger Coleman as the perpetrator. When Jack Davidson placed him under arrest and informed him of the additional charge, Coleman denied he was the man in the library, and claimed he had records that would prove he was at work at the time. Ultimately, the indecent-exposure charge was dismissed. In years to come, however, the library incident would reemerge as a major issue in the state's effort to put Roger Coleman in the electric chair.

Nicholas E. Persin was appointed circuit judge of Buchanan County in 1974, and held that position for more than twenty years, until his retirement in 1995. He had presided over Roger Coleman's trial for attempted rape in 1978, and he would preside over his trial for murder.

Today, Nick Persin looks and sounds like the Hollywood model of a good judge. In his sixties, he is tall, erect and firm-bodied, with white hair and a friendly voice. He was the kind of judge lawyers liked to appear before, because he did not berate or embarrass them the way some judges will, and he did not frighten their clients. He also knew the law, and how to run a trial so it didn't last forever. According to one leading defense lawyer in the area, like many judges who are former prosecutors he was somewhat prosecution-minded in criminal cases, but not so much as to cause him to rule in ways that might cause a reversal. Judge Persin was very seldom reversed. Throughout his career he was widely viewed as a decent and honorable man and one of the best trial judges in Virginia.

On April 14, the day after his arrest, Roger Coleman was brought before Judge Persin for arraignment, the occasion when a defendant is given formal notice of charges against him and the opportunity to enter a plea. When Coleman said he had no lawyer and could not afford to hire one, Judge Persin ordered that he be held without bond, and began the process of finding a lawyer who could be appointed to represent him.

Mickey McGlothlin had already foreclosed one obvious source of competent representation for Coleman. In a case of this importance, McGlothlin felt that he needed an assistant, and Tom Scott, an energetic young lawyer with the Street firm, had agreed to serve, thus eliminating from Judge Persin's consideration not only Scott himself but the entire firm. There were other lawyers in Grundy and the surrounding area who had the experience and ability to defend a capital-murder case, and Persin spoke to several of them. Given the huge financial sacrifice that an experienced lawyer is required to make in taking on an appointed murder case, not to mention the intense public feeling that had been aroused by this murder, and especially by the news that the accused was the victim's brother-in-law and had already been convicted once for attempted rape, Judge Persin was not surprised when all of them begged off.

Whether he believed their excuses were legitimate or simply didn't want to saddle them with the burden, Judge Persin did not appoint any of these experienced criminal defense attorneys to represent Roger Coleman. Rather, he called on one of the newest lawyers in Grundy, Terry Jordan. Jordan was no more anxious to take the case than his more experienced colleagues, and pointed out to the judge that, unlike the prosecutors, he had very little criminal-trial experience of any kind, and had never represented anyone for murder or even a serious felony, much less a murder for which the Commonwealth was seeking the death penalty. With Terry Jordan, however, Judge Persin was insistent, while at the same time reassuring him that he would also appoint a second, more experienced attorney for the case.

Fifty miles from Grundy in Tazewell, seat of the county that adjoins Buchanan to the east, Judge Persin found his second lawyer, Steven Arey. Arey had been in practice two years longer than Jordan, but he too had little criminal-trial experience and had never tried a murder case. He had, however, tried a case before Judge Persin, and the judge thought he had done a good job. On April 16, Terry Jordan and Steven Arey were officially appointed to represent Coleman.

Most cases, criminal or civil, are decided on the basis of which side has the best facts, not which side has the better lawyers, but when the case of *Commonwealth* v. *Roger Keith Coleman* went to trial, with Mickey McGlothlin and Tom Scott for the prosecution, assisted by Jack Davidson, against Steven Arey and Terry Jordan for the defense, assisted by no one, the playing field was tilted dramatically in favor of the prosecution. And while no one would suggest that Judge Persin had created this mismatch intentionally, at least one local lawyer says that if the balance of skill had turned out to be tilted the other way, Judge Persin would have taken steps during the trial to level the field, but since it was tilted in favor of the prosecution, he didn't.

Even so, a judge can react only to what he knows, and it is unlikely that Judge Persin knew the facts that would have revealed how bad the mismatch really was. If he had, he might have insisted that a more experienced lawyer accept his appointment, or done something to help the defense bring out important information during the trial.

News travels fast in small towns, and the news that the police had made an arrest in the Wanda McCoy murder case was big news indeed. A whole lot of people in Grundy had known for some time that the police thought they knew who did it, and that the suspect was Roger Coleman, the victim's own brother-in-law, the one who had been convicted of trying to rape Brenda Rife, the mayor's daughter. Roger was arrested on a Monday evening, and by the time *The Virginia Mountaineer* came out with the news on Thursday, just about everybody in Buchanan County had already heard it, and all the details of his prior record and the library incident as well. In case anyone missed hearing about it from a neighbor, or at the barbershop, or in the *Mountaineer*, the daily papers published in Bluefield, West Virginia, and Bristol, Tennessee, also covered the story.

Some folks talked about how much they would like to get on the jury and help send the son of a bitch to the electric chair, while others took the position that they shouldn't wait around and take any chances with what the courts would do, but instead drag him out of the jail and take care of him right away.

One proponent of a swifter brand of justice was Preston Rife, Brenda's husband. By happenstance, he was in a position to do more than just mutter threats to his cronies. In 1981 Preston no longer owned the car lot in Vansant. Instead, he had two gas stations, and one of them was located right next to the courthouse on Main Street. In the front of his property, next to the street and less than fifty feet from the courthouse entrance, Preston Rife erected a four-foot-by-eight-foot lighted advertising sign. It read TIME FOR A NEW HANGING TREE IN GRUNDY.

Sheriff Auburn Ratliff thought it was probably all talk, but the jail was attached to the courthouse and he didn't have a whole lot of men to protect it, so after some telephone death threats and a bomb threat that vacated the courthouse as well as the jail, he decided to ship Roger Coleman off to Bristol, where Sheriff Honaker had constructed a large modern jail that accepted prisoners from all over the state and the federal government as well, to the considerable profit of the county, at least according to the sheriff. Years later Honaker committed suicide when auditors discovered he had embezzled nearly a million dollars from the jail account.

The death threats and Preston Rife's hanging-tree sign were simply the most visible manifestations of an attitude among the Buchanan County citizenry which seemed pervasive to Roger Coleman and his family. Not long after Roger was arrested, even his wife, Trish, turned against him after the police worked on her for a while, claiming that the blood type and hair comparisons were scientific proof positive that he was guilty.

Fearing it would be impossible to get a fair trial in Grundy, Coleman asked his lawyers to file a petition for change of venue to move the trial out of Buchanan County. The motion was filed in September, and finally came up for hearing on December 2, 1981.

Steve Arey was going to take primary responsibility for preparing and presenting the motion to Judge Persin, but at eight-thirty that morning he called Terry Jordan to say he could not appear. He had forgotten a National Guard meeting he was committed to attend that day.

Rather than seek a continuance, Jordan decided to argue the motion himself. The defense had done almost nothing to collect evidence in support of their contention that Coleman could not get a fair trial in Buchanan County, although Coleman's uncle Roger Lee did have two newspaper clippings and a photo of the hanging-tree sign, which Jordan filed in support of his motion. On the other side of the courtroom, Mickey McGlothlin had before him a pile of some fifty affidavits from county residents attesting to their own lack of prejudice about the case, and that of many of their acquaintances.

After the two sides presented their arguments, Judge Persin asked whether, under the circumstances, Jordan would like time to present additional evidence. When Jordan declined the offer, Judge Persin denied the change of venue.

In truth, even if Coleman's lawyers had made the best possible record in support of their motion, it would probably have been denied and its denial affirmed on appeal. Nevertheless, the preparation and performance of Roger Coleman's lawyers on the venue motion did not bode well for the future.

In the early weeks of his imprisonment, Roger's spirits were buoyed by the frequent visits and vigorous support of his friends, his uncle and most of all, his wife, Trish, whose insistence on his innocence to all who would listen was reported to him by Roger Lee. And then, suddenly, Trish's visits stopped and the truth of a rumor that she was now persuaded of his guilt became too obvious to ignore.

Roger fell into a deep depression, and on June 4 he tried to commit suicide. He remained depressed for several months, and then gradually began to regain his spirits. The credit largely belonged to the Reverend Michael Trent, pastor of the Little Prater Baptist Church which Roger's grandparents attended regularly and where he had occasionally gone to Sunday school as a child. As Roger would say later, he had a negative attitude about religion before his arrest, but as the magnitude of his situation began to overwhelm him, he turned to religion for the strength to cope with his problems on a daily basis. Soon he was a regular attendant at jailhouse services, began writing for a monthly church publication and started a correspondence Bible course. By the time of his trial, he had completed 136 lessons.

With his spirits revived, Roger Coleman also began to take an active interest in his defense. He was not happy with what he observed.

Following the denial of Coleman's motion for change of venue, Judge Persin had continued the trial date to March 15, 1982. On February 15, Roger wrote a two-page letter to Judge Persin asking him to reconsider his denial of the venue motion. In his letter Coleman said he thought his lawyers had been ill prepared for the motion, and described why. He also told the judge that his family had circulated a petition that had been signed by a lot of people who said they did not believe he could get a fair trial in Buchanan County. Judge Persin did not change his mind, but it could be said that Coleman's handwritten letter was more persuasive than anything his lawyers had presented in support of the venue motion.

Two weeks later, on March 2, Roger wrote a letter to his sister-in-law Peggy Stiltner in which he once again declared his innocence of Wanda's murder. He enclosed the experts' reports and other papers the prosecutor had turned over to his lawyers and supported his denials with a long, logically constructed argument that the evidence as a whole showed he did not and could not have committed the crime.

Coleman addressed the letter to Peggy because he knew Trish had turned against him and he hoped Peggy would be more receptive to his plea. In conclusion Roger wrote:

> Please show these papers to your family, and Brad if you want to, so they can see I'm innocent. I don't have any hard feelings against Brad because I know he can only believe what the police say, I'd feel the same way if I were in his shoes. . . . I've done everything I know to do. I've tried to fire my lawyers because they're not doing the best they can and the judge won't let me. I've tried for a change of venue and the judge turned me down. I've done a lot of research and other things. I believe I've done more than my lawyers have. In 17 more days it will be over and I hope for the best. . . . I hope more than anything that if I get out that Trish will give me another chance. I love her more than anyone will ever know and it has been real hard without her. I know that her and all of you have suffered alot also. I just hope that soon the suffering will be over for all of us. . . .
>
> Peg, I just ask that you do me one favor, write me and tell me what you and your family think of these papers, please, because it's important to me.

Peggy never wrote. Shown a copy of Roger's letter that turned up in the Commonwealth's Attorney's file fifteen years later, she says she never received it.

Chapter 7

Trial

At 9:26 A.M. on March 15, 1982, the case of *Commonwealth* v. *Roger Keith Coleman* was called for trial before Judge Nicholas Persin in the Buchanan County Courthouse. It was exactly one year from the day Wanda Fay McCoy was buried.

After denying a defense motion for separate trials on the rape and murder charges, Judge Persin went to work selecting a jury.

Of forty-nine prospective jurors questioned by the judge and the lawyers, twenty-four admitted they had heard, read or talked about the case. Fourteen admitted they had already formed an opinion on Coleman's guilt, and were excused. Additional jurors were excused because they opposed the death penalty. The rest assured the court they had no opinion on the case, and could be impartial. By six-thirty that evening the jury was seated.

At the beginning of every trial the lawyers for each side are given an opportunity to tell the jury what they think the evidence will show. Like an overture, opening statements provide a preview of the evidence to come, with each side emphasizing the facts they consider the most helpful. Experienced lawyers believe this is likely to be their most important performance during the trial. Studies have repeatedly shown that jurors often make a judgment about how a case should turn out on the basis of opening statements, and that about 80 percent of the time they vote the same way when it comes time to render a verdict.

Mickey McGlothlin presented the opening statement for the prosecution. He began dramatically, describing Wanda McCoy, her youth, her large family and the gruesome scene that greeted her husband when he arrived home from work almost exactly a year earlier. He proceeded to describe in detail the investigation that followed the murder in terms that made it seem careful and complete in every respect, while emphasizing those facts which supported the state's theory of the case. He said that the murderer had been admitted to the house voluntarily, and that Roger Coleman was one of the few people whom Wanda would have admitted. He told the jury of Coleman's visit to the Stiltners' trailer, and asserted that when Coleman arrived that night, Sandy Stiltner had looked at a clock and saw it was 10:20 P.M. McGlothlin described, with great emphasis, the scientific evidence, and especially the comparison of the pubic hairs, asserting that "it would be extremely unlikely that anyone else would have hair that would be consistent with this hair." In conclusion, McGlothlin hinted that there would be some evidence that Coleman had admitted involvement in the crime, and told the jury that at the end of the case he would ask them to find Coleman "guilty of the capital murder and rape of Wanda Fay McCoy."

McGlothlin's opening statement was well calculated to leave the jury with the impression that Roger Coleman was guilty, and that the evidence of his guilt was overwhelming. Thus the burden fell on defense counsel to counter that impression by describing the warm and friendly relationship between Roger and the McCoys before the murder, by demonstrating the weak and circumstantial nature of the state's scientific evidence and by presenting in detail Coleman's alibi, with special emphasis on the testimony of Philip VanDyke—the irreconcilable conflict between his observations about time and that attributed to Sandra Stiltner, the improbability that VanDyke could be wrong, given the time card showing when he clocked in at his job, and the impossibility of Coleman being the murderer if VanDyke was right. Other details the prosecutor left out would not only suggest the defendant's innocence but also tend to weaken McGlothlin's credibility: the pry mark on the door; the fact that the victim's fingernails were broken but no scratches were found on Coleman; and the fact that while Coleman's clothes were covered with coal dust, the state's own expert found that the substance found on the victim's body was soil, not coal dust.

Given the facts, a well-crafted opening for the defense would at least even the field, and perhaps leave a majority of the jury believing that Coleman might well be innocent. Instead, Steve Arey delivered a brief opening statement that started by telling the jury, almost apologetically, that he and Jordan had been appointed by the court and so had the duty "to do the very best job we can for him, to see that the truth is out here"; moved on to an apology for taking so much time on the jury selection; reminded the jury about the presumption of innocence and that what McGlothlin had said was not evidence; and then gave a short, vague description of Coleman's alibi and the theory that he had had no time to commit the crime, without, however, mentioning any names or even telling the jury that most of the defense testimony about when the witnesses saw Coleman on the night of the murder was undisputed. Philip VanDyke's name wasn't even mentioned; nor did Arey tell the jury about VanDyke's time card or emphasize the crucial importance of his testimony. The scientific evidence was ignored altogether, leaving unchallenged McGlothlin's exaggerated claim about the importance of the pubic hairs. Also unanswered was McGlothlin's enigmatic statement that there would be evidence that Coleman had admitted the crime.

The presentation of witnesses began with Roger Coleman already in a deep hole.

The Case for the Commonwealth

Mickey McGlothlin called Brad McCoy as his first witness. The jury sat transfixed as the slight, soft-spoken young man, widowed for a year at age twenty-one, described what he had seen when he came home from work at about 11:15 P.M. on March 10, 1981.

On cross-examination, the defense had two obvious choices—to ask Brad McCoy nothing at all, since nothing he had said was seriously disputed and nothing he had said implicated Coleman in the horrible crime he described; or to ask him a few carefully crafted questions to demonstrate that he probably arrived home closer to 11:05 than his estimate of 11:15. The earlier Brad arrived home, the less likely it was that Roger Coleman had time to commit the crime, and, given the events Brad described before his father called the sheriff and the fact that the call to the sheriff was logged in at 11:21, it seems clear that he arrived home well before 11:15. Hezzie McCoy would testify that about ten minutes elapsed between the time he received Brad's call and the time he called the sheriff, and Brad didn't call his father until after he checked around the outside of the house, unlocked the door, discovered his wife and looked around the house for the killer.

A second, more dangerous, but more important subject of possible cross-examination was the fact that some months earlier Wanda McCoy had received obscene phone calls which she believed were coming from Danny Ray Stiltner, her sister Peggy's ex-husband. The calls stopped when Brad and Wanda changed their phone number. Roger and Trish clearly had the new number; Danny Stiltner didn't. Certainly it would be safer to elicit this information from a friendly witness, rather than on cross-examination of Brad McCoy, who by now had been persuaded that Roger was guilty, but in the absence of such a witness, one way to bring out those facts was on cross-examination of Brad.

For the defense, Steve Arey chose neither course, instead engaging McCoy in a rambling cross-examination with no discernible purpose, which served only to highlight the state's claim that there was no forced entry into the house, that the door had been locked and that Roger Coleman lived close by—facts that perfectly fit Mickey McGlothlin's theory of the case. Arey never challenged Brad's estimate of when he arrived home, nor did the defense at any time in the trial elicit evidence of the obscene phone calls and the Thompson family's belief that they had come from Danny Stiltner. Wanda's belief that she recognized the voice of Danny Stiltner could have been difficult to prove since she was not alive to testify, although the judge might well have admitted her statements on the subject to Brad and others, and the fact that the calls stopped when Brad and Wanda changed their phone number was surely admissible. Certainly the totality of circumstances would have provided the defense with an argument that the killer was not Roger Coleman but probably the person who had made the obscene phone calls.

Brad McCoy was followed to the stand by his father, by the sheriff's dispatcher who received Hezzie's phone call and by a succession of town policemen and deputy sheriffs who thereafter arrived at the murder scene and entered the house. Each described what he saw and did and swore he had not touched or moved anything. Each was subjected to a brief, purposeless cross-examination.

After the lunch recess the state called Grundy Police Chief Randy Jackson, who told of his arrival at the scene, his sense that the murder had occurred so recently that the killer might still be in or near the house, his call to Jack Davidson, and also of clearing the house while waiting for the arrival of the evidence van. According to Jackson, there was no sign that the house had been broken into, and while he was inside he had checked all the windows and found them nailed or locked. Mickey McGlothlin ended his direct examination by eliciting from Jackson the odd statement that at dawn the next morning, March 11, he measured the water in Slate Creek at the point closest to the McCoy house and found it to be ten to twelve inches deep.

Randy Jackson's testimony that he measured the depth of Slate Creek at dawn the morning after the murder and found that it was the same depth as the dampness Jack Davidson says he found the next day on the legs of Roger Coleman's blue jeans was odd for two reasons. First, there was no water or wet footprints found in the house, and Roger Coleman's pants were not obtained by the police until the next afternoon, so one wonders what could have prompted Jackson to measure the creek that morning. Second, Jackson's own report of his activities that night says nothing about measuring the creek. Indeed, none of the available reports refer to such a measurement at any time during the investigation. Nor does there appear to be any report that anyone checked the windows in the murder house and found them locked or nailed. Years later Jackson said it was someone else who measured the creek, and conceded that his testimony that the creek was measured the morning after the murder was a mistake—it was done after Coleman's wet pants were turned over.

What the written police reports did or did not include is significant for several reasons. Police forces routinely train their officers on the importance of recording everything they do in the course of an investigation in detail, with special emphasis on activities and observations that might be important to the solution of the crime.

The discrepancy between Randy Jackson's testimony and the only known police report of his activities on the night Wanda McCoy was murdered and similar discrepancies affecting other prosecution witnesses raise a host of questions about the conduct of the police and prosecutors and the performance of Roger Coleman's trial lawyers that have confused the case for years, and have never been fully resolved.

One reason for the confusion is that, unlike the rule in most state and federal criminal cases, Virginia does not require prosecutors to provide the defense with the statements or interview reports of its witnesses, even those who actually testify. Only reports that contain information suggesting the defendant may be innocent or evidence that contradicts the testimony of a state witness must be turned over, and those requirements are subject to a great deal of leeway when prosecutors and judges decide just what is covered. Thus, a prosecutor might conclude that Jackson's report of his activities on the night of the murder did not have to be turned over to the defense, even though an experienced defense lawyer would surely argue that its omission of any reference to measuring the creek or checking the windows was impeaching of Jackson's testimony that he had done those things.

The only contemporaneous evidence that any witness statements at all were turned over to Roger Coleman's defense team is the state's written response to a defense discovery motion in which McGlothlin turned over three reports relating to the obscene phone calls received by Wanda McCoy and the Thompson family's suspicion of Danny Stiltner. Apparently these were the only statements the prosecutors thought they were required to produce as exculpatory or impeaching. However, rather than take a chance that a judge will later hold that a statement was withheld improperly, some prosecutors will simply turn over all witness statements to the defense, and the state has asserted that additional statements were in fact shown to the defense in this case.

Long after Roger Coleman's trial was over, the question of which, if any, additional police reports or witness statements had been shown to the defense would remain in dispute. If additional statements and reports were produced, no written record was made of it at the time, although years later Terry Jordan would support the state's claim that he had been shown some additional reports.

In any event, whether it was because he had not seen the report, or did not know how to use it, or considered it unimportant, when Terry Jordan cross-examined Randy Jackson, he made no effort to impeach Jackson's testimony about measuring the creek and examining the windows. Nor did he establish with Jackson or any other witness that the banks and bed of Slate Creek are lined with slippery rocks and boulders, which would make it almost impossible to cross without slipping, splashing and in all likelihood falling, especially at night and in a hurry. Jordan did establish that Jackson had not measured the creek on the night of the murder, and inferred that the water level could have changed by the next morning, but otherwise his cross-examination seemed as purposeless as Arey's had been with the earlier witnesses.

In truth, the state's theory that the bottom ten inches or so of Roger Coleman's jeans were wet because he had parked his truck along the road across Slate Creek from Longbottom and waded the creek to reach the McCoy house was ludicrous. For one thing, the worst imaginable place for someone to park if he were trying to avoid being seen in the vicinity of Longbottom is across the creek on the shoulder of Route 83. There, parked alongside the busiest road in the area, where every passing car could see it, and in a place where a parked car would seem unusual, Coleman's blue pickup truck would almost certainly have been seen and remembered after the murder was discovered. Conversely, there were several places to park in the Longbottom area itself that were out of sight of any house or street, and much closer to the McCoy house. Moreover, if the killer had for some inexplicable reason parked on the other side of the creek and waded across in the dark, he then would have had to walk or run several blocks, past a number of occupied houses, exponentially increasing the possibility of detection. And finally, if he had done so, he would inevitably have left some trace of water from his wet pants and shoes in Wanda McCoy's house, but none was found.

On March 20, 1988, Jim McCloskey, an investigator who was trying to test the plausibility of the state's theory, waded Slate Creek at the point nearest the McCoy house and found that no matter how hard he tried, it was impossible to avoid splashing water on his pants up to his crotch and buttocks. The state later belittled that finding by saying that the water level could well have been different on the night of the murder, and they were right.

The Corps of Engineers maintains equipment to monitor the water flow on Levisa Fork at Big Rock, downstream from where Slate Creek enters the river. The Corps maintains daily records of water flow going back for many years, as well as information on rainfall in the area. Those records show that water flows in the area rise and fall significantly, depending on rainfall upstream from the measuring station, and that rain in Grundy begins to register at Big Rock between eighteen and twenty-four hours later. When the rain stops, a similar delay occurs before the river starts to fall. There was a heavy rain in the Grundy area on March 5, 1981, which pushed water flow at Big Rock from 289 cubic feet per second on March 4 to 1,320 cubic feet per second on March 6. There was no more rain between the fifth and the tenth, and water flow decreased each day. Water flows on March 10, 11 and 12, 1981, were 366, 314 and 249 cubic feet per second respectively. On March 20, 1988, when McCloskey waded the creek, flows at Big Rock were 136 cubic feet per second, and they fell to 124 on the twenty-first and to 113 on the twenty-second. In other words, the water flow on Slate Creek was more than twice as high on the night of the murder as it was on the day Jim McCloskey conducted his experiment and found he was unable to avoid splashing water up to his waist and getting it down inside his sixteen-inch boots. However the bottom of Roger Coleman's pant legs got wet on the night of March 10, 1981, it was not from wading across Slate Creek in the dark.

Apart from its improbability, the theory that Roger Coleman had waded Slate Creek to murder Wanda McCoy was a double-edged sword for the state. To park on the highway shoulder, wade the creek in the dark, make your way through the Longbottom neighborhood to the McCoy house and retrace your steps after committing the rape and murder would take much more time than simply driving into the subdivision and parking close to the house. So much longer, in fact, that if it had occurred, it would be unlikely that Coleman had time to commit the murder even if the Stiltners were right about when he was at Boyd's Trailer Park.

In the hands of a skillful defense lawyer, the state's theory could have been used both to undermine the credibility of the prosecution's arguments and to emphasize the lack of time for Coleman to commit the murder. Instead, the defense left Jackson's testimony unchallenged, never brought out the numerous facts that demonstrate the improbability of the prosecution theory and, worse, failed to demonstrate to the jury that if Coleman had waded the creek, there would have been no time left for him to commit the murder. The case went to the jury with the creek theory unchallenged except by Coleman's claim that he may have gotten his pants wet at the bathhouse.

If the state's creek theory was silly, and should have been turned to Coleman's advantage, the theory that Wanda McCoy was killed by someone she knew and admitted to the house at night was more troublesome. If the jury believed it, it was an important circumstantial link in the case against Roger Coleman, which the defense needed to attack in every way possible. If the defense knew about it, the attack should have begun with proof that Jackson's report made no mention of checking the McCoys' windows.

When Randy Jackson left the stand, the state called Dr. Thomas McDonald, who testified that the time of death had been about 10:30 P.M., give or take a half hour, and Mary Smith, the neighbor who took out her garbage at 10:30 and told police the McCoys' porch light had been on. Steve Arey conducted short, pointless cross-examinations of each, failing to bring out that when McDonald first came to the murder house at about 11:40 P.M., he told Randy Jackson that Wanda had been dead only about a half hour. That would place the time of death at about 11:10, and the autopsy report showed that the killer was still there—at least one and probably both of the stab wounds was inflicted after Wanda McCoy was dead. If Coleman had arrived home at 11:05, as he and his grandmother later testified, he would have been home well before Wanda McCoy's throat was slashed, according to McDonald's first estimate. Even if McDonald was able to explain the revision of his opinion about the time of death, in a case in which the state was relying so heavily on scientific evidence, any demonstration of fallibility on the part of the "experts" would have been helpful.

To Arey's credit, however, he did bring out for future reference another fact in McDonald's report—that he had come back to the house the next morning, before Wanda's body was removed, and rolled her over to check for wounds on her back. As a result, the pubic hairs found on Wanda could as easily have come from the floor as from the killer.

Proceeding in chronological order, the prosecutors next called the state's investigators, Kelly Andrews and Jack Davidson, to describe the search of the crime scene they conducted after Andrews arrived from Wytheville with the evidence van.

Andrews testified first, and through him the state placed in evidence the photographs he had taken at the scene, including gruesome pictures of Wanda McCoy lying dead on the floor, naked from the chest down, with stab wounds in her breast and abdomen and her head surrounded by a large pool of blood. Although such photographs are of little relevance to any issue in most murder cases, they are almost always allowed in evidence despite their prejudicial impact on the jury. While Judge Persin kept out some of them as repetitive and unnecessary, most of the pictures the state offered were admitted over defense objection.

There was not much of value for the defense to accomplish with Andrews on cross-examination, but Arey's cross did raise an issue that added to the mystery over which police reports had been provided to the defense. Andrews had prepared a brief report of his collection of evidence at the murder scene. The only piece of evidence specifically identified in the report is "one latent fingerprint . . . lifted from the outside front door screen." On cross, Arey asked Andrews if he found any fingerprints, and Andrews mentioned the print found on the door screen. Arey then asked if any prints were found inside the house. Andrews said there were none, and Arey abandoned the subject. He never again mentioned the print on the screen. It was almost as if he didn't know about the print in advance, and didn't hear or process Andrews's answer. Arey now thinks he did know about the print, but cannot recall seeing any report of the state's effort to identify it. No such report was turned over to the defense, nor do the available records contain such a report, or any indication that the defense lawyers specifically requested its production. Andrews, who now lives in Arizona, cannot recall what happened to the print, although he concedes that normally some report would have been made, even if the print turned out to be too smudged to identify.

One thing is certain. The fingerprint on Wanda McCoy's front door was not identified as belonging to Roger Coleman, or it would have been a featured part of the state's case. The print may not have been clear enough to identify, or it may have belonged to Wanda or someone else who could not have been the killer, but if it belonged to a stranger, or someone whose prints were not on file, the defense could have used it to create doubt.

Following Kelly Andrews, Jack Davidson took the stand for the first of four appearances in the trial. With the permission of the court, Mickey McGlothlin had divided up Davidson's testimony into segments that fit the chronological order of the state's case and made it easier for the jury to follow. The first segment of his testimony was a perfunctory description of his participation in the search of the murder house, and the cross-examination was equally perfunctory.

Although Davidson said that he, Kelly Andrews and Roger Owens had searched the house thoroughly, starting at the front door, Mickey McGlothlin carefully avoided asking him what they had found. Davidson, however, had prepared a written report describing the search of the crime scene in some detail, and that report contained a nugget of pure gold for the defense, a statement that cast doubt on the central theme of the state's case against Roger Coleman—that the murderer had to be one of the few people Wanda McCoy would have admitted to her house at night because there was no sign of forced entry.

Randy Jackson had established the foundation for the state's theory by testifying that when he entered the house he saw no sign of forced entry, but he did not claim to have made a careful inspection. Jack Davidson did, and his official investigation report revealed that on the front-door molding, three feet two inches from the floor, "a pressure mark which appeared to be a pry mark was found. This mark appeared to have been made with very little pressure." Attached to Davidson's report was Roger Owens's sketch of the crime scene, which made specific reference to the pry mark and included a separate drawing to illustrate where it was found.

Roger Coleman's lawyers did not bring out the existence of the pry mark, either with Jack Davidson or later with Roger Owens, and the jury never learned that these experienced investigators had found evidence that someone may have tried to pry open Wanda McCoy's front door.

When Jack Davidson took the stand for the second time, an incident occurred that again raised a question of whether the defense had seen the state's witness interview reports, or knew how to use them if they had. This time Davidson's testimony centered on his interviews of

Roger Coleman on March 11 and 12, and on the physical evidence Coleman provided at Davidson's request. Coleman had told his lawyers that when he was first interviewed Davidson had examined his face, hands and chest for scratches, and found none. On cross-examination, Steve Arey asked Davidson: "Were you looking for anyone with scratches particularly or anything like that?" Davidson replied: "No, sir. We were not."

As unartful as was Arey's question, Davidson's response was misleading. The photographs of Wanda McCoy's body showed that her fingernails were broken and jagged, a sure sign that she had tried to fight off her attacker, and Dr. Oxley's autopsy report also mentioned the broken nails. Moreover, while Davidson's report of his interview with Roger Coleman does not mention checking for scratches, the report of his initial interview with Brad McCoy demonstrates that the police were indeed looking for scratches, stating specifically that Brad did not have any fresh wounds. If Coleman's lawyers had seen the Brad McCoy interview report and knew how to use it, they could have demonstrated that Davidson's answer was disingenuous, and even without the report they could have cast doubt on it by reference to the broken nails and their investigative significance. Furthermore, if the lawyers had interviewed Wanda McCoy's neighbors, they would have known that the police also searched two neighbors for scratches. Jordan and Arey did none of these things, and Davidson's answer went unchallenged. While the defense did raise the broken fingernails in its closing argument, they lost an important opportunity to damage Jack Davidson's credibility. Years later, Davidson would concede that his answer "was a misstatement on [his] part." He said he probably made the misstatement because by the time of the trial he knew the autopsy report said that no appreciable material was found under Wanda's nails.

Meanwhile, Davidson was able to suggest that Coleman had lied about how he got his pants wet, pointing out that he had first claimed they probably got wet at the mine and then changed his story to the shower room when Davidson informed him that there was no water at the mine site. In fact, there is evidence suggesting there may in fact have been wet areas around the mine site, but the defense lawyers had not gone to the mine, and thus could not counter the state's inference that Coleman had deliberately lied.

Davidson was also allowed to recite what Coleman had told him about his activities on the night of the crime, and a typed version of the statement, prepared from Davidson's notes, was received in evidence. The point, as McGlothlin would remind the jury in his closing argument, was that Coleman had "left out" his visit to the Stiltners at Boyd's Trailer Park. The tape recording that Davidson made of his first interview of Roger Coleman should have revealed whether Coleman in fact left out the visit to the Stiltners, inadvertently or deliberately, or whether Davidson, inadvertently or deliberately, left it out of his report. Unfortunately, Davidson testified, the recorder had malfunctioned.

With the stage thus set, Mickey McGlothlin and Tom Scott moved to the central part of their case—the presentation of scientific evidence that they hoped would persuade the jury that Roger Coleman was guilty.

The first scientific expert to testify was the pathologist who had performed the autopsy, Dr. David Oxley. Oxley had little to contribute to the case other than a description of the evidence he collected and forwarded to Elmer Gist and Elmer Miller for analysis, consisting of blood and hair samples, swabs from Wanda's mouth, rectum and vagina, and a swab of the black substance from her hands. The state, however, was able to use him to offer in evidence some additional photos of the victim on the theory that they supported his testimony on the wholly uncontested question of the cause of Wanda McCoy's death. Like most autopsy photos, these were especially gruesome, but Judge Persin admitted them over defense objection.

On cross-examination Steve Arey elicited one important fact that McGlothlin had steered away from—that the two stab wounds were each about four inches deep. The blade of the pocketknife that Roger had turned over to the police and that the state would characterize as the murder weapon was only three inches long. Arey failed, however, to elicit the fact that when a victim's fingernails are broken it may result in the victim having either human tissue or clothing fibers under the nails, which can help to identify a killer. Oxley said in his report that there appeared to be "no appreciable quantity of material beneath the nails," but there is no indication that any microscopic examination was done by Oxley or any other forensic expert.

The defense also failed to point out several apparent errors in

Oxley's autopsy report, especially the statement that there were no injuries to Wanda's extremities—photographs show what appear to be a bruise on her upper arm and cuts on her hands. Failure to bring out these apparent errors was another mistake. For one thing, the bruise on Wanda McCoy's arm fits nicely into a theory that would have explained one of the oddest things about the case—the fact that although Wanda was clearly killed in the bedroom after a struggle in the living room, and although there were neighbors at home and close by on three sides of the house, no one heard any screams or noises. It seems almost impossible that Wanda was unable to scream if there was only one killer, especially since her broken fingernails and cut hands indicate that at some point during the struggle she was facing her killer with her hands free. But if there were two killers, and one of them seized her from behind, with one arm around her head and mouth to muffle her screams, and the other grasping her upper arm, she might well have been subdued and dragged into the bedroom unheard. And that would also explain why the struggle was apparently so brief—barely disturbing the angle of the coffee table; and how someone—a second man approaching her from the front—could have cut her throat from ear to ear with a single, uninterrupted stroke, as Dr. Oxley interpreted the wound in his testimony.

At the very least, pointing out the apparent omissions in the report of one expert might have helped lessen the credibility of the state's next witness, Elmer Gist.

After establishing Gist's credentials, Tom Scott led him through his identification of the blood type of the sperm found in Wanda McCoy's vagina and Coleman's blood, both type B; his comparison of Wanda McCoy's blood with the tiny blood spots found on Coleman's blue jeans, both type O; and his comparison of the pubic hair found on Wanda McCoy with Coleman's pubic hair.

Years later, in response to the author's question about what evidence in the case he thought had the most powerful impact on the jury, Judge Persin said it was Elmer Gist's testimony about the comparison of the pubic hairs. It was, Judge Persin observed, the first and only testimony that seemed to tie Roger Coleman to the murder specifically. The blood comparisons meant only that Coleman, along with a huge number of other people, *might* be guilty, but the hair comparison seemed to deal with Roger Coleman alone. The jury, Persin said, was on the edge of their chairs from the start of Gist's testimony, and Gist made an effective and persuasive witness as he explained the characteristics of hair, and how hairs are microscopically compared, using a chart he had prepared to illustrate his testimony.

Gist's chart, however, dealt with hair comparison in general. It did not show anything about the hair found on Wanda McCoy, or about Roger Coleman's hair—and Elmer Gist never did present the jury with any enlarged photographs or other depiction of the hairs in question. Nor did he compare the pubic hairs found on Wanda with anyone other than Coleman and Wanda herself—not even her husband Brad. Nevertheless, when he asserted that he had made a comparison of those hairs with Roger's pubic hair, and that the hairs were "consistent" with each other, meaning, he said, that it was "possible, but unlikely" that the hairs found on Wanda could have come from anyone other than Roger Coleman, the jurors exchanged glances and settled back in their seats.

Terry Jordan undertook Gist's cross-examination. He had never examined a blood or hair expert before. He was apparently unaware of the commonly available PGM test, which, if Gist had performed it, would have substantially narrowed the field of people who could have produced the sperm in Wanda's vagina. He also seemed not to know about the three additional enzyme tests that could be performed on blood but that Gist, for some reason, failed to perform on the blood found on Coleman's pants. Those tests would have reduced the people who could have produced the blood from 45 percent of the population to a tiny number.

The failure of the prosecution to perform important investigative procedures that might have cleared the defendant is one of the most common reasons that juries cite for finding "reasonable doubt" in criminal cases.

If Gist failed to perform those tests without a valid explanation, it could have been devastating to the state's case, but apparently the defense lawyers did not interview Gist before trial or even attempt to obtain the contemporaneous notes he had made as he performed his work, notes that are essential to the adequate preparation of the cross-examination of an expert witness. Thus, even if he knew about the other tests, Jordan did not know if there was any reason for not performing them, and the jury was never informed about this important investigative omission.

Jordan was also apparently unaware of the fact that many hair experts believe it is impossible to make a judgment that hairs are consistent on the basis of as few hairs as were available to Gist in this case, or that most experts believe that even if sufficient comparison hairs are available to find consistency, it is an exaggeration to say it is unlikely the hairs came from different people. Indeed, in the 1970s the Law Enforcement Assistance Administration sponsored a laboratory proficiency testing program which, among other things, tested the accuracy of hair analysis by approximately 235 state, local and private crime laboratories nationwide. So imperfect was the "science" of hair analysis that the laboratories failed more than 50 percent of the time on four of the five tests. On one test the misidentification rate was 67 percent! If Jordan knew these things, he did not confront Gist with authoritative writings on the subject, nor did he call a hair expert of his own to testify to these facts. Indeed, he did not talk to any hair expert, or have any of Gist's results checked by another expert. His preparation for the cross-examination of Elmer Gist on the crucial hair and blood testimony was to read articles about hair and blood evidence in a book for lawyers called *Proof of Facts*.

Jordan's cross-examination of Elmer Gist was as good as could be expected under those circumstances, but it left the jury with the unchallenged impression that Gist had done all he could to determine whether the semen came from Coleman and the blood from Wanda McCoy, and that it was unlikely that the pubic hair found on Wanda's body could have come from anyone other than Coleman. The heart of the state's circumstantial case against Coleman was unshaken and essentially uncontested.

Following the testimony of Elmer Gist, the state recalled Jack Davidson and through him tried to put into evidence the blue jeans Roger Coleman had worn the night of the murder, on which Gist had found traces of type O human blood. The pants were contained in a paper bag, which, it turned out, had been unsealed a few days earlier so that the lawyers could personally examine the evidence. Because they had remained unsealed between then and the time they were brought into court, Steve Arey objected to their admission, and despite Davidson's testimony that they had been in his possession the whole time and had not been tampered with, Judge Persin somewhat surprisingly denied their admission.

As it turned out, it was a Pyrrhic victory for the defense. As the photographs of Wanda McCoy's body had shown, there was a smear of blood on the front of her right thigh, and in closing argument, without objection, Tom Scott told the jury that it was that blood which got on Coleman's jeans when he was on top of her, raping her. Elmer Gist, Scott said, had testified that there was blood on the left leg of the jeans, which would match up with Wanda's right leg. In fact, Gist had said nothing about the location of the blood he had found on the blue jeans, and a photograph reveals that with one tiny exception all the blood spots Gist tested were on the right leg of the jeans, not the left. If the blue jeans had been admitted in evidence, the jury could have seen for itself that Scott's argument did not fit the evidence.

Next on the witness stand was Scott Stiltner. As he had told Jack Davidson a year earlier, Stiltner testified on direct examination that Coleman had come to his trailer sometime between 10:15 and 10:30 on the night of the murder, a time he estimated from the TV show he was watching. At the end of Steve Arey's cross-examination, however, Stiltner narrowed the time even further—his wife, he said, had looked at a clock and seen that it was 10:20.

Sure enough, when Sandra Stiltner was called as the state's next witness, her testimony about what time Coleman knocked on the door was as follows: "As I looked at the door, the clock is kindly [sic] over the stove right along side the door. I just automatically looked up at the clock to see what time it was. . . . It was about twenty after 10:00 P.M."

Sandy Stiltner's statement that she could positively place Coleman's visit at 10:20 P.M. was crucial. If the jury believed that she had looked at a clock when Coleman arrived and somehow saw that it was 10:20, there would have been time, although not much, for Coleman to commit the murder and be out of the McCoys' house a few minutes after 11:00 P.M. If instead they believed that Coleman was more than eight miles away at Looney Creek until about 10:30, as Philip VanDyke would testify, and then drove to Boyd's and visited the Stiltners, there was not.

It is not clear whether prior to McGlothlin's opening statement the defense lawyers knew that Sandy Stiltner was going to say she had looked at a clock when Roger arrived. In any event, they made no effort to question or weaken her testimony on cross-examination. The defense failed to bring out the fact that Coleman's visit could have been much later and still have occurred during *Hart To Hart*, which is an hour-long program. Nor did they lay the foundation to question whether someone sitting in a room lit only by a television set could have accurately read the clock from across the room. But, then, the defense had apparently never conducted an in-depth interview with these two crucial witnesses, and even after McGlothlin's opening statement, neither Jordan nor Arey visited the Stiltners' trailer to see if they had a clock "over the stove, alongside the door," much less whether it could be read in the dark. Sandy Stiltner's assertion that she knew exactly when Roger arrived at Boyd's Trailer Park was left essentially unchallenged by the cross-examination.

Next Brad McCoy was recalled to testify that Wanda McCoy had begun menstruating the day before she was killed, that they had not had intercourse since before then and that in any event Brad was blood type A, all for the apparent purpose of proving that the sperm found in Wanda was not her husband's. Ironically, the time would come when the state would have to argue that some of her husband's sperm *was* in fact in Wanda's vagina when Dr. Oxley made the vaginal swab during his autopsy.

The state's last witness was Roger Matney, a habitual criminal who had been in the Buchanan County Jail with Roger Coleman after Coleman's arrest. On May 29, 1981, Matney, who admitted he had been convicted of four felonies in Virginia and one in Kentucky, was in jail awaiting sentencing on one of the felony charges when he told his jailers that he wanted to talk to Jack Davidson. Roger Coleman, he claimed, had confessed that he had been involved in Wanda McCoy's murder. His story, which he repeated on the witness stand, was that Coleman had said he and another man had been at Wanda's house when Brad called at nine o'clock, that after she got off the phone the other man cut Wanda with a knife when she started screaming, and that the two of them had then raped her. The knife, he said, was supposed to have been hidden under a bridge in a paper bag. McGlothlin concluded his examination of Matney by eliciting the statement that Coleman had also said something about a paper towel that was in the bathroom. In an effort to support Matney's credibility, the prosecutors would later tell the jury that the yellow tissue found next to Wanda's body in the bedroom was the paper towel, that Matney could not have known about it except from

Coleman and that Coleman could not have known about it except by being there.

On cross, Arey established that Matney had failed to mention additional convictions, and that although he had been sentenced to four years in jail the prior spring, he was already out, thus suggesting he had received favorable treatment in return for his testimony.

It is not clear whether Steve Arey had a handwritten draft of Matney's statement to Davidson, in which Matney also claimed that Coleman had drawn him a diagram of the murder scene, which Matney believed was back in his cell. Davidson left that part of Matney's statement out of his typewritten report, and if Arey knew about it he didn't bring it out on cross, despite the fact that no such diagram had been found. Indeed, no report has been found relating to looking for either the diagram or the knife under the bridge. Arey was also apparently unaware that at the very same time Matney testified, he was facing serious additional charges, including beating and threatening to kill a fellow inmate in order to force him to perform fellatio.

In years to come, both Jack Davidson and Randy Jackson would concede that they gave little credence to Roger Matney's testimony, but, as Jackson put it, we figured we had to give it to Mickey, and Mickey figured he should put it before the jury and let them decide whether to believe it. Of course, the jury would have been better able to make that judgment if they had known more about Mr. Matney.

With the testimony of Roger Matney, the state rested its case.

The Case for the Defense

As its first witness, the defense called Elmer Miller, the soils expert from the Virginia Bureau of Forensic Science who had examined the material found on Wanda McCoy's hands. Although the prosecutors knew that Mr. Miller had determined that the material was soil, not coal dust, during the state's case witnesses had frequently referred to the dark substance that had covered Wanda's hands, thighs and sweater as a black, dusty substance, and the state had brought out that Coleman's coveralls were covered with coal dust and that his blue jeans also showed a "black stain" on the upper legs.

The Buchanan County jurors could hardly have failed to make the connection the state desired between the "black dust" on Wanda and the coal dust on Roger's clothes, and now the prosecution objected to allowing Miller to testify on the grounds that the defense had not proved a chain of custody, that is, they had not proved that the material Miller studied had come from Wanda McCoy. If the prosecution's objection had been sustained, the jury would have been left with the impression that Wanda McCoy was covered with coal dust from Roger Coleman's clothes, even though the state's own expert had found that it was not coal dust at all. It was a daring, if shameless, ploy—but Judge Persin was not buying. Miller was allowed to testify that he had examined the swab sent to him by Dr. Oxley and found no coal dust, but rather a small lump of soil and bits of vegetation. "Definitely not coal. That's what I was seeking."

On cross, Tom Scott could only bring out that the swabs Miller studied had come from Wanda's hands but no other part of her body. Of course, that was because the hands were the only area that had been swabbed by Dr. Oxley. The substance also covered Wanda's sweater, which the state could easily have submitted to Miller if they were not satisfied that his report of "no coal dust" applied to all of the black material.

It was a good start by the defense on an important issue, and provided substantial ammunition for the defendant's closing argument, but it could have been made even stronger. Miller had testified that from 1959 through 1977 he had been employed as a forensic scientist by the FBI, retiring in 1977 as chief of the Mineralogy Unit. As described by John McPhee in a 1996 *New Yorker* article titled "The Gravel Page," the FBI Mineralogy Unit was and is the world leader in forensic mineralogy, often using its expertise to locate the exact scene of a crime by careful analysis of a few grains of recovered dirt or sand. While the substance sent to Miller was a small amount, the state never sent him the sweater, which was covered with it, or asked him to try to determine the source of the material. Could it have come from the area around the house, thus showing that Wanda had been assaulted outside and destroying the central theory of the state's case? Miller would have to say that he didn't know because he was never asked. If the defense had established these facts, and displayed the photo of Wanda McCoy's sweater to the jury, the value of Miller's testimony would have been greatly enhanced. Once again, the defense attorneys either did not realize the full value of what they had or did not know how to use it.

Following Miller, the defense called the men Coleman had seen and talked to on the night of the murder, starting from the time he left home for work and ending with Philip VanDyke. Hour by hour their undisputed testimony traced Coleman's movements, corroborating the story he had told Davidson and would soon repeat for the jury. When it was VanDyke's turn, he testified that his conversation with Coleman at the mouth of Looney Creek had lasted until 10:25 or 10:30, and that he based that estimate on the fact that he clocked in to work at 10:41. Arey brought out that the Black Watch Coal Company tipple where VanDyke worked was only a quarter of a mile from where he and Coleman had talked, and that he had left before Coleman and went straight to work. Unfortunately, Arey did not have VanDyke describe in detail the routine he had gone through upon arriving at work and clocking in, which would have emphasized the reliability of his time estimate.

Nor did Arey introduce VanDyke's time card into evidence. That Philip VanDyke had clocked in at 10:41 was undisputed, but the time card itself, had it been received in evidence, would have been in the jury room during the jury's deliberations and served as a constant reminder of the likely accuracy of VanDyke's crucial testimony about when Roger Coleman left Looney Creek. No experienced trial lawyer would fail to appreciate the value of such an exhibit.

With adequate support and embellishment of VanDyke's testimony and even a moderately effective cross-examination of Sandra Stiltner's testimony about the clock, at least some of the jurors would likely have concluded that VanDyke was right, and that Roger Coleman simply did not have time to commit the murder of Wanda McCoy. As it was, however, Mickey McGlothlin would assert in closing argument that Philip VanDyke had simply "guessed" about the time, while Stiltner had been able to place it exactly.

Next on the witness stand were Roger Coleman's wife, Patricia Thompson Coleman, and his grandmother, Garnett Coleman. Calling them was a mistake.

Trish Coleman testified first. Roger had always claimed that he got home at about 11:05 P.M. on the night of the murder, and his wife had supported that estimate in interviews with Coleman's lawyers. By the time Roger went on trial a year later, however, as the defense must have known, the police had persuaded Trish Coleman that her husband had in fact murdered her sister. On the witness stand, she denied knowing when Roger arrived home, and the defense lawyers succeeded only in displaying her hostility to their client. That his own wife no longer believed him was sure to injure his credibility with the jury.

Garnett Coleman did support Roger's time estimate, but she was effectively impeached by her earlier statement that he had arrived home at about the time the eleven o'clock news ended. Her explanation that she had just gotten out of the hospital and was "all mixed up" was unconvincing, and her repeated, volunteered statement that "he had not been drinking and he wasn't nervous" served to suggest that Coleman might have been both, or at least that he had a problem with drinking that worried his grandmother.

In truth, it is difficult to believe that Coleman arrived home as early as 11:05 if he left Boyd's at 10:45 and then went to the bathhouse to shower and change clothes, as he would assert. The defense would probably have been better off leaving the subject alone, except for a rough estimate by Coleman of when he arrived.

It was now time for Roger Coleman to try to save himself.

Shortly before 11:30 A.M. on Thursday, March 18, Roger Keith Coleman took the witness stand to testify on his own behalf. Whether the defendant in a criminal case will testify is often the most difficult strategic question faced by the defense. If the defendant does not testify, lawyers fear the jury will assume he has something to hide. If he does testify, he will be subjected to cross-examination that may destroy his credibility in the eyes of the jury and assure his conviction.

The decision of whether the defendant will testify is especially hard when the defendant has a prior felony conviction, because if he testifies, the conviction will usually be made known to the jury, some of whom will feel that if he committed one crime it is likely he committed another. Since most of Roger Coleman's alibi was corroborated by other witnesses, many lawyers would say it was foolish for him testify in this case. It would be unfair, however, to criticize the defense decision for Coleman to take the stand. It was a judgment call on which the finest lawyers could differ, especially since in the small community of Grundy, most of the jurors probably already knew about Coleman's prior conviction.

Those who saw him say Coleman was neither an exceptionally good witness nor an exceptionally bad one. He told his story without hesitation or difficulty. Steve Arey had prepared well for this part of the case and took Coleman through a detailed description of his conduct on the evening of the murder, ending with a flat denial that he had raped or murdered Wanda McCoy or knew who did. He avoided stating unequivocally that his pants had gotten wet at the bathhouse, but said that was probably how it happened since the room was small and the only place to put his clothes was on the floor, which was wet and uneven. Unfortunately, neither Arey nor Jordan had visited the bathhouse to see whether that testimony could be effectively supported with a photograph or a jury visit.

Coleman denied telling Matney that he had been involved in the murder, but said he had given some of the people he was in jail with information about the crime that he had learned from his wife, his uncle and his in-laws. All in all, at the end of his direct testimony, Roger Coleman had reason to feel he had given a good account of himself.

Mickey McGlothlin's cross-examination was argumentative and hostile, full of innuendos that Coleman had planned to rape Sandra Stiltner until he found her husband at home, and direct accusations framed as questions:

Q. You didn't think she [Wanda] was pretty?
A. No, I didn't.
Q. Was this before you killed her or after you killed her that you
   didn't think she was pretty?
A. I didn't kill her.

Coleman remained calm, and for the most part handled the badgering well. One problem arose when McGlothlin asked Coleman how he got type O blood on his pants and Roger speculated that it might have come from someone who got scratched by his cat. McGlothlin effectively ridiculed the suggestion and turned it to his advantage even more by having Tom Scott call Trish Coleman as a rebuttal witness to say she had never seen the cat scratch anyone. The prosecution thus made it clear to any juror who had missed it the first time that Roger's wife had turned against him. To drive the point home, Scott closed his questioning by asking Mrs. Coleman: "How do you feel about your husband right now?" It was a grossly improper question and a defense objection was sustained, but no one could have missed the implication. Coleman would have done well to forget the cat. His other suggestion that he could have brushed up against someone who had cut himself in the coal mine was far more credible. Miners suffer cuts all the time, and whether working or crammed together in the carts that carry them around inside the mine, it is not at all unusual for them to get a small amount of blood on their work clothes.

With the completion of Coleman's testimony, the defense rested. After the state's brief rebuttal testimony all that remained was for the lawyers to present closing arguments. In closing argument the lawyers are free for the first time in the trial to engage in the kind of hyperbole and flamboyant speech the television public associates with the role of a trial lawyer. Apt analogies, colorful language and appeals to emotion all have their place, and many lawyers use them to good effect, but every accomplished trial lawyer knows that a careful weaving of the facts and the law into a logical theory of the case supporting the desired verdict is far more important than verbal pyrotechnics. Cases are often won without brilliant argument, but they cannot be won without the presentation of a logical theory, supported by evidence.

For the prosecution, presenting such a theory was easy. There was no breaking and entering—the killer was voluntarily admitted. Roger Coleman was one of a small number of people who could gain such admission. He was in the vicinity when the murder took place, and had time to commit it. Philip VanDyke was only "guessing" about when Coleman and he parted company, but Sandra Stiltner was certain—she saw a clock. The water on Roger's pants matched the depth of the creek—he waded it, and then changed his story about how he got wet. Most important, the man who raped Wanda had type B blood and so did Roger. Type O blood—the same as Wanda's—was found on Roger's pants at a location that matched a bloodstain on Wanda's thigh and pubic hairs that matched Roger's were found entwined with Wanda's. To top it off, although he didn't tell the exact truth, Coleman had confessed involvement to his fellow inmate in jail.

Tom Scott presented the prosecution theory in full detail, interspersed with emotional appeals for justice and references to Wanda's youth and beauty, to the pain caused Brad and her family by her death and to the killer as inhuman, an animal. If Scott made any mistakes it was in a few exaggerations which, if pointed out by the defense and recalled by the jury, might have cost the prosecution some credibility. His assertion that Coleman had left his audio tape at Sandy Stiltner's to provide an excuse to go back and gain entrance to the house, and that pursuant to that plan Coleman's original intent on the night of the murder had been to rape her, was pure fantasy, unsupported by evidence or logic. Coleman had no idea he was going to be laid off until the night of the murder, and but for that unexpected fact would have been at work that night and every other night when he might expect Sandy's husband to be gone. Philip VanDyke was not just "guessing" about the time—he had established it within a narrow range from his time clock at work. There had been no testimony that the type O blood was on the left leg of Coleman's pants—in fact, most if not all of it was on the right leg. And while Elmer Gist had claimed that it was "unlikely" that the pubic hairs came from anyone other than Roger, he had not said, as Tom Scott did, that it was "highly unlikely."

Although he began slowly, with a disjointed and unfocused discussion of the law, Steve Arey's responding argument for the defense improved when he got to the facts, and was his best work of the trial. If he didn't call the state on all of its exaggerations, he called them on some, and presented a number of logical reasons for the jury to have reasonable doubt about Coleman's guilt. In particular, he emphasized the proof that the substance found on Wanda was dirt, not coal dust, as it surely would have been if Coleman had raped her in his work clothes; the fact that the blade on the knife taken from Coleman and claimed by the state to be the murder weapon was only three inches long while both stab wounds were four inches deep; the fact that Coleman was not scratched despite Wanda's broken fingernails; the fact that something (he should have but didn't specifically mention the pubic hairs) could have gotten on Wanda's body when Dr. McDonald rolled it over on his second visit to the house; the illogical and incredible nature of Matney's testimony; and the lack of time for

Coleman to commit the crime. One could say that he gave insufficient attention to the time issue, and especially to the importance of the dispute between Sandy Stiltner and Philip VanDyke, but, all in all, Arey did well with what he had. His problem was the important, exculpatory evidence he did not have. Among other things, the pry mark on the McCoy's door; the discrepancies between the testimony of prosecution witnesses and the reports they prepared; the important tests that the state's experts had not performed; and the highly subjective nature of the hair comparison went unmentioned, because those facts had not been brought out during the testimony. Nor could Arey urge the jury to examine Philip Van Dyke's time card while considering the time issue—it was not in evidence.

Still and all, after Mickey McGlothlin closed by delivering a well-crafted, emotional but unexceptional rebuttal for the prosecution, it was not at all certain what verdict the jury would return. Years later, Judge Persin said he thought the case could have gone either way. The lawyers must have thought so too—when the jury retired to deliberate, Mickey McGlothlin offered to drop his demand for the death penalty if Coleman would plead guilty. Roger Coleman refused. He was innocent, he said, and if the jury couldn't see it, he would as soon be executed as spend the rest of his life in jail.

The jury retired to begin its deliberations at 6:01 on the evening of March 18, 1982. At 8:15 P.M. Judge Persin sent them to dinner, and they resumed deliberating at 9:35. One hour and fifteen minutes later they had reached a verdict. Roger Keith Coleman was found guilty of rape, and under Virginia law the jury fixed his punishment at life in prison. He was also found guilty of capital murder. A separate hearing would begin the next day to determine the jury's recommendation of the sentence for murder: life in prison, or death in the electric chair. If the sentence was life, it would be final. If it was death, the judge would have the power to review it and substitute a life sentence if he chose to do so.

Under Virginia law, in order to recommend a sentence of death the jury must find beyond a reasonable doubt either that there is a probability that the defendant will commit additional criminal acts of violence constituting a serious threat to society or that his conduct in committing the murder was "outrageously or wantonly vile, horrible or inhuman, in that it involved torture, depravity of mind or aggravated battery to the victim."

Addressing the jurors, Mickey McGlothlin began the sentencing hearing by asserting that the second standard had been met by the evidence the jury had already heard, and that the prosecution would prove the first as well, through the testimony of Mrs. Rife, the woman Roger Coleman was convicted of assaulting five years earlier. The jury had already learned that Coleman had a prior conviction but had not been told the nature of the charge. Now Brenda Rife would be called as a witness to tell her story in detail, and McGlothlin set the stage by describing it himself, in the most inflammatory terms. Steve Arey's brief opening statement told the jury they had a simple but terrible choice, and asked them to listen. The imbalance between the effectiveness of the two opening statements in the penalty phase of the trial mirrored that which had left Coleman in such a deep hole after the opening statements on the guilt phase of the trial.

After Brenda Rife recited her story, the defense lawyers, over their client's objection, called the Reverend Michael Trent and another minister, who testified that they believed Coleman's religious conversion was sincere. Roger Coleman also testified:

> Really, I feel there is nothing the jury can do to me. . . . Last night when the verdict of guilty came back, I lost the only thing that ever meant anything to me, my freedom, my life and my wife, whom I love very much. At that point, the death penalty or life. It doesn't matter. It's up to the Lord now, anyway. I didn't request that those ministers come up here. I told my lawyers last night I didn't want them to come. . . . It's not in their hands anymore. There is nothing more you can do to me. It all happened last night. . . . I don't feel that the Lord should be drug into this. I don't.

At 2:33 P.M. on March 19, after listening to brief closing arguments, the jury retired to choose between life and death for Roger Coleman. It took them a little longer to decide on the penalty than it had to decide guilt or innocence. At 6:17 P.M. they returned to the courtroom and announced they had chosen death.

While Judge Persin had not been surprised by the jury's finding of guilt, he was surprised by their recommendation of a death sentence. The rape and murder of Wanda McCoy had been a terrible crime, but Nicholas Persin did not think the state's circumstantial evidence had created the absolute certainty that would be required to persuade twelve of his fellow citizens to approve the killing of another human being.

If Coleman was shocked or surprised by the jury's decision, he did not show it in the courtroom. Later he was asked to provide a written statement on the subject for Judge Persin, who would have the final say on whether the death penalty should be imposed. In his neat hand, on lined yellow paper, Coleman wrote his response:

> . . . I see very little difference between two life sentences and the death penalty. . . . Considering all that I've already lost I have very little left that matters to me to lose. There's no way I can fear the death penalty, I can't live in the future. I can only continue as I do now, live one day at a time and take whatever comes to me the best way I can.

Judge Persin had never sentenced anyone to death before. He had never given a great deal of thought to the matter, but he guessed that if he had to declare a position, he would say he opposed capital punishment. But he had taken an oath to uphold the law, and to Persin that meant that his personal opinion on the wisdom of the death penalty was irrelevant. It was on the books, and the jury had recommended it. He had the power to overturn their recommendation, but only, he thought, if the jury's findings on the two "aggravating factors" were unsupported.

It was the hardest decision he ever made. The date Persin had set for sentencing was April 23, 1982. Well before the appointed hour the courtroom was full, including members of the Thompson, McCoy and Coleman families. When the lawyers arrived in the courtroom, the judge had his clerk ask them to come back into chambers. Judge Persin said that under the circumstances he thought it would be appropriate to tell them of his decision so that they would be prepared for it when it was announced in open court.

Persin went on to say that he had agonized over the decision day and night since the jury verdict, but had been unable to find any principled basis for overturning the jury recommendation. Therefore, he said, I am going to sentence him to death. As Nicholas Persin spoke, tears rolled down his cheeks.

In the courtroom, Judge Persin quickly announced his sentence, ending with the traditional words: "May God have mercy on your soul."

Book III

—

Death Row

———

Chapter 8

Life on the Row: Mecklenburg

With his conversion from defendant to condemned convict, Roger Coleman's life was about to change in ways even he could not imagine, despite having been in prison before. Judge Persin's benediction had invoked God's mercy when the sentence of death was carried out, but if that was ever to occur, it was years away. Roger Coleman's needs were more immediate.

Two days after he was sentenced to death, Coleman was transported by prison van to the Virginia State Penitentiary in Richmond. It was a seven-hour drive, and Roger was kept in handcuffs and leg irons for the entire trip. Leg irons are steel ankle cuffs joined by a heavy metal chain barely long enough to permit the wearer to walk— with practice. Roger would get plenty of practice.

At the penitentiary Coleman was placed in an isolation cell for a period of evaluation. The cell was in the basement of A Building, where the electric chair was located and where men were brought for deathwatch, a period of about two weeks before a scheduled execution, when the condemned man was kept under constant observation to prevent suicide or escape. Virginia had reinstated the death penalty in 1977, and although no one had yet been executed, several prisoners had been brought to Richmond for deathwatch before their execution dates were continued.

Coleman's evaluation presented no reason to keep him in isolation or assign him to a psychiatric unit, so he was soon transferred to Mecklenburg Penitentiary. About an hour and a half southwest of Richmond, close to the North Carolina border, in 1982 Mecklenburg housed Virginia's most violent criminals, including its death row. It was supposedly the state's most secure prison, and it was a cauldron of violence and corruption.

While most of the guards were honest, hardworking and underpaid, a few were not. According to reports in the *Virginian-Pilot* newspaper, some guards at Mecklenburg allegedly specialized in smuggling drugs, money, alcohol and even weapons to the inmates. Others brutalized the prisoners, who in turn would throw feces at a hated guard, and protest the terrible food they were served by throwing it out of their cells or stopping up their toilets to flood the corridors.

On death row everyone had his own cell. Strangely, that made it easier for the handful of inmates who were vicious sexual predators. Once a predator had raped his victim and so thoroughly intimidated him that the victim no longer had the will to resist, the victim would become known as the predator's "punk," and a corrupt guard might accommodate the arrangement by letting the victim out of his cell and putting him in with his "husband."

Roger Coleman had worked hard to keep in shape during the year he was in jail awaiting trial, and he was strong for his size, but at five feet nine inches and 155 pounds he was sure to be a target for the predators, and he knew it. The only organized recreation on death row was basketball, played on the cement surface of a small, fenced-in exercise yard attached to death row. Games were intense, and very rough. Roger was a good player despite his size, and he joined the games eagerly, both for the exercise and for the opportunity to show he could not easily be intimidated.

Coleman also quickly recognized that the men who ran death row were not the guards but two inmate brothers, James and Linwood Briley. On the basketball court, and through an offer to include them in a project he had in mind, Coleman made friends with the Brileys and obtained their protection. James Briley made it clear to the other inmates that Coleman was to be left alone.

One thing Roger could do nothing about was the termination of his marriage. Even before he was convicted, the police had persuaded

Trish that Roger was guilty of killing her sister, but Roger had always believed that somehow, someday, she would change her mind. Not long after his trial ended, however, she had filed for divorce, and on August 27, 1982, Terry Jordan wrote to tell him that three days earlier the divorce had been granted. It was no surprise, but it still hurt. The statements he had made in his letter to Peggy Stiltner and during the sentencing hearing were true. He still loved Trish, and her loss was an awful blow.

The problems on Virginia's death row when Roger Coleman arrived were not limited to physical conditions. Equally frightening, especially to inmates whose execution dates were approaching, was the absence of qualified lawyers to represent the condemned men once they lost their direct appeals to the Virginia Supreme Court, as they usually did. The shortage of competent lawyers willing to represent death-row prisoners was a problem all over the country, but it was especially acute in Virginia. The NAACP Legal Defense Fund was the largest provider of lawyers for death-penalty cases, but its efforts were necessarily concentrated in states with an even higher number of death cases than Virginia, especially Texas, Florida and Georgia.

Representing clients who have been sentenced to death is a complex, time-consuming and emotionally draining process for which a private lawyer receives little or no compensation, or even reimbursement of expenses. Nowadays he is also likely to be vilified by the public, and sometimes even by the judges who hear the cases and ought to praise the effort to provide access to justice for the poor as well as the rich.

Without the help of an organized group of full-time death-penalty lawyers, death-row inmates in Virginia either represented themselves or depended on a few tireless lawyers who volunteered for such cases. Even those who had lawyers found that prison rules made access for consultation and assistance extremely difficult.

When Roger Coleman arrived on death row in the spring of 1982, these poisonous conditions had caused one death-row inmate to decide he had had enough. Frank Coppola was not like Gary Gilmore and other men who have asked to be executed. Coppola wanted to live, but by early 1982 he had decided it was no longer worth the effort. Another death-row inmate, Joe Giarratano, had been helping him with his appeals, but Coppola told him to stop—he wanted to get it over with.

Joe Giarratano was the jailhouse lawyer for Virginia's death row, and one of the best in the country. He had made it his mission to keep Virginia from executing anyone, including himself, and he did not take kindly to Coppola's request, but he could not dissuade him. Through the grapevine Giarratano knew of an organization called the Southern Coalition on Jails and Prisons, which was providing assistance to death-row prisoners in thirteen states of the Deep South. He wrote them for help, and shortly thereafter a man from the coalition named Joe Ingle came up to Mecklenburg from Tennessee. He tried, but failed, to persuade Coppola to resume his appeals. In late July Coppola was transferred to Richmond for deathwatch.

Coppola would be the first person executed in Virginia since the death penalty was reinstated in 1977. On August 10, 1982, as the hour of Coppola's execution approached, tension swept through the death-row cell blocks like a thick summer fog, turning the inmates' skin sticky and hot and making it hard to breathe. At 11:32 P.M., when Coppola died, the men in general population at the state penitentiary in Richmond shouted and banged on their cell doors, but on death row at Mecklenburg it was deathly quiet.

Chapter 9

Death Row Angel

The events surrounding the execution of Frank Coppola had one positive result for the men on death row, and especially for Roger Coleman. Joe Ingle had failed to persuade Coppola to resume his appeals, but as a result of his efforts he had become familiar with conditions on death row, and when he returned to Tennessee he asked a woman who worked as a volunteer for the coalition to go to Virginia, investigate further and write a report on whether they should try to do something to help. The woman was Marie Deans, a forty-two-year-old native of Charleston, South Carolina.

Marie and her husband, Bob Deans, had become involved in prison reform work after Bob's mother, Penny, was murdered in 1971. Marie and Penny had become close friends, and the murder devastated both Bob and Marie. Instead of seeking revenge, however, their reaction was to try to understand why so many innocent people are murdered without any apparent motive. Their studies soon convinced them that one answer was the fact that most American penitentiaries produce inmates who leave prison more violent and antisocial than when they entered.

Marie Deans's trip to Virginia persuaded her that the coalition's help was desperately needed there, and when she submitted her report, Joe Ingle obtained the approval of his board to create a coalition branch in Richmond and asked Marie to run it. Bob and Marie had already decided to separate, and in January 1983 Marie accepted the job and moved to Richmond with her 11-year-old son, Robert. The Virginia Coalition of Jails and Prisons opened its office in February.

Two months later Marie Deans met Roger Coleman for the first time. According to Marie, in their initial encounter he did little but whine, reciting a litany of complaints about conditions on death row and all he had lost as a result of a conviction he insisted was unjust—his wife, his family, his job and so on. Marie Deans responded in typical fashion. "Okay," she said, "you're right. Conditions are miserable and you've lost all those things. So, what are you going to do now? Sit here and complain, or do something for yourself?" For a while, Coleman mostly continued to complain.

On September 9, 1983, the Virginia Supreme Court decided the direct appeal of Coleman's conviction, which Terry Jordan and Steve Arey had filed after his trial. Jordan and Arey had done a creditable job, raising a number of promising issues in support of reversal, but the court rejected each of them. Coleman's conviction and death sentence were affirmed.

Roger then wrote to the ACLU asking them to find him a lawyer to file a state habeas corpus petition. Such petitions seldom succeed, but they are a required predicate to filing a petition for a writ of habeas corpus in federal court. That procedure allows federal courts to review state criminal convictions for violations of the United States Constitution. Since reinstatement of the death penalty, about 50 percent of all death sentences not set aside at an earlier stage of the proceeding have been reversed in federal habeas corpus proceedings. It was Coleman's best remaining chance. However, Coleman's letter to the ACLU went unanswered, and he could not find a lawyer to take his case.

Not long afterward, Roger and seven other death-row inmates followed the lead of Frank Coppola by dropping their appeals. Without a lawyer there was little hope of success, and it seemed better to die than to continue enduring the conditions on death row.

Marie Deans, however, had made it her first priority to improve inmate access to legal assistance, and to that end had been contacting law firms that might be willing to provide assistance on a pro bono basis. She concentrated on firms large enough to handle a case without the extreme hardship imposed on small firms and sole practitioners by the massive expenditure of time and money required to handle a capital case properly. She also worked with a group of students at the University of Virginia Law School to provide legal research for lawyers who would accept death-penalty cases.

In late 1983 Marie Deans made arrangements to talk to Roger Coleman again. By this time the prison authorities had decided that Marie's role as a kind of unofficial ombudsman for the inmates was an asset to the orderly administration of death row, and she was permitted to talk to prisoners on the cell block. When Marie arrived in front of Coleman's cell, he gave her a look that signaled indifference. She began explaining her efforts to find competent lawyers for the death-row inmates. Roger was the next person on her list to try to help. If he would cooperate, she was certain she could find a good lawyer to represent him.

Roger Coleman had moved up to the front of his cell while Marie talked. Suddenly, she realized he was crying. He was desperately ashamed of himself for crying in front of her and, worse yet, his fellow inmates. Marie Deans reached her hand between the gray steel bars of Coleman's cell door and touched him on the arm. He did not pull away, as she had half expected. Instead, he moved closer to her. Before she left he had agreed to resume his appeals. From then on, the relationship between Roger Coleman and Marie Deans grew. They became friends. Roger came to trust her. He even began to talk to her about being afraid to die.

In late 1983 the University of Virginia Law School students had finished reading the transcript of Roger's trial and begun research for a state habeas corpus petition. A few weeks later Marie persuaded Arnold & Porter, a large, prestigious Washington, D.C., law firm, to represent him.

Chapter 10

—

Sharon

At about the time Marie Deans was looking for a lawyer for Roger Coleman in the winter of 1983, Coleman placed an ad in the University of Virginia student newspaper seeking a "pen pal." His budding friendship with Marie had cracked his shell of depression and resentment and he wanted to begin establishing contact with the outside world. Uncle Roger Lee occasionally wrote, but it was nearly impossible for him to make the long trip from Grundy, and no one else even tried.

Roger's ad was short and direct:

> Thirteen steps from eternity. Death Row prisoner seeks sincere people to correspond with and for possible visits. White, 24 years old, 5′9″ tall, 155 pounds, brown hair and green eyes. Photos appreciated but not necessary. Sincerity is what counts. Roger Coleman 128287/Death Row—MCC/Box 500/ Boynton, VA 23917.

At least one person who saw Coleman's ad responded. Her name was Sharon Paul, and she was a sophomore at the University of Virginia in Charlottesville.

Sharon Paul came to the University of Virginia from the working-class town of Thorofare, New Jersey, where her father had been a rail-road worker until injuries compelled his retirement. Sharon had schol-arship assistance and worked during the school year and in the sum-mer for the four years it took to earn her bachelor's degree in early childhood development. She is five feet three inches tall, slim, with a quiet voice, an easy smile, long brown hair and bangs. After Roger met her he told Marie she was "like the girl next door." Marie thinks he meant that she seemed classically wholesome, and she does.

After she saw Roger's ad, Sharon wrote to him the next weekend. Just bare facts—I'm a sophomore at the University of Virginia, my classes are x, my interests are y, and so on. No picture. Her letter was mailed on Monday; she had a response in her mailbox on Thursday. It was a long letter describing Roger's life in Grundy and in prison. He told of the crime that had put him on death row, and ended the letter by saying, "I know everyone says it, but for what it's worth, I really didn't do it."

Sharon was amazed at how well written Roger's letter was. She wondered if someone had written it for him. As for whether he had "done it," at that point she didn't really care. She was a "saved" Christian, and her motive in writing him in the first place was to try to "save" him. Several letters later, when she learned he had been bap-tized in jail while awaiting trial and considered himself already saved, she was a little disappointed. By then, however, the correspondence had become a weekly ritual, and she enjoyed it. As far as guilt or inno-cence was concerned, she decided to afford him a "presumption of innocence"—believe him until something occurred to make her disbe-lieve. By that she did not mean proof of his guilt, but evidence that he would lie to her. In her opinion, he never did.

When Sharon went home for Christmas, she told her parents about her pen pal. In fact, it was almost the only thing she talked about. In his letters Roger had been asking her to visit him, and she decided that when she got back to school she would go down to Mecklenburg to see him. Her parents were concerned. "What's going on with you two?" they asked. "What if he escapes and comes after you?" Sharon laughed. "He's on death row, Mom. People don't escape from death row."

Sharon talked her roommate into going with her to visit Roger for the first time. She was afraid they might run out of things to talk about, and with two of them it would be easier to keep up the conversation. Besides, her roommate had a car.

Visitors to death-row prisoners at Mecklenburg sit in one of a number of cubicles in the visitors' room. The prisoner sits behind a thick glass partition that separates him from the visitor. There is a telephone receiver on each side of the partition. The prisoner and the visitor can see but not touch each other. If the visitor has brought something for the prisoner, it must be given to a guard.

The conversation between Sharon and Roger went easily. It was hard for Sharon's roommate to participate, given the telephone setup, and her participation wasn't really necessary. Across the visiting room the reverse situation had developed, with two death-row prisoners trying to "share" a single visitor. The prisoners were James and Linwood Briley. Sharon's roommate saw what was happening, and with the permission of a guard moved to another cubicle and began a conversation with James Briley.

After the visit, Sharon's roommate began to correspond with Briley, and the two women made several more trips to Mecklenburg that spring. Then, on the night of May 31, 1984, James and Linwood Briley led the largest death-row escape in American history.

The escape had been in the planning stage for months, and almost everyone on death row knew about it. The Brileys offered to include Coleman in the plan, but he declined. He was innocent, he explained, and now he had lawyers who might be able to prove it. If he joined in the escape, it would be like admitting he was guilty, and if he was recaptured, it would not only mean a long prison term for escape but would also probably ruin any chance of a court believing his claim of innocence. Besides, although Roger didn't say so, he thought the chance the escape would succeed was slim at best.

But it did succeed. The prisoners executed a series of intricate and unlikely steps in their plan, beginning with the capture of a death-row guard and culminating in the prison motor pool sending a van to death row for what was thought to be the emergency removal of a bomb. When the van arrived at the entrance to death row, six inmates wearing guards' uniforms overpowered the driver, drove out an open prison gate and disappeared into the surrounding countryside.

All six fugitives were apprehended within three weeks. James and Linwood Briley were the last, arrested by the FBI on June 19 in their uncle's apartment in Philadelphia. By the time the Brileys were caught, Sharon Paul was out of school for the summer, and was home visiting her parents in Thorofare, only a few miles from Philadelphia, across the Delaware River. Sharon was able to persuade her mother and father that the Brileys were close by because of their uncle, not her, but she had to change her tune about nobody ever escaping from death row.

Actually, she had come to realize that talking about Roger made her parents uncomfortable, so she stopped. But she didn't stop writing or visiting him.

By now Sharon had also read the transcript of Roger's trial in the office of the prisoner-assistance project at the law school. She didn't know anything about trials, but it seemed obvious to her that Roger's lawyers had made a lot of mistakes. Even so, she couldn't understand how the jury could have found him guilty.

During the next two years, while Sharon finished her degree, her correspondence and visits with Roger Coleman grew more frequent. After graduation, Sharon began teaching first grade at a school in Woodbury, New Jersey, not far from where she grew up, but each vacation period she would use part of the time to drive down to Mecklenburg to visit Roger. Their letters now went back and forth two or three times a week. Mostly, they just told each other every detail of what was going on in their lives.

Each summer, when her regular school job was over, Sharon returned to Charlottesville and worked as a counselor in a summer enrichment program for gifted children. From there she could drive down to see Roger and return on the same day, so she made the trip every few weekends.

It was sometime in late 1987 or early 1988 that Sharon realized her feelings for Roger were more than friendship. She thought he was the most sensitive and caring person she had ever known. Despite the vastly greater magnitude of his own problems, he always seemed more concerned about hers, or Marie's, or some other friend's. When she visited, they would talk nonstop on the visiting-room telephone for as long as the rules permitted. Neither of them ran out of words. The visits were the highlight of her life. She looked forward to them for weeks, and dreaded the moment when the guard would finally say visiting hours were over and she had to leave. She had fallen in love.

Over the years Sharon had become friends with Marie Deans. When she finally realized she was in love, she confided in Marie and asked what she should do. Marie said she should just tell Roger how she felt, but Sharon couldn't do it. What Marie didn't tell Sharon was that she had had almost the same conversation with Roger not long before. For several months Marie heard from Roger and Sharon on a regular basis, each declaring their love for the other but unwilling to announce their feelings for fear they would be rejected. Marie, the confidante, was enjoined to secrecy. Finally she got sick of it and told both of them that if they didn't confess, she was going to tell on them. It was the summer of 1988, and Sharon had made arrangements to visit Roger a week or two later.

Roger still could not bring himself to declare his love for fear Sharon would be offended and reject him. Instead, he wrote a letter saying he was worried that he had become too dependent on her. He thought about her all the time, he said, and he knew that wasn't good. He thought they should back off, write less often. She should cancel her planned visit.

Rather than being devastated by Roger's letter, Sharon correctly read between the lines. She wrote back that she understood what he was saying, but disagreed with his suggestion about what to do about it. She thought about him all the time too, and she now realized that she was in love with him. Unless he insisted, she was going to keep her appointment for a visit.

Roger did not insist. He could barely contain his happiness, and wrote her at once, saying so. When she arrived at Mecklenburg and they could talk, they agreed that it was an odd, impossible situation, that most people would think they were crazy and that all they could do was see how it went, what would happen next. There would be no impetuous effort to have a prison engagement or wedding, no foolish planning of impossible events. They would just keep on doing what they had been doing, and hope that somehow, someday, things would work out. And that is what they did.

Sharon didn't tell her parents that her relationship with Roger had changed from pen pal to romance—she knew they wouldn't understand—but she did tell a few of her closest friends. They didn't understand either. "You what?!" they would say, and look at her as if she had announced she had been visited by creatures from outer space.

She quickly decided to stop talking about it to anybody except Roger and Marie. Later, Roger's lawyers and some other friends were included. By then, Sharon Paul no longer had any doubt that Roger was innocent, nor did she doubt that his innocence would one day be recognized and he would be released from prison. Then they could make real plans.

Chapter 11

The Choice Is Yours

While Roger Coleman was trying to adjust to conditions on death row, gradually opening up to Marie Deans, falling in love with Sharon Paul and trying to help his new lawyers find a way to get his conviction reversed, he was also working on a project he had started and called The Choice Is Yours.

Originally, the program was simply a letter addressed to young people of high-school and junior-high-school age. It described in direct and pungent language the misery of life in prison, and especially life on death row. The idea was to have the letter distributed to young people who had been getting into trouble, in the hope that the vivid description of the horrors of incarceration would "scare them straight." The name of the program was taken from the last line of Roger's letter, which read: "And remember, there is always room for one more on DEATH ROW, so the choice is yours!"

According to Coleman, the idea for the letter had come to him while he was in jail in Grundy awaiting trial and trying to figure out how to help other young men avoid what was happening to him. Others have suggested that Roger started the program when someone on death row advised him that if he wanted to beat the executioner, he should start laying the foundation for a claim of rehabilitation. In any event, by October 1982 Roger had composed his letter and sent it off to a list of juvenile court judges with the suggestion that if they thought it might be valuable, they should find a way to have it distributed to young people in the community who were at risk. As he had promised them, Roger included the Brileys as coauthors and cosponsors of his program. Quite a few judges responded favorably to the letter and found ways to have it distributed. Before long Roger was receiving mail from kids who had read the letter and wanted to learn more, or thank him, or ask his advice.

Whatever Roger's original motivation for the program, it soon became something he deeply believed in. When his lawyers learned of it and asked him to keep them advised of any favorable commentary in the press or from judges, youth counselors and others who made use of the letter, Roger was reluctant. His lawyers were building a file for a clemency petition. Roger was afraid it would appear that his purpose all along was to seek clemency, and that the program would lose credibility. He made them promise not to mention his efforts in anything they filed without clearing it with him first.

After the death-row escape, Roger took the Brileys' name off his letter, and when they were recaptured they agreed to the change. The project probably wouldn't have done them any good in the first place, and it certainly wasn't going to help them now, they grimly agreed. Having them associated with it after all the publicity about the escape would just mean fewer people would give the project credence.

The Brileys were right that neither association with Roger's program nor anything else was going to do them any good. Linwood Briley was sent to the electric chair in October 1984. James Briley had to wait until March 1985.

By the end of 1985, The Choice Is Yours letter had been widely distributed to troubled teenagers across Virginia and featured on two nationally syndicated radio shows. It had attracted the attention of several newspapers and received favorable write-ups. Then, in 1986, the communications director of the Catholic Diocese in Richmond became aware of the program and asked the prison authorities for permission to make a videotape of Coleman and another death-row inmate in their cells, presenting The Choice Is Yours concept and demonstrating what prison is like in pictures as well as words.

Coleman was enthusiastic and the authorities agreed. Soon the videotape was produced and distributed around the country.

The administrators of several school programs for troublesome
teenagers received permission for their classes to come into the prison
and meet Coleman. The students were brought into the prison audito-
rium, where Roger spoke to them, standing on the stage in manacles
and leg irons. As Roger developed his presentation, several guards
were added to the program to describe life in other parts of the prison
system. These sessions were featured on several television programs,
including *Good Morning America*.

Not everyone was impressed. One prison official referred to
Coleman's description of prison life as a blatant effort to gain sympa-
thy. Contacted by the press, Mickey McGlothlin remarked on the programs's essential theme that young people should behave themselves
in order to avoid the horrors of prison: "The main reason a person
should not commit crime is because of its effect on society. A young
girl, with hopes, dreams and aspirations—he took all those away from
her without reason. He has not expressed any remorse for it, or any
sadness. The real reason he should not have killed Wanda McCoy is
not because he could go to prison but because she had a right to live."

If you thought Roger Coleman was guilty, as Mickey McGlothlin
did, it was hard to disagree with McGlothlin's sentiments. Nevertheless, substantial numbers of school and youth corrections administrators, job corps supervisors, religious counselors and other men and
women working with troubled young people thought that The Choice
Is Yours video and lectures were helpful. By 1988 Coleman said he was
receiving and answering nearly a hundred letters a week from young
people who had been exposed to the program and administrators who
wanted to use it.

The glare of publicity that resulted from the spectacular death-row
escape had exposed conditions at Mecklenburg and throughout the
Virginia penal system. Governor Charles Robb had promptly moved
to bring in new management from outside the state. For warden of
Mecklenburg a man named Tony Bair was recruited from Utah. Bair
set out at once to improve security at the prison while also making
Mecklenburg a more humane environment for the inmates. Contrary
to previous policy, he made it a practice to welcome outsiders into the
prison to see what was happening.

Tony Bair's new policy was important to the expansion of The Choice Is Yours program, and it impacted on Roger Coleman in another way as well. In 1985 a newspaper reporter had received permission to interview several Mecklenburg inmates including Roger Coleman. He found Coleman's discussion of his youth program intelligent and interesting, and thought a friend of his would like to meet him. The friend was a forty-six-year-old French and music professor at Lynchburg College named Robert White. In addition to teaching at the college, White was an accomplished classical pianist who played regularly in chamber music concerts and served as a volunteer teacher at a prison near Lynchburg. The reporter arranged for White to visit Coleman on death row. The two men hit it off and White became a regular visitor. Like Sharon Paul, Robert White saw Roger Coleman as a man of great sensitivity and compassion. He thought Roger had an extraordinary understanding of people and events. Whether or not he was guilty, White wondered how anyone from Roger's background had acquired those attributes.

Chapter 12

A Day Late

By the middle of 1984, lawyers at Arnold & Porter had read the transcript of Coleman's trial, visited him at Mecklenburg and were well on the way to filing his state court petition for writ of habeas corpus. Under the leadership of a newly conservative majority of the United States Supreme Court, both state and federal courts were anxious to limit the legal rights of criminal defendants, especially in habeas corpus cases. Recent decisions had created increasingly technical barriers to the consideration of a prisoner's claims on the merits of his case. Nevertheless, Coleman's lawyers had identified several arguments that seemed promising.

Among the claims that would be raised were the failure to grant Coleman a change of venue due to excessive pretrial publicity and community bias, the improper exclusion of jurors who were opposed to the death penalty, the state's failure to provide the defense with exculpatory documents and the excessively prejudicial nature of the prosecutor's closing argument. There was also a legal argument that the Virginia death-penalty statute was unconstitutional. But the argument Coleman's lawyers presented in greatest detail, and with the greatest hope, was the claim that Coleman had not received effective assistance of counsel, as required by the Constitution.

In September 1984, Arnold & Porter filed Coleman's petition in the circuit court of Buchanan County. Since the petition claimed that Judge Persin had made errors in conducting the trial, the case was assigned to Judge Glyn Phillips, from neighboring Dickenson County. After a number of delays, a hearing was set for November 12, 1985, in Judge Phillips's courtroom. It would be an evidentiary hearing in which the parties would be permitted to call witnesses to support their claims.

In preparation for the hearing, David Green, the Arnold & Porter lawyer most involved in Roger's representation, made several trips to Grundy to line up local counsel and seek out witnesses who might be helpful. The issue in the habeas case was not whether Coleman was guilty or innocent, and Green had always assumed he was probably guilty, but when he returned from his first trip to Grundy he sought out Marie Deans. "You know, Marie," he said with surprise in his voice, "I think he might even be innocent. I drove around down there and I don't think he had time to do it."

With the help of Roger's uncle, Arnold & Porter had developed some helpful evidence to supplement the arguments presented in the petition. In particular, a husband and wife had come forward to say that a relative of theirs, who became one of the jurors in Roger's trial, had told them before the jury was selected that he hoped he would be chosen because he thought Coleman was guilty, and he "wanted to help burn the S.O.B."

Also, a prominent local lawyer had read the trial transcript and agreed to testify about the deficiencies in the representation Roger had received from his trial lawyers. On the same subject an expert witness was engaged to discuss the scientific evidence and what should have been done to attack it if the lawyers had been properly prepared.

The most important witnesses on the issue of inadequate representation, however, were Steve Arey and Terry Jordan themselves. Johnny Farmer, a respected trial lawyer from nearby Norton, Virginia, had agreed to become local counsel for Coleman, and it was wisely decided that he would question Arey and Jordan. The purpose of the examination, as Arey and Jordan knew, was to show that their representation of Coleman had been inadequate, and they were likely to be less disingenuous on the subject under questioning by a respected local lawyer than by some Washington big shot they would probably never see again.

Farmer did a masterful job. Terry Jordan was examined first, and to his credit seemed entirely straightforward in describing what he had and hadn't done. Before the Coleman case he had never tried a murder case, a rape case, any case involving blood or hair analysis or a criminal case of any kind that lasted more than a day. He had expected that Arey would handle the motion for change of venue until the morning it was heard, when Arey called to say he couldn't make it. He had also expected Arey to cross-examine the state's blood and hair expert, Elmer Gist, but for a reason he could not recall he ended up doing it himself.

As far as preparation was concerned, since he practiced in Grundy while Arey was from Tazewell, it was understood that Jordan would do most of the local witness interviews and investigation. However, he did not interview all the investigating police officers, he did not interview Hezzie McCoy, he did not interview Dr. McDonald, who first examined Wanda's body and estimated the time of death, he did not interview Kelly Andrews, the evidence expert, he did not interview Dr. Oxley, who did the autopsy, and he did not even interview or try to interview Elmer Gist. He thought he might have spoken briefly to either Sandy or Scott Stiltner, but if so it was in the courtroom at the time the case was originally set for trial in December 1981, and he was not sure which of them he spoke to.

Jordan said that his only preparation for the cross-examination of Elmer Gist had been reading Gist's report, a single article about hair comparisons and another on blood analysis. He did not know about more sophisticated blood tests, he did not read any books about blood or hair analysis, he did not try to hire or even talk to any expert on either subject. In short, he had done almost none of the things necessary to conduct a truly effective cross-examination of the state's most important witness.

Regarding the physical locations that were important to the case, he looked at the murder house from the street, but never went inside or even up to the door to see if there was any evidence of forced entry. He did not go to the bathhouse. He did not go up to the mine where Roger worked. He never drove the route Roger took the night of the murder with a watch to see how long it took and whether there was time for him to go everywhere he indisputably went that night and still commit the murder. He drove to Boyd's Trailer Park, but he did not go into the Stiltners' trailer, or canvass the area to try to locate other witnesses at Boyd's who might have seen Roger and been able to corroborate his estimate of when he was there. He did not take any photographs anywhere; he did not specifically inquire of the police about fingerprints; and although he knew about Philip VanDyke's time card and was told that the police had it, he never asked that it be turned over to him so it could be put into evidence. As far as Terry Jordan knew, Steve Arey had not done any of these things either, or talked to any other witnesses.

On examination by the assistant attorney general handling the case for the state, Jordan was asked if it were not true that he had the prosecutor's file available, with witness statements and reports. He answered: "Yes. We made a discovery motion and had the exculpatory statements turned over to us. The file and the various pieces of clothing and the knives . . . we had access to." It was not clear what reports or witness statements were contained in the file he "had access to," but Jordan's answer would play an important role in Roger Coleman's case in the years ahead. From that point forward, whenever some report or witness statement helpful to the defendant was discovered, the state would contend that the defense lawyers had had access to it as part of the "prosecutor's file."

Steve Arey was more vague about the witnesses he had interviewed, saying he may have talked to some that Jordan did not talk to, but the only witnesses he actually recalled interviewing were the defense alibi witnesses, Jack Davidson, Randy Jackson and a man named Stiltner, though he wasn't sure if it was Johnny Lee (the van driver from the mine where Roger had worked), Danny Ray (Wanda's ex–brother-in-law) or Scott (from Boyd's).

Arey also said he had seen some police reports and statements the police had obtained, but he did not recall having access to the prosecutor's file itself. Again, what he did or didn't see was not specifically identified, although he said that by the time of the trial, "[the prosecutor] gave us pretty much everything."

At the conclusion of the hearing before Judge Phillips, Roger Coleman's lawyers felt they had made as good a record as possible, especially on the effective-assistance-of-counsel issue. They had no illusions about their chance of success before Judge Phillips, whose demeanor had signaled that he was not about to order a new trial for one of the most notorious convicted murderers in the recent history of southwestern Virginia. The important thing was that they had made a good start toward building a record for presentation to the federal courts after the likely rejection of their required appeal to the Virginia Supreme Court.

Roger Coleman had been present throughout the hearing, and had testified briefly himself about what he had or hadn't told his lawyers or asked them to do. When the hearing was over he felt sure he had been correct in what he told James Briley before the death-row escape. Now he had good lawyers, lawyers who could win his case.

In June 1986, Judge Phillips finally informed the parties that he intended to rule for the state, and asked the assistant attorney general to prepare an appropriate order. Judge Phillips signed the order on September 4, 1986. It rejected all of the defense contentions.

September 4 was a Thursday. Because Judge Phillips was in Clintwood and the order had to be filed in the circuit court of Buchanan County, the judge had his secretary mail it to the circuit court clerk in Grundy. On September 9 the order was officially entered into the record of the Coleman case by the court clerk, who mailed certified copies to the lawyers. The clerk's certification and transmittal letter were both dated September 9.

On September 15, 1986, David Green at Arnold & Porter prepared a memo for his fellow attorneys working on the Coleman case. "As predicted," the memo said, "Judge Phillips signed the Commonwealth's Order without changing a word. The order is dated September 4, but entered September 9. We have thirty days to file a Notice of Appeal with the Court."

The Arnold & Porter lawyers prepared a notice of appeal and sent it to their local counsel, Johnny Farmer. On October 6, Farmer mailed the notice to the clerk in Grundy. The notice of appeal, which is a simple half-page document, said Coleman was appealing from a decree "entered on September 9, 1986."

If Johnny Farmer had sent the notice by registered or certified mail, under Virginia law it would have been deemed filed on the day it was sent, Monday, October 6. Since he didn't, the notice was deemed filed on the day it was received, October 7.

Some time later, the attorney general's office informed Roger Coleman's lawyers that they intended to argue that the thirty-day filing period began not on September 9, when the clerk in Grundy had entered the order, but on September 4, when Judge Phillips signed it. Thirty days from September 4 was October 4, but that was a Saturday, and under Virginia law, if the thirty-day period expired on a Saturday or Sunday it was extended to Monday; in this instance, Monday, October 6. If the attorney general was right that the time ran from September 4, when the order was signed, the notice of appeal had been received one day late.

If this would seem to any sensible person like nitpicking of the worst sort, Coleman's lawyers recognized at once that it was a deadly serious issue. Under Virginia law the time for filing a notice of appeal is jurisdictional, meaning that if it is missed, even by a day, the appeal will be dismissed without consideration of its merits. If the attorney general's argument was accepted by the Virginia Supreme Court and the appeal dismissed for that reason, the major problem was not the loss of the tiny chance that the Virginia court would reverse Judge Phillips; it was the potential impact on Coleman's chances in federal court.

Until a few years earlier, there would have been no problem. Since at least the late 1950s, the federal courts had made it clear that they would not deprive someone of their right to consideration of a petition for habeas corpus just because some lawyer made an innocent mistake that the defendant had nothing to do with. And that was especially so in death-penalty cases. But times had changed. The Supreme Court had embraced and begun to expand on the theory that if a state prisoner fails to exhaust his state-court remedies, that is, have his arguments considered first by every available state court, he loses his right to have them considered by a federal court. If Coleman's appeal was dismissed by the Virginia court without consideration of its merits because of a procedural mistake in filing the notice of appeal, under recent decisions a federal court might hold that he had lost his right to pursue federal habeas corpus as well. It seemed incredible that a court would apply a rule so egregiously unfair to a defendant facing the death penalty, but that was the way the law was moving.

On December 4, 1986, Arnold & Porter filed Coleman's brief on appeal with the Virginia Supreme Court. On December 9 the state moved to dismiss the appeal on the ground that the notice of appeal had been filed a day late. Although the Virginia Supreme Court required the state to brief the case on the merits rather than deciding the motion to dismiss first, four months later the court entered an order granting the state's motion to dismiss.

As everyone understood, whether that series of events meant Roger Coleman had lost his right to consideration of his constitutional arguments on federal habeas corpus was an issue that would have to be resolved by the federal court in which Coleman filed his federal habeas corpus petition.

Since Arnold & Porter and Johnny Farmer were responsible for the alleged filing mistake, someone else now had to be brought into the case to argue the issue, both because there was a potential conflict of interest and because of the old adage that whoever represents himself has a fool for a lawyer. In a sense, the conduct of Arnold & Porter and Johnny Farmer was the issue—so they were the last lawyers who should be responsible for defending the correctness of their belief that the time for appeal had not started running until September 9, or, in the alternative, that the mistake should be excused.

At Debevoise & Plimpton, a large law firm in New York City, an experienced trial lawyer named John Hall received a telephone call from a friend at Arnold & Porter. Although most of Hall's work involved litigating securities cases for large corporations, he had a record of accepting federal habeas corpus cases for men who had been sentenced to death. Hall agreed that he and his firm would take over the Coleman case for as long as necessary to resolve the issues raised by the late-filed notice of appeal. Arnold & Porter would continue to work on the merits of the case, and take back primary responsibility for the case when the notice issue was resolved. Arnold & Porter also found an independent lawyer to advise Roger Coleman on whether that arrangement was in his best interests, and whether any action should be brought by Coleman against either Arnold & Porter or Johnny Farmer. After receiving advice from his independent lawyer, Coleman decided to accept the arrangement. Arnold & Porter's knowledge of the case and expertise, he decided, was a lot more valuable than anything he would gain by suing them.

Book IV

Jim and Kitty

Chapter 13

—

The Centurion

In the fall of 1980, six months before Wanda McCoy was murdered, a thirty-seven-year-old former management consultant named Jim McCloskey entered his second year in the graduate program at the Princeton Theological Seminary in Princeton, New Jersey. The son of an executive in a family-owned construction company, McCloskey grew up on Philadelphia's Main Line. After college he pursued a successful consulting career until he awakened one day to the realization that his life seemed empty. He had always been casually religious, but now he felt the need for a deeper religious commitment. A bachelor with few obligations other than his business, he applied for admission to the seminary. His application was accepted, and after winding up his business he moved to Princeton to begin his studies.

Part of the second-year curriculum at the seminary involved field work, and McCloskey chose to work as a student chaplain at Trenton State Prison, a maximum-security institution in the state capital, just ten miles away. The assignment changed his life.

There were forty prisoners in the cell block where Jim McCloskey was assigned that fall, all of them serving long sentences for serious crimes. While many of them complained from time to time about the fairness of their trials or the competence of their lawyers, only two persistently claimed they were innocent of the crimes for which they were imprisoned. One was an ex-heroin addict who had been sentenced to life in prison in 1975 for the murder of a Newark car salesman. His name was George De Los Santos, and his protestations of innocence were so insistent that Jim McCloskey finally agreed to read the record of his trial.

What McCloskey found confirmed what De Los Santos had said: There was no significant evidence to tie him to the crime, with one exception—an inmate of a jail where De Los Santos had been held on a drug charge claimed that De Los Santos had confessed the murder to him. For his trouble, it appeared that the inmate had received favorable treatment from the prosecutor. Jim McCloskey had no familiarity with criminal law, but he immediately sensed what any experienced prosecutor or defense lawyer could have told him—of the types of evidence commonly used in criminal prosecutions, none is more likely to be false than the claim of a fellow inmate that he heard a jailhouse confession. Jim McCloskey agreed to reinvestigate the case to see if he could verify or refute George De Los Santos's claim of innocence. To do so, McCloskey put his seminary studies on hold and began working on the case full-time.

Slowly, but with infinite patience and determination, McCloskey learned the ropes of criminal investigation and the intricacies of federal habeas corpus, the process by which state prisoners can have their cases reviewed for constitutional error in a federal court. Three years later McCloskey's work paid off. In July 1983, United States District Court Judge Frederick Lacey granted George De Los Santos's petition for writ of habeas corpus, finding that the testimony of the jailhouse witness was false, and that the prosecutor in the case knew or should have known it. Stripped of its only significant witness, the state decided not to reprosecute. George De Los Santos was a free man, and Jim McCloskey had found the purpose in his life. That same year he obtained his degree from the seminary, but rather than proceed to ordination and assignment to a church, he founded Centurion Ministries, named for the soldier who said of Christ on the cross, "Surely this one was innocent."

Of average height, slightly pudgy, double-chinned, with fringes of brown hair on each side of an otherwise bald head, Jim McCloskey looks more like a monk than a private investigator. Wearing a clerical collar, as he often does when conducting the door-to-door digging for information that is the stock-in-trade of any good investigator, he makes a convincing cleric. It is a valuable tool for opening doors, and no private eye, real or fictional, applies himself more diligently or effectively to his chosen work.

In 1986 two more convicts were exonerated and released from prison as a result of McCloskey's efforts. When they were freed, Rene Santana had served ten years of a life sentence for murder, and Nathaniel Walker had spent three years as a fugitive and eight years in prison for a rape which blood tests showed he could not have committed.

By 1987 the fame of Centurion Ministries had spread beyond New Jersey, and McCloskey was receiving hundreds of requests for help from prisoners who claimed they were innocent. By then he had seen enough cases to devise a rough but effective set of criteria for determining which cases were worthy of further investigation and which were not. Not surprisingly, he looked for cases in which the prosecution relied heavily on a jailhouse confession. He also looked for cases in which the conviction depended on uncorroborated eyewitness identifications, which are also famously unreliable. If the convict had always maintained his or her innocence, if any additional evidence was circumstantial and if a review of the record satisfied Jim McCloskey's sixth sense that the convict's story was true, McCloskey would interview him face-to-face, and cross-examine him closely. If the prisoner survived that encounter with McCloskey believing him, Centurion Ministries would begin a reinvestigation of the case. Or rather, they would do so if one other standard was met—so many requests for help were pouring in, and Centurion's resources were stretched so thin, that McCloskey would consider only those cases in which the sentence was death or the practical equivalent of life in prison.

Applying those criteria, McCloskey has compiled a record that is unparalleled, and a shock to anyone who thinks that wrongful convictions seldom occur. By the end of 1995, operating on a shoestring, Centurion Ministries had obtained freedom for sixteen wrongly convicted men and women, an extraordinary achievement in a system that ferociously resists admitting a mistake once direct appeals are over and a defendant's conviction has become "final."

In April 1987, Jim McCloskey heard about Roger Coleman almost by accident. Earlier that year Kate Hill, who had previously done volunteer work for Centurion Ministries, became McCloskey's first full-time assistant. Among her duties was screening requests for assistance to eliminate those which did not meet McCloskey's criteria for further study. One such request had come from a woman named Denise Haase, who claimed her brother was wrongly incarcerated in Virginia. The story she told was heart-wrenching and quite convincing, but it did not meet Centurion's criteria—the prisoner's sentence was for a term of years that was long, but not long enough. Kate Hill wrote a sympathetic letter to the sister, explaining why they could not take the case, but providing advice and encouragement on other ways to pursue her brother's freedom. On April 29, 1987, Mrs. Haase wrote back thanking Ms. Hill for her concern and enclosing a news clip about Roger Coleman's youth program and his claim of innocence. Mrs. Haase asked Kate Hill to contact Coleman and see if his case was one that Centurion Ministries might be willing to pursue. She did, and on May 15 Coleman wrote back, enclosing a packet of information about his conviction.

The material Coleman provided showed that his case fit almost perfectly into McCloskey's profile. From the circumstantial nature of the state's evidence to the jailhouse informant to the logical and well-supported alibi to Coleman's persistent and unwavering claim of innocence, it was the kind of case that might well have produced a miscarriage of justice.

To Jim McCloskey, it seemed at least worth reading the transcript of the trial, especially since the death penalty was involved. Coleman provided a copy, and McCloskey saw that it was consistent with Coleman's description of the evidence on which he had been convicted. The next step was a personal interview, which McCloskey arranged to conduct at Mecklenburg. At the interview the fervor of Coleman's claim of innocence was impressive, and his answers to the hard questions McCloskey posed about the murder were logical and articulate. Centurion Ministries would take the case.

To Coleman's lawyers at Debevoise & Plimpton in New York, the issues that needed to be pursued were whether his right to consideration of a petition for habeas corpus had been lost by the state-court filing delay and, if they won on that issue, whether an error of constitutional magnitude had occurred in Coleman's trial. For Jim McCloskey, however, there was a different question, one that none of the lawyers was pursuing—the question of guilt or innocence. While it was an unusual question to pursue at this stage of the case, to McCloskey it was the only question. If Roger Coleman was in fact innocent and he could prove it, McCloskey believed he could save his life. If not, he doubted that anyone could.

Coleman's lawyers were preparing to file their federal habeas corpus petition, and before they did, McCloskey wanted to see if he could turn up any new information that might be helpful. Thus, in the first week of March 1988, McCloskey set out for Grundy to reopen the investigation of the murder of Wanda Fay McCoy. Living with Roger's uncle to save money, McCloskey remained in the area for nearly a month, knocking on doors, talking to witnesses and reviewing scores of documents. It was quite different from the inner-city investigations Jim McCloskey was accustomed to conducting in most of his cases:

From the day I first arrived in Grundy in 1988, the thing I noticed was how extraordinarily courteous and open the people were. Without really knowing who you were, or even why you were there, they would invariably invite you into their homes. And when you explained why you were there, no matter what they thought about Roger Coleman, they would almost always tell you whatever they knew. After they thought about it they might pull back, but they almost always started out open and trusting. I'd had experience with Southern hospitality, but I came to think that Appalachian hospitality was different—even warmer and more gracious, at least to strangers. It seemed like they wanted very much for you to think well of them, to appreciate them for who they were, rather than as some kind of stereotypical "hillbillies."

The problem you sometimes have in the inner city is that people won't talk to you—or even open their doors—but here, except for a few people who were flat out hiding from me, that almost never happened. The main problem was finding where someone lived among all those mountains and hollows. You couldn't go to some numerical address on a street map, you had to learn to follow country directions—"Go up over yonder mountain to the third holler on the right, and then up the holler a piece" and so on. The good thing was, when you got lost you could always knock on someone's door and whoever answered usually knew who you were looking for and could give you a new set of directions.

For all the difficulties, McCloskey's trip to Grundy proved fruitful.

Chapter 14

New Records, New
Science and a New Court

By coincidence, Jim McCloskey arrived in Grundy seven years to the day after Wanda McCoy's murder. In meetings with the authorities who investigated the crime and prosecuted Coleman, McCloskey first sought to locate the state's physical evidence and examine it for himself. When the police refused his request, McCloskey went to see Judge Persin in his chambers at the Buchanan County Courthouse. The judge listened as Jim explained his mission. When he finished, Judge Persin picked up the phone and told Jack Davidson to gather the evidence and have it available for inspection the next morning.

The offices of the state police were located in a small brown brick building on the outskirts of Vansant. When McCloskey arrived and Jack Davidson directed him to a table piled with documents and other materials, Jim was relieved to discover that among the materials were the actual slides and swabs that had been collected by Dr. Oxley during his autopsy of Wanda McCoy. The science of DNA comparisons had recently arrived on the forensic scene, and McCloskey knew that if enough sperm was left, there was a real possibility that DNA testing could prove Roger Coleman's innocence by excluding him as the donor of the sperm found in Wanda McCoy's vagina and rectum. In a report to Coleman's lawyers prepared after his trip to Grundy,

McCloskey urged them to try to obtain a court order for such a test.

Closely examining the other physical evidence and photographs from the autopsy and crime scene, McCloskey made a number of significant observations.

Examination of Coleman's blue jeans revealed the fallacy of the prosecutors' claim that the blood on Roger Coleman's pants was on the left leg and got there from the blood on Wanda's right thigh when he was raping her. McCloskey saw that virtually all of the tiny holes made when Gist tested the blue jeans for blood were on the right leg, not the left.

From the photographs, McCloskey noted that both of Wanda's hands had been cut with what he believed were X-shaped patterns. Like Davidson, McCloskey saw that a coffee table and end table were askew, showing there had been a struggle in the living room before Wanda was taken into the bedroom and killed. The fact that china figurines and a photograph on the coffee table had not been knocked over showed that the struggle was brief and not very violent, leading McCloskey to conclude that at least two assailants had probably been involved. That theory was bolstered in McCloskey's mind by the X-shaped cuts, which he felt were made deliberately, and by the fact that sperm had been found in her rectum as well as her vagina, suggesting she had been sodomized as well as raped vaginally, probably by two separate men. McCloskey's belief that there was more than one killer also seemed supported by the fact that no one had heard any screams or other noise on the night of the murder despite the proximity of several neighbors and the evidence that Wanda had been able to struggle, albeit briefly.

McCloskey was also interested in the black dirt that covered Wanda McCoy's hands, the arms of her sweater and her upper thighs. Oddly, it did not appear on her lower legs nor was it found anywhere else in the house. Perhaps, he thought, someone had dragged her by the feet through the dirt. That might account for the pattern of the stains. McCloskey also theorized from his study of Dr. Oxley's autopsy report that the killer was left-handed, and that the pocketknife taken from Roger was probably too small to have been the murder weapon, as Coleman's lawyers had argued.

An examination of the Longbottom neighborhood persuaded him that the theory that the murderer had parked his car alongside the highway and waded Slate Creek was ludicrous, given the distances involved and the exposure of both vehicle and person that would have occurred had he approached the house that way. Timing the route Coleman had to have taken if he was the killer, McCloskey realized how little time there was for Coleman to commit the crime, even accepting the state's time line. And it was Jim McCloskey who waded the creek himself and found the water much deeper than the trial testimony had indicated.

But as valuable as were McCloskey's insights from examining the state's evidence, they were dwarfed in importance by a packet of papers he obtained at the end of his second week in Grundy.

Among the first people McCloskey interviewed in Grundy was a man who had been in law enforcement at the time of the murder but was now retired. Hoping he would have helpful information he would now share, McCloskey knocked on the man's door and introduced himself. The man was willing to help if McCloskey would protect his identity.

While it turned out that McCloskey's source had no useful information himself, he had a friend who was still in law enforcement and had doubts about Coleman's guilt. Upon receiving Jim's solemn promise never to reveal that name either, the man agreed to provide copies of some of the investigative files on the case. One evening a few days later, McCloskey received a phone call from his original source. There was a package for him. Jim drove immediately to the man's house, where, without a word spoken, he was handed a thick tan envelope closed with a metal clasp. The front of the envelope was blank and bore no indication of its origin.

Jim McCloskey could barely wait to open the package. When he did, he recognized at once the potential value of its contents. The first several pages were a copy of the report Police Chief Randy Jackson had prepared to summarize his activities and observations on the night of the murder. That report was followed by a lengthier document that bore on its front page the following legend:

COMMONWEALTH OF VIRGINIA
DEPARTMENT OF STATE POLICE
BUREAU OF CRIMINAL INVESTIGATION
October 26, 1981

REPORT OF INVESTIGATION CONCERNING
WANDA FAY THOMPSON MCCOY—Victim
ROGER KEITH COLEMAN—Accused

Attached was a letter to Mickey McGlothlin, also dated October 26, which identified the document as Jack Davidson's report of his investigation. Included were copies of Davidson's typewritten reports of his own activities and of interviews with many of the witnesses who had testified for the state at trial.

Leafing quickly through the document, McCloskey saw that it was not a complete set of witness interviews, but only those which Davidson believed would support the case against Coleman. Even so, he saw that the reports contained much valuable information. They had not been among the material turned over to Arnold & Porter by Coleman's trial lawyers, and there was no indication in the court file that they had ever been produced for the defense by the prosecutors.

While Virginia law did not require that all witness statements be turned over to the defense, under Supreme Court decisions beginning with a famous case called *Brady* v. *Maryland,* information that is exculpatory of the defendant or impeaching of significant state witnesses must be turned over to the defense as a matter of constitutional law, and while the line is not always clear, McCloskey believed some of the information he had just received fell within that requirement.

The first thing that caught McCloskey's attention was Davidson's report of his investigation of the crime scene, which revealed the existence of the pry mark he had found on the front door of the McCoy house. Given the state's heavy reliance on the proposition that the murderer had been voluntarily admitted to the house by Wanda McCoy and that Coleman was one of only three men she would have admitted, McCloskey believed the pry mark was an extremely important piece of exculpatory evidence that surely should have been made known to the defense.

The crime-scene report also specifically mentioned the latent fingerprint Special Agent Andrews had lifted from the "outside front door screen," but surprisingly, there was no reference to the result of any effort to identify the print. McCloskey again wondered if the defense lawyers had seen the report, since they had apparently done nothing to follow up on it before trial.

Three more items in the October 26 reports provided obvious and important opportunities to impeach the testimony of state witnesses during the trial, but the defense lawyers had not used them. Both Randy Jackson and Jack Davidson had reported Dr. McDonald's statement, made at about 11:40 P.M., that in his opinion Wanda McCoy's death had occurred "about" or "no more than" a half hour before, while at trial McDonald had said the time of death was "about 10:30 P.M."

And contrary to his testimony at trial, Jack Davidson's report of his initial interview with Brad McCoy showed that he was indeed looking for someone who had been scratched.

The most important impeachment document, however, involved the testimony of Sandy Stiltner that she had looked at a clock when Roger Coleman came to her trailer the night of the murder and noticed that the time was 10:20 P.M. The material McCloskey received from his informant in March 1988 contained both a report of Jack Davidson's interview of Sandy Stiltner on March 12, 1981, and a summary of the testimony he expected to obtain from Scott and Sandy Stiltner. The summary had been prepared shortly before October 26, 1981, seven months after the murder. Neither the interview report nor the summary mentioned anything about Sandy Stiltner looking at a clock, or observing that it was 10:20 P.M.

On the crucial issue of whether the Stiltners or Philip VanDyke were correct about the time of Coleman's visit, Sandy Stiltner's testimony had been the state's most important evidence. If properly presented to the jury, the fact that Sandy Stiltner had apparently not mentioned looking at a clock in her interview with Davidson the day after the murder, and indeed had apparently failed to mention it until sometime after October 26, would have seriously damaged the credibility of her story and might well have caused the jury to accept Philip VanDyke's time estimate instead. If so, Roger Coleman would almost certainly have been acquitted, as he would have had no time to commit the crime.

The information in Jack Davidson's investigative report was so important and useful to Coleman's defense that Jim McCloskey did not think it possible that Coleman's trial lawyers had the information but failed to use it. McCloskey knew Terry Jordan had testified that he had access to the prosecutors' files, but he also knew that meant whatever the prosecutors chose it to mean. As inexperienced as Arey and Jordan were, Jim thought, they would not have passed up the opportunity to tell the jury about the pry mark on the McCoys' front door, or to impeach Davidson about looking for someone with scratches, or to bring out Sandy Stiltner's apparent failure to mention anything about looking at a clock when she was first interviewed.* The reports did not prove that Roger Coleman was innocent, but a jury who knew about them certainly might have had a reasonable doubt about his guilt.

While obtaining the investigative report by itself justified McCloskey's trip to Grundy, the bulk of his time was spent on the kind of shoe-leather investigation a good policeman conducts when first presented with an unsolved crime. He interviewed witnesses—not just those who saw Coleman the night of the murder but neighbors of the McCoys who might have seen or heard something, state witnesses who might now change their stories or recall something new or different and others who for one reason or another could have relevant information.

McCloskey's effort to find new evidence and new witnesses resulted in a multitude of leads that would be explored further in years to come, but two contacts from this first trip to Grundy turned out to be especially useful. One involved Coleman's alleged jailhouse confession to Roger Matney. McCloskey was able to learn the names of a number of people who knew Matney, including his mother-in-law, Goldie Owens. After considerable effort McCloskey tracked her down. She lived in an old log cabin several miles east of Grundy. It was a plain and primitive place, with simple furniture and a concrete floor, but it was as clean and orderly as any house could be. Several renderings of Jesus adorned the walls, and a large, well-worn Bible was displayed on a table near the door.

Mrs. Owens was a friendly woman whose several missing teeth and wrinkled, sun-weathered skin made her look older than she really was. She invited Jim into her home without hesitation, and when he

---

* As discussed in more detail below, the question of which documents had been turned over to the defense before trial was a subject of continuing dispute between Coleman's lawyers and the state. Ultimately Terry Jordan supplied the state with an affidavit that essentially supported the state's position that Coleman's trial lawyers had access to all witness summaries in the prosecutors' file, including, specifically, the pry-mark report.

told her why he was there, Goldie Owens turned out to be no fan of the honesty or intelligence of her son-in-law. He "would steal a penny off the eyes of a dead man," she said, "and stick his head in flames of fire for ten dollars."

According to Goldie Owens, on one occasion when his testimony against Roger Coleman came up, Matney said, "If you use your head for something more than a hat rack, you can avoid a lot of jail time." Asked if "that boy really owned up to it," Matney had said no.

Two other men who were trustees at the Buchanan County Jail when Coleman and Matney were incarcerated there supported Goldie Owens's poor opinion of Roger Matney. Both said that Coleman had always maintained his innocence to them, and both found it hard to believe he had confessed anything to Roger Matney, who, they said, was widely known to be a liar and a snitch who would inform on anyone to avoid prison time.

As it would turn out, however, McCloskey's visit to one of Wanda McCoy's neighbors was even more important than his interview with Goldie Owens. On March 23, 1988, near the end of his trip, McCloskey climbed a set of stairs behind the murder house that led to a ramshackle frame structure on the hill above. There he found and interviewed Mrs. Helen Ramey, her husband, Bobby, and two of their children, Bobbie Donald, known as Donnie or "Trouble," and his sister Portia.

The story the Rameys told to Jim McCloskey was in some respects helpful, and in others simply puzzling. According to Helen Ramey, who did most of the talking but whose account was confirmed verbally or with nods of agreement from the others, the first the Ramey family knew of Wanda McCoy's murder was when the police came to their door the next morning. Mr. Ramey had already gone to work and Donnie's younger brother Michael had left for school. Mrs. Ramey and Donnie thought it had been Jack Davidson, Randy Jackson and some other men who came to the house. Donnie was still in bed, and when the police arrived he emerged from the bedroom wearing nothing but his undershorts. The police surrounded him and inspected his face, arms, chest and back. He had no scratches. Later, Mrs. Ramey said, Police Chief Randy Jackson came to the house and told her the police were going to the high school to interview Michael. They did, and also inspected Michael's upper body, apparently finding no scratches.

Thus, one thing the Ramey interview confirmed was that the police were indeed looking for someone who had been scratched by Wanda McCoy's broken fingernails.

While the Rameys denied having seen or heard anything from the McCoy house the night of the murder, their description of the evening was startling. According to Helen Ramey, Donnie and Michael had been out, she thought at a movie, and returned home around 9:00 or 9:30. Shortly thereafter, around 9:45 or 10:00, Michael Ramey went out onto the porch to recover some clothes that his mother had washed and left on a line to dry. He rushed back into the house and grabbed a poker from the fireplace, exclaiming that there was a figure lurking under the porch. Before he could run out of the house to "beat the shit out of him," his mother intervened, saying the man might have a gun and he should stay inside. Mrs. Ramey herself went out on the porch to look, but by then the figure was gone.

The story of a man lurking near the Ramey house between 9:45 and 10:00 P.M. was significant news. It could not have been Roger Coleman, who had been placed at the mine on Looney Creek at that time by several independent and undisputed witnesses as well as his own testimony. Surely, McCloskey thought, here was the real killer. Moreover, the police had apparently not told the defense about this, and if they knew about it, it was probably a violation of their obligation to reveal exculpatory evidence. Had the Rameys told the police about this figure? No, Mrs. Ramey said, he was the first person they had ever told. McCloskey raised his eyebrows.

If it made little sense that the Rameys had failed to tell the police about seeing a figure lurking so close to the McCoy house, what Donnie Ramey said next was even more puzzling. According to Donnie, when he and Michael arrived home on the night of the murder there was a pickup truck in his parking place at the bottom of the hill, across the street from the side of the McCoy house. He recognized it as belonging to Roger Coleman. Moreover, Ramey said, when Jack Davidson came to the house the next morning, he told Davidson about Coleman's truck having been there the night before.

When McCloskey expressed amazement at Donnie Ramey's story, Mrs. Ramey confirmed it, saying she remembered Donnie coming into the house and cursing, "That damn Roger Coleman has his truck down there in my parking place."

McCloskey did not know what to make of the Rameys. The lurking-figure story was helpful, but the Rameys' claim that they had not told the police about it detracted from its constitutional significance—the police couldn't be faulted for not disclosing something they didn't know. Moreover, the Rameys' failure to report it impacted on the credibility of the story.

Even more puzzling was the claim about Roger Coleman's truck. McCloskey knew that if there *was* a truck in the Rameys' parking area between 9:30 and 9:45 P.M., it couldn't have been Coleman's. Yet, when pressed, the Rameys said they were certain about the time. McCloskey also knew the Rameys had to be wrong about telling the police. If anyone had told the police they saw Roger Coleman's truck parked next to the McCoy house on the night of the murder, it surely would have been brought out at trial. The police would have persuaded the Rameys that they could have been wrong about the time, or, failing that, the prosecutor would explain it that way to the jury. One way or the other, in a case this difficult and important, the prosecutor would not fail to use testimony placing Roger Coleman at the scene of the crime that night. When he left the Ramey home, Jim McCloskey was puzzled. He could not reconcile their story with the facts as he knew them, but neither could he fathom any reason for them to lie.

When Jim McCloskey departed Grundy in early April, he had not solved the murder of Wanda McCoy, but everything he had learned strengthened his belief that Roger Coleman was innocent. Everything, that is, except for Donnie Ramey's claim about seeing Roger's truck. That was a puzzle that remained to be solved.

When McCloskey called Coleman to report the results of his trip, Coleman was pleased, but subdued. Death row, he explained, was in the mood of deep, quiet tension that always marked the approach of an execution. Earl "Goldie" Clanton was on deathwatch in Richmond. He was executed on April 14, 1988.

On April 22, 1988, John Hall and his associates at Debevoise & Plimpton in New York filed Coleman's federal petition for writ of habeas corpus. The petition had been prepared using the arguments and evidence gathered for the state habeas corpus petition a year and a half earlier and held pending the outcome of McCloskey's investigation. Now, in addition to the claims previously made in the state petition, Coleman's lawyers were able to strengthen the claim that the state had violated its constitutional duty to provide exculpatory evidence to the defense. In particular, they charged the state with failing to produce the pry-mark report and the Scott and Sandy Stiltner interviews.

Of course, there was a problem that had nothing to do with the merits of Coleman's petition for habeas corpus—the question of whether the one-day "delay" in filing the notice of appeal in the state court would foreclose consideration of his constitutional claims.

Twenty-five years earlier, in *Fay* v. *Noia*, the Supreme Court held that a prisoner whose confession was coerced was entitled to habeas corpus relief in federal court even though his counsel had failed to file a state court appeal. In ringing language the court declared that no fair-minded person or civilized society would permit a citizen who had been deprived of his liberty in violation of the Constitution to nevertheless languish in prison because of his lawyer's mistake.

As irrefutable as the logic and humanity of the *Fay* decision seemed, to the dour judges of the Reagan/Rehnquist revolution it was simply another example of liberal criminal mollycoddling and federal court interference with the rights of the states. If the principle of *Fay* was applied to the issue in Coleman's case, he would win, and *Fay* had not yet been expressly overruled. However, in recent years the Supreme Court had decided a number of cases in a manner that was inconsistent with *Fay*'s holding, and most lawyers agreed that the case was all but dead.

Coleman's best chance was for his case to be assigned to a federal judge who believed that human life and adherence to the Constitution were more important values than a state's interest in strict adherence to its procedural rules. Such a judge could use what was left of the *Fay* decision and the unusual facts that had led to the state's claim of late filing to justify considering Coleman's case on the merits. If the district judge granted discovery and a hearing, and the facts of the case worked out as well as the lawyers hoped, there was a good chance that a writ of habeas corpus would be granted, upheld by the court of appeals, and allowed to stand by the Supreme Court. A case in which the lower court specifically found that a man was facing death as a result of a trial in which his constitutional rights were violated was not the kind of case the Supreme Court would prefer as the vehicle for declaring the death of the *Fay* decision. There would be plenty of opportunities for that in circumstances that were not so starkly unfair.

Coleman's petition was filed in the United States District Court for the Western District of Virginia, headquartered in Roanoke. The case was assigned to the Honorable Glen Williams in the Abingdon Division.

When Jim McCloskey returned from Grundy he had been greeted by a tremendous workload of other cases that were reaching a critical stage. By the end of 1989 Centurion Ministries had obtained freedom for three more prisoners. While commitments to those matters had diverted his attention from Coleman, McCloskey kept in touch with Roger and his lawyers and followed the progress of the pending habeas corpus case. He also renewed his suggestion that the lawyers try to obtain an order for DNA testing of the blood and semen evidence. For the most part the lawyers were opposed to the idea. They had lots of reasons, all logical. It was unlikely, especially at this stage, that a judge would order such a test. If he did, it was unlikely, based on existing technology, that the test would prove anything, given that the crucial evidence had been sitting unprotected in a box in Jack Davidson's office for eight years. And, in any event, the issue before the courts, assuming the late filing could be overcome, was not guilt or innocence but whether constitutional error had occurred at Coleman's trial. A jury had already decided that Coleman was guilty, and under the American criminal justice system it was unlikely that any court would reconsider that finding unless the conviction was set aside for legal reasons, especially given the law in Virginia that prohibited the introduction of newly discovered evidence more than twenty-one days after the entry of a judgment of conviction. If it comes down to where nothing is left but executive clemency, the lawyers said, maybe then we can get the governor to order a DNA test.

McCloskey understood the arguments, and disagreed with them. If Coleman was innocent, and McCloskey believed he was, DNA testing was the best, and perhaps the only, way to prove it. McCloskey knew from past experience that if convincing proof of innocence could be presented to a court, most judges would find a way to set the defendant free, whatever procedural barriers might exist. Still, Coleman himself was inclined to follow his lawyers' advice. The federal habeas corpus petition was pending and had at least some chance of success, and there would be time later to seek testing from Judge Persin, who everyone agreed was a decent man.

McCloskey suspected that an unspoken reason for the lawyers' opposition to DNA testing was their own doubt that Coleman was innocent, and a fear that the test would simply confirm his guilt. Judges are human, and just as proof of innocence was likely to motivate a judge to find a way around any legal barriers to granting relief, further proof of guilt might motivate him to ignore trial errors that would otherwise provide a basis for habeas corpus relief and a new trial. Jim McCloskey was not interested in anything other than guilt or innocence, but there was no urgent need to press the issue further at this time. If the lawyers somehow succeeded on the petition for habeas corpus, the state would have the option of trying Coleman again, and he had no doubt that at that point an effort would be made to subject the evidence to DNA testing. If not, McCloskey would raise the issue again.

Meanwhile, on death row Roger Coleman was wrestling with a development in his relationship with Robert White. Over the years their visits and correspondence had become more frequent. On paper and over the visitors' telephones at Mecklenburg they enjoyed discussions covering a broad range of topics, with particular emphasis on their relations with other people and the problems and dreams they were confronting on a day-to-day basis in their own lives. Roger thought White had an unusual understanding of what he was experiencing and trying to describe about life on death row. For his part, Robert White thought Roger had an extraordinary ability to observe people and events objectively and from a variety of perspectives, rather than exclusively in light of his own interests.

In the summer of 1988, during a visit to Roger at Mecklenburg, Robert White said he would like their relationship to be more than an intellectual dialogue. He thought they should regard each other as friends. Roger was hesitant. He said he wanted to be sure White knew what he was getting into. Being the friend of a man who has been condemned to death, Roger said, is not an easy prospect, and Roger did not take such commitments lightly. He asked White a number of questions, and after White answered them in a letter, Roger concluded that White *did* know what he was getting into. From that time on they treated each other as friends. In fact, they became best friends, and finally came to think of each other as brothers.

Later that year two events occurred that potentially lessened Coleman's chance of avoiding the electric chair. In November, George Bush was elected president, creating the strong probability that one or two of the most liberal, anti-death penalty members of the Supreme Court would soon be replaced with pro-death penalty conservatives. William Brennan and Thurgood Marshall were both in their eighties and both had been hanging on to their seats on the Supreme Court through the Reagan years, hoping that a Democratic president would be elected and replace them with someone more in tune with their judicial philosophies. It was unlikely that either could hang on for another four years. With either Brennan or Marshall replaced, Coleman's case would be almost hopeless at the Supreme Court level. Moreover, a district court judge like Glen Williams might feel even safer in dismissing the petition on procedural grounds with the prospect that Brennan or Marshall or both were likely to be replaced.

A month after the election, on December 6, 1988, Judge Williams in fact dismissed Coleman's case, holding that the mistake in allegedly filing the notice of appeal in the Virginia Supreme Court one day late precluded consideration of a federal petition for writ of habeas corpus. At the same time, in what Coleman's lawyers saw as a cynical effort to ensure against the possibility that his procedural ruling would be reversed, Judge Williams also purported to consider and reject Coleman's arguments on the merits.

In due course Coleman's lawyers appealed Judge Williams's decision to the United States Court of Appeals for the Fourth Circuit, albeit without much hope of success, given its reputation as one of the most conservative circuits in the country.

Jim McCloskey again raised the DNA issue, but the lawyers continued to resist. Now, however, McCloskey decided to press harder. The later an issue is raised in a death-row prisoner's legal battle, the more likely it is that a court will see the claim as last-minute desperation and question its good faith. McCloskey was afraid the time was approaching when that factor would come into play with respect to asking for DNA testing. He wanted to ask for the tests before Coleman's legal avenues were so nearly exhausted that the state could claim that the very fact of the testing would delay his execution.

Since the lawyers seemed unmovable, McCloskey tried to persuade Coleman to overrule them. If the client insisted, his lawyers would have no alternative but to seek the test—it was Coleman, after all, who was facing the electric chair. Now, however, Roger himself came up with a reason to oppose the test: While he was in jail awaiting trial, he told McCloskey, he had sexual intercourse with a female attendant who came on to him one night, and he now believed that she was a plant and that the state had substituted the sperm from that coupling for the sperm from Wanda McCoy in order to convict him. If he was right, the swab in the evidence box would be his, and the DNA test would suggest his guilt rather that prove his innocence.

McCloskey was furious. People who are sent to prison often develop paranoid ideas, especially if they are sentenced to death, and even more so if they are innocent, but McCloskey had long realized that because an inmate's paranoia is understandable doesn't mean he had to abandon his own sanity. Coleman's story was utterly ridiculous, McCloskey knew it and he told Coleman so. Even if it was true that Coleman had intercourse in the jail, unless a number of people with no apparent motive to do so had lied under oath, the semen swabs had been taken from Wanda McCoy's body and tested by Elmer Gist before Coleman was even arrested. It was Gist's finding that the semen was from someone with type B blood like Coleman's that had played a major role in McGlothlin's decision to charge him.

Jim McCloskey was inclined to blame Coleman's story on prisoner's paranoia and to continue to believe in his innocence, but he could not deny that his belief was shaken. An obvious alternative was that Coleman was guilty and did not want the DNA test because he knew it could only hurt him. When Coleman and his lawyers persisted in refusing to seek DNA testing, McCloskey gave him an ultimatum. "I still believe in you," he said, "but I've got lots of other people who need my help. When you decide to go for the DNA test, I'll be back, but until then, I've got to use my time helping people who cooperate with me."

In March 1989, Coleman told a newspaper reporter that he thought that if his appeals were denied, he was likely to be the next person on death row to be executed. "I'm afraid of dying," he said, "but the fear doesn't rule me. Today, I'm dealing with it good. When they take me to shave my head, though, I don't know how I'll be. I hope I'll deal with it like a man, but I don't know."

Coleman was wrong about being next. On August 30, 1989, Virginia electrocuted 34-year-old Alton Waye.

Also that summer, the subject of innocent men being sentenced to death intruded on the public's attention when Texas finally released Randall Adams, the subject of the widely praised documentary *The Thin Blue Line*. Adams had been on death row for thirteen years before Texas was forced to concede that the true murderer was probably the state's star witness against him. Many of the men on death row in Virginia had also followed the highly publicized saga of Joseph Brown, who was fifteen hours away from execution in Florida when a federal court stayed his execution to consider new evidence. In 1988 Florida finally released Brown when his accuser recanted and his recantation was corroborated by other witnesses and evidence.

None of the men Virginia had executed up to that point had made a serious claim that they were innocent of the crime that had sent them to death row, but in addition to Roger, several other men who remained on the row did proclaim their innocence. None of them doubted that it was possible for an innocent man to be executed.

The previous year, two prominent death-penalty researchers had published the results of a four-year effort to quantify the number of innocent men and women who had been convicted of capital crimes in America. They were able to identify 350 such cases, 139 of which had resulted in the defendant receiving a death sentence. Twenty-three of the defendants had been executed. And those were only the highly unusual cases in which proof of innocence emerged after the execution.

The advent of DNA testing soon began to produce additional examples of the conviction of innocent men. In June 1996, the National Institute of Justice, the research arm of the United States Department of Justice, published a study entitled "Convicted by Juries, Exonerated by Science," in which the authors described twenty-eight cases in which a defendant had been convicted of rape or rape/murder and later proved innocent by DNA analysis. Three of those men had been sentenced to death, and all but one had spent long years in prison before their exoneration. In every instance, if the victim was alive she had mistakenly identified the defendant as her attacker, and in most cases the defendant had become a suspect because of a prior arrest or conviction. In many of the cases, like Coleman's, the prosecution had relied on blood-type evidence and/or hair comparisons.

The most startling information in the Justice Department study, however, involved some ten thousand cases that had been submitted to the FBI laboratory for analysis before trial after a prime suspect was identified and often arrested and charged with the crime. Of those eight thousand cases in which DNA analysis was successfully completed, some 25 percent resulted in a finding that *excluded* the suspect as the perpetrator. The implications of that finding are staggering for convictions obtained where no conclusive DNA test is possible. But for the DNA tests, statistics suggest that most of those two thousand suspects would have been tried and erroneously convicted.

In October 1989, Coleman's case was argued in the Fourth Circuit. Everyone understood that time was running out. If the Fourth Circuit ruled against him, Coleman's lawyers would ask the Supreme Court to hear the case by filing a petition for writ of certiorari, but certiorari (full review by the Supreme Court) is granted in only a tiny percentage of cases. The strong probability was that the Court would exercise its discretion *not* to hear the case by denying certiorari, either before the Supreme Court term ended in June 1990 or, more likely, when they resumed hearing cases in October. At that point, Coleman would be left with a series of "successive" petitions, which almost never succeed and which, in recent years, were being dismissed by the courts with increasing rapidity and disdain.

After that there would be nothing left but a petition to the governor for clemency—never a likely source of relief, and even less so in recent years, as politicians increasingly sought to outdo each other in pledging support for more use of the death penalty. Even if a clemency plea is based on a claim of innocence, it suffers the further difficulty that in most states, including Virginia, there is no viable mechanism for resolving factual disputes. State law-enforcement agencies almost never concede that they made a mistake, and politically governors are a lot safer accepting the police version of events than those advanced by the condemned.

It is said that the prospect of execution marvelously concentrates the mind, and it concentrated Roger Coleman's. The time had come to put aside his own paranoia and his lawyers' reluctance and move ahead. "I want to go for the DNA test," he told his lawyers, "and I want you to find witnesses down in Grundy who know the truth. There has to be someone."

Coleman's lawyers could hardly deny that the time had come to begin examining the innocence question, but looking for further witnesses in Grundy at this late date seemed to them like a waste of time, and Roger's suggestion that they put an ad in the local Grundy paper asking for witnesses to come forward only seemed likely to stir up community resentment and lessen any chance of clemency. If Coleman wanted to pursue the DNA issue, however, they would now do so. Dr. Edward Blake and his company, Forensic Science Associates, were conducting tests known as polymerase chain reaction amplification (PCR testing). If the samples taken from the body of Wanda McCoy contained enough remaining sperm to conduct a successful PCR test, and if the state would agree to the testing or a judge would order it, it might prove Coleman's innocence.

Among the characteristics of human DNA are six traits, or markers, called alleles. They are known as 1.1, 1.2, 1.3, 2, 3 and 4. Everyone has two alleles, although they can be the same two. In other words, your two alleles may be 1.1 and 1.1, or any other combination of the six alleles; there are twenty-one combinations in all. A PCR test might reveal the alleles of the person whose sperm was left on Wanda McCoy by her rapist, and if they were not the same as Roger Coleman's alleles, it would prove that he could not have been the rapist. That would not necessarily mean he was not the murderer, but the state's case so heavily depended on the proposition that the two crimes were committed by one and the same man that prosecutors would be hard-pressed to adopt some other scenario now.

On the other hand, if the rapist's alleles were the same as Coleman's, it would not prove him guilty, since, unlike more sophisticated tests commonly known as DNA "fingerprinting," PCR testing cannot make a positive identification but only reduce the field of persons who could have produced the DNA. It would, however, add significantly to the chain of circumstantial evidence that had resulted in Coleman's conviction.

After obtaining clearance from his firm to spend what was bound to be a substantial sum of money as well as time on PCR testing, Chris Painter at Arnold & Porter asked the attorney general's office to agree to have the blood and semen evidence sent off to Dr. Blake for testing. The attorney general refused, and on January 2, 1990, Coleman's lawyers filed a motion with Judge Persin in Grundy, asking that he order the tests.

If the reluctance to seek DNA testing previously displayed by Coleman and his lawyers suggested some concern about the outcome, vigorous opposition to testing by the Virginia attorney general's office indicated that they too were less certain about the result than their public insistence on Coleman's guilt would admit. Indeed, one may wonder why the state's chief law-enforcement officer would oppose a scientific test that might result in saving the state from executing an innocent citizen.

Nevertheless, Donald Curry, the deputy attorney general assigned to oppose Coleman's legal maneuvers and hustle him to the electric chair, argued that the proposed test was unlikely to prove anything, that the request was simply another effort to delay Coleman's execution and that in any event Judge Persin had no jurisdiction to order it.

As a matter of law Curry may have been right about the last point. Fortunately, however, unlike the attorney general's office, Judge Persin was more interested in justice than in legal technicalities. After a series of arguments and briefs, on April 26, 1990, Judge Persin held that the swabs should be sent to Dr. Blake in California. The state can appeal if it wants to, he said, but I am not going to be the one to refuse a test that might prevent the execution of an innocent man.

Meanwhile, on January 31, 1990, the Fourth Circuit Court of Appeals had affirmed Judge Williams's order dismissing Coleman's petition for writ of habeas corpus. Unlike Judge Williams, however, the court of appeals did not pretend to resolve the merits of Coleman's claims, ruling only that the one-day delay that had occurred four years earlier had indeed resulted in a waiver of Coleman's right to seek federal habeas corpus. After rehearing was denied in late May, Coleman's lawyers filed their petition for certiorari in the Supreme Court. It probably would not be ruled on until October, when it probably would be denied.

—

Chapter 15

Starting Over: Kitty Behan

On Monday, July 2, 1990, Kathleen "Kitty" Behan began work as Arnold & Porter's newest associate lawyer. Tall, slim, with auburn hair and Irish freckles, Kitty had graduated from Columbia Law School a year earlier and worked for the ACLU before joining the firm.

Kitty Behan was born in Milwaukee, Wisconsin, on July 28, 1963, the third child and second daughter of Peter and Marie Behan. Two more boys and another girl would follow. Peter and Marie are one of those couples who produce exceptionally smart children. In a family that lived most of the time in educated, genteel, but very real economic hardship, three of their six children became lawyers, one is a psychologist, and another is a business executive. The sixth recently graduated from college.

Kitty's father, Peter, is a libertarian. His strong opinions, deep interest in public affairs and insistence that his children learn to think for themselves provided an atmosphere of learning and intellectual excitement in the Behan household.

When Kitty was a young girl her mother and father were dedicated Catholics, and Kitty had the usual little girl's fascination with the ritual and drama of the Church. As her father's libertarian views grew stronger, however, he decided that his belief in freedom of thought and action was inconsistent with the Church's emphasis on faith and acceptance of doctrine. The year Kitty was eight, her father left the Church altogether. Kitty followed her father in rejecting Church dogma, but retained her belief in the importance of good works and the possibility of redemption.

As a teenager Kitty's interests turned to science, and her academic achievements earned her a job at the United States Centers for Disease Control, where research done while she was still in high school resulted in the publication of two articles in the *Journal of Clinical Microbiology*.

When Kitty won admission to Yale on a full scholarship, she began by taking math, physics and chemistry courses, but her growing interest in social issues soon resulted in her adopting a new goal of attending law school and practicing public-interest law. She wanted to live in New York City and study at Columbia University. In 1985 she was admitted to Columbia Law School.

While a scholarship covered her law-school tuition, Kitty still had to provide for expenses, and, like most law students on scholarship, she did so with a combination of student loans and work. When her first-year grades confirmed her ability, Kitty obtained the job she had most wanted—as a research assistant to Professor James Leibman. Leibman was writing a treatise on habeas corpus, and part of Kitty's job was to do research for the book.

In addition to his other work, Professor Liebman often accepted court appointments to represent prisoners in death-penalty cases, and during the second year she worked for him, Leibman asked Kitty to help with one of them. For Kitty it was work that struck powerful chords of past experience and beliefs. The concepts of reverence for life and belief in redemption which Kitty retained from her Catholic heritage seemed violated by a legal system that would countenance killing a helpless person in cold blood, regardless of his crime. Kitty Behan resolved to include death-penalty work in her professional life, and as graduation approached, she applied for a job handling death-penalty cases for the NAACP Legal Defense Fund Inc. Unfortunately, the "Inc. Fund" was at the limit of its budget and unable to hire her.

Disappointed, but determined to work in a public-interest position rather than succumb to the blandishments (and reputed horrors) of the large corporate practice law firms that pursue law graduates with her qualifications, Kitty accepted a job with the ACLU in Washington, D.C. Her work involved contesting the government's denial of Freedom of Information Act requests. The work was boring, and Kitty kept her eyes open for a chance to move on to something more satisfying.

Soon a more urgent problem presented itself. Kitty was sick, and no one could tell her why, or what to do about it. The illness had started in law school with occasional headaches and a feeling of fatigue. Now it was progressing to slurred speech, an intermittent limp and loss of memory. Her illness was finally diagnosed as lupus—a strange disease that, for scarcely understood reasons, can cause an inflammation of the brain. There is no known cure for lupus, but sometimes its symptoms can be treated successfully with drugs. On the advice of her doctors, Kitty took three months off.

Kitty's lupus responded to drug treatment, and in the spring of 1990 she began looking for another job, this time with large Washington law firms where she could earn enough to care for her medical needs properly. The offer that was most attractive was Arnold & Porter, a firm with a good reputation for allowing its young lawyers to spend some of their time on pro bono work—including death-penalty cases.

During her employment interviews Kitty had disclosed her interest in working on death cases, so it was not surprising that a few weeks after she joined the firm the assignment partner asked if she would like to work on the Roger Coleman case.

At first, Kitty was reluctant, since the partner's description of the case made it seem unlikely to amount to much more than a death-watch, prolonged briefly by a series of unsuccessful efforts to persuade some court to consider Coleman's arguments on the merits. On reconsideration, however, Kitty decided that such a case would at least give her a chance to refamiliarize herself with the rapidly changing law applicable to death cases, and to participate in the kind of massive, sophisticated effort a firm like Arnold & Porter can bring to even a hopeless case. Besides, she wanted to work on death-penalty cases, and this was apparently the only one the firm was handling that needed additional staffing. Thus, in early August 1990, Kitty Behan became the latest in a line of new Arnold & Porter associates to become the junior lawyer on the Coleman case.

If Kitty joined the Coleman team without much enthusiasm, from Roger Coleman's perspective it was a familiar and equally uninspiring event. Older lawyer quits case, younger lawyer assigned, not much happens—except that the string of available appeals continues to grow shorter, along with Roger's life expectancy.

But at that point, Kitty Behan didn't know anything about the facts of Roger Coleman's case, and Roger Coleman didn't know anything about Kitty Behan. It was not long before both of them were greatly and gratefully surprised; Kitty because she soon came to believe that her new client might actually be innocent, and Roger because he soon observed that the new lawyer on his case was attacking the state's evidence with unprecedented energy and determination.

Chapter 16

A New Suspect and Other Mysteries

Back in April when Judge Persin ordered the state to send forensic samples to Dr. Blake for PCR testing, Donald Curry had vowed to appeal. Someone in the attorney general's office apparently thought better of it, however, and after some bickering about procedures, on July 17, 1990, Judge Persin signed a final order providing for the tests.

To most of his lawyers, the question of whether Roger Coleman would ever be able to prove his innocence began and ended with the results of Dr. Blake's testing. But to Kitty Behan, newly assigned to the case, it didn't make sense to do nothing while waiting for the result of a test that Dr. Blake himself said was likely to be inconclusive.

After reading the transcript of Coleman's trial and the report of Jim McCloskey's investigation in 1988, Kitty went down to Mecklenburg to meet with her new client. She thought Roger was surprisingly articulate for someone with his background. He thought Kitty looked awfully young for someone who was supposed to save his life—but the new lawyers on his case always looked young.

Two things about Kitty did impress Roger: first, the fact that she had taken the time to come and see him—some lawyers had worked on his case for years without ever meeting him; second, the fact that she seemed genuinely interested in what he had to say about the evidence in the case. She asked him several questions that showed she was well acquainted with the trial record and was trying to figure out how she could prove that he was innocent. Also, she was the first lawyer Roger had talked to who was open to his idea of advertising for information in the Grundy newspaper. When she left, Kitty promised she would try to get permission to place the ad.

When Kitty returned to Washington, she began planning a trip to Grundy to reopen the investigation of Wanda McCoy's murder. First, as she had promised Roger, she reraised the issue of a newspaper ad. The other lawyers thought it was a waste of time, and might do more harm than good by rekindling passions against Roger in the community. Kitty finally persuaded them that it was unlikely Roger would suffer more harm from aroused passions in Grundy than the state had already planned for him in the basement of the penitentiary in Richmond. The firm finally agreed to place an ad in the August 9, 1990, issue of the *The Virginia Mountaineer*, Grundy's weekly paper. In substance, the ad claimed that Coleman was innocent and asked anyone with information about the murder of Wanda McCoy to call his lawyers collect at Arnold & Porter. It cost thirty-five dollars.

To everyone's surprise, a response to the ad came on the first day it ran. Chris Yukins, one of the other lawyers on the case, took a call from a woman who refused to give her name. She said she knew who killed Wanda McCoy, and it wasn't Roger Coleman.

There are many problems in trying to prove the innocence of someone who has already been convicted of a crime. For one thing, it is always difficult to prove a negative—that someone didn't do something. For another, neither the police nor the courts like the idea that they made a mistake, and both are extremely resistant to evidence that they did. Moreover, to accept that the convict is innocent is to turn a solved case into an unsolved one, an unhappy result for all but the convict. Thus, the task becomes a little easier if the innocent defendant can, at the same time, provide the identity of the real perpetrator.

It was therefore with special excitement that Coleman's lawyers learned that the anonymous caller not only said Coleman was innocent but also claimed that the real killer had confessed the crime to her. The caller said that several years earlier a young man had attacked her at a friend's house, forced her into a bedroom and tried to rape her. When she screamed and struggled, he put his hand over her mouth and said if she didn't shut up, he would "do [her] like he did that girl on Slate Creek." At the time, the caller said, she didn't understand the reference, but later a friend told her the man was referring to Wanda McCoy. Moreover, sometime later she confronted the man and asked him point-blank about the murder and he admitted it.

The woman's identification of the man she was accusing was so startling that when Yukins heard it, he was hardly able to contain his excitement. It was Donnie Ramey, also known as Trouble, one of the brothers who, at the time of the murder, lived in the house immediately above the McCoys' house.*

Donnie Ramey was born in 1962, one of nine children of Bobby Ramey, a coal miner, and his wife, Helen. Donnie left school and went to work when he was sixteen, first as a carpenter's apprentice, and a year later as a coal miner. At age sixteen he had been in the seventh grade, and he could neither read nor write. According to Donnie, the nickname "Trouble" was given him by the manager of a local skating rink where he hung out as a kid. If so, it was prophetic. Before he was sixteen he spent a month in a detention center for selling stolen merchandise. Not counting using and selling illegal drugs, which he has admitted but never been charged with, Donnie's "troubles" included misdemeanor convictions for assaulting a police officer and destruction of property.

In March 1981, Donnie, his sister Portia and his younger brother Michael lived with their parents in the house that perched on a hill above Brad and Wanda McCoy's. Two years earlier the Rameys had told Jim McCloskey the story of seeing Coleman's truck parked next to the McCoys' house on the night of the murder and of Michael seeing someone lurking in the shadows below their porch at about the same time. Kitty had read McCloskey's report as part of her introduction to the case, and, like McCloskey, she was puzzled by the implausibility of the Rameys' claim that they had not reported the "shadowy figure" to the police. Kitty did not know Donnie's even stranger story about Roger Coleman's truck, which Jim had not included in his report.

---

* In affidavits later provided to the state and a deposition taken in a later civil case, Donnie Ramey has denied the sexual assault charges made by Teresa Horn and the other women referred to below; denied any involvement in Wanda McCoy's murder; and denied ever saying he was involved in the murder.

If the anonymous caller's claim seemed extremely promising, it was also problematical. It was hard to imagine anyone freely admitting to a vicious murder, especially to someone who might well report him to the police. Moreover, the caller had refused to give her name. Yukins told her how important her information was, and that it was essential that he come to Grundy and talk to her in person. The woman had promised to think it over and call back, but there was no telling if she would.

Late in the afternoon of the first call, the anonymous caller called again. She said her name was Teresa Horn, and she was living with her boyfriend not far from Grundy. She agreed to meet with Kitty and Chris the following Friday at her mother's trailer on Dismal Creek, east of Grundy. She said her mother knew the story, but her boyfriend did not, and she didn't want him involved.

On Monday morning, August 13, Chris and Kitty called Jim McCloskey and told him what Teresa Horn had said. McCloskey remembered interviewing the Rameys and now told them Donnie's story about Roger Coleman's truck being parked by the McCoy house at a time when the undisputed evidence showed he had been else-where. That Ramey might have been involved in the murder was emi-nently logical, McCloskey said. From his house he had easy access to the McCoys' house without being seen, and he was in a position to escape the murder house and return home undetected in the short time available between the time Wanda's throat was cut and Brad McCoy's arrival home.

Everyone agreed that on their trip to Grundy, Kitty and Chris should concentrate on building the confidence of Teresa Horn and checking the reliability of her story. They would stay away from the Rameys until later.

On Friday, August 17, Kitty Behan and Chris Yukins flew from Washington to Roanoke, Virginia, rented a car, and drove the 175 addi-tional miles to Grundy to meet with Teresa Horn. Teresa was an attrac-tive but hard-looking, dark-haired woman who had just turned twen-ty-two the day before. Her mother, Brenda Keene, welcomed Kitty and Chris into her home and directed them to a sofa in the living room of the neatly maintained trailer. Teresa's father, who worked a night shift, was asleep in a bedroom, and her chubby, cheerful one-year-old son, Derek, played at her feet as she sat across the room from the two lawyers.

In plain, unabashed language, Teresa Horn repeated the accusations she had made on the telephone. The attack, she said, had occurred in 1987 at a trailer owned by Jeff Chaffles's mother, who was out of town. At the time, Teresa was working at Clancy's Bar near Grundy, and when the bar closed, Chaffles, who was drunk, asked her to drive him home. She did, and two other men also left the bar and drove to Chaffles's trailer. They were Mark Helton, who Teresa had known for some time, and Donnie Ramey, who she knew only slightly. Shortly after they arrived at the house, Chaffles went to bed while Teresa and the two men sat around and drank. According to Teresa, Donnie suddenly grabbed her and started taking off her clothes while Mark Helton held her. Ramey then picked her up, carried her into a bedroom, locked the door and threw her on the bed, hitting her face on the nightstand. He knelt on top of her, trying to kiss her and force her legs apart with his knees. Teresa struggled and screamed, and it was then, she claimed, that Donnie said if she didn't shut up he would "do [her] like he did that girl on Slate Creek."

Finally, Teresa said, Mark Helton broke into the bedroom, pulled Donnie off her and hit him. After the attack, Teresa immediately drove to the house where her ex-boyfriend Kenny Clevenger was living and told him about what happened. Clevenger knew Ramey and told Teresa he knew of another time when Ramey had sexually attacked a woman, reaching into her vagina with his hand. Kenny Clevenger said that was why he had started calling Trouble Ramey by a second nickname, "The Hand."

Teresa Horn went on to claim that sometime after the attack she saw Mark Helton again, and at that time he explained Donnie's reference to the girl on Slate Creek. Mark said Donnie had also admitted to him that he had killed Wanda McCoy, and as a result Mark had moved out of Donnie's trailer, where they had been living. Moreover, Teresa said, she herself had seen Donnie on two subsequent occasions and asked him about the murder. The first time was at the Acapulco Club, where she asked him directly if he had killed the girl on Slate Creek. At first, she said, he wouldn't answer, but finally he hung his head and said, "Yeah." Later, when she saw him again, she asked if he wasn't afraid the police would find out what he did, and he said no, because the case was closed.

At the conclusion of Teresa's recitation, her mother said that Teresa

had told her the same stories. According to Teresa, she was now vol-
unteering her information because she had been receiving obscene
and threatening phone calls that she thought might be coming from
Donnie Ramey. Teresa and her mother believed the calls were the
result of recent newspaper articles about Coleman's effort to prove his
innocence, and were intended to warn Teresa to keep quiet about what
Ramey had told her. The most recent call had come just three days earlier. Teresa's mother had answered the phone, and the caller, apparently thinking it was Teresa, had made an obscene remark. Teresa said
she picked up the phone shortly after her mother, and heard enough
to believe she recognized Donnie Ramey's voice.

Kitty and Chris asked Teresa Horn if she would put her charges in
writing. Teresa hesitated, but said she would.

When Kitty Behan and Chris Yukins left the Horn trailer, they were
elated. If Teresa Horn's story was true, and they could support it, there
was a chance it would save Roger Coleman's life and earn him freedom. Moreover, there were several reasons the story seemed credible,
including the logic of Ramey's involvement based on his proximity to
the McCoy house; his poor reputation; her mother's claim that Teresa
had told her the stories years earlier; and the fact that Teresa had given
them the names of two men who, she said, could verify parts of the
story.

On the other hand, although Teresa had impressed both lawyers as
honest and forthright, they could see that her story would be easy to
attack. She had failed to report Donnie's alleged attack to the authorities, and her willingness to meet and talk to Ramey on later occasions
seemed odd if he had tried to rape her. On one of the occasions she
described, when Donnie had allegedly admitted the murder, Teresa
had even accepted his offer to drive her home from the Acapulco Club
after a night of drinking.

Teresa Horn's story could be the key to saving Roger Coleman's life,
but it would need to be carefully checked. In that mood, the two
lawyers made the long trip home.

When Chris and Kitty got back to Washington, they learned that the
advertisement in the *Mountaineer*, which ran again on Thursday,
August 16, had produced another lead. While they were in Grundy, a
woman had called Arnold & Porter and said she had been working at
a mine site the day after Wanda McCoy was murdered when one of

the coal-truck drivers discovered a plastic garbage bag containing a shirt, a sheet, a map and a pair of scissors. They called the sheriff, who said it wasn't in his jurisdiction but he would send the police. When the police didn't come, the men threw the bag and its contents into a ravine near the mine. The woman would not give her name, but said another person who would know what happened was named Keester Shortridge. She provided phone numbers for Shortridge and said she thought he would be willing to talk.

At first it was not clear whether the caller's information was significant, but it seemed worth following up, and the next week, after several unsuccessful efforts, Chris Yukins reached Keester Shortridge on the telephone. Shortridge confirmed and clarified the story. In fact, he said, he was the owner of the mine and had found the bag in the back of his own pickup truck. His wife, Nell, often put garbage from his house in the truck, which he would discard at the mine site. A day or so after the murder he found such a bag. Before throwing it away he decided to check its contents. His wife, he said, was a little crazy, and sometimes threw away perfectly good things, like his blue jeans. What he recalled seeing were two sheets, some pillowcases, a clock, a flashlight and a pair of scissors.

Thinking the contents of the bag had come from his house, Keester said, he shoved them back in the bag and took it home. That night when he questioned his wife she denied knowing anything about the bag.

Shortridge confirmed that he and his wife had thought the bag might have something to do with the McCoy murder, so his wife had called Sheriff Ratliff, but when no one came to pick it up he took the bag and its contents back up to his mine and threw them away. The house where Keester and Nell Shortridge lived, and where the pickup truck was parked on the night of the murder, was directly across Slate Creek from Longbottom, about a quarter-mile from Brad McCoy's house.

The proximity of the Shortridge and McCoy homes made it seem worthwhile to try to find the contents of the bag, and Keester Shortridge said he thought he could point out where he had dumped it.

A week later the Coleman defense team received more good news. When the state was fighting DNA testing, one of their arguments had been that there probably wasn't enough material left for a successful test, and Dr. Blake had conceded that prospects were not favorable. Now the laboratory had completed its gross examination of the evidence, and on August 30 Dr. Blake's assistant reported that sperm had been found on the vaginal swab taken from Wanda McCoy and on the vial in which it was stored. Based on past experience, she thought there was enough to conduct a successful PCR analysis.

In the scant three weeks since Teresa Horn had responded to the advertisement in the *Mountaineer*, three avenues of investigation had appeared, each bearing the potential to prove Roger Coleman's innocence. Dr. Blake expected to have his results in late fall. To pursue the investigation in Grundy, Coleman's lawyers decided on a two-pronged attack. First, they would hire a private investigator from southwest Virginia who had good connections in Buchanan County to conduct a separate investigation of his own. At the same time, Kitty and the others would follow up the information they had received from Teresa Horn and Keester Shortridge. McCloskey agreed to return to Grundy in mid-September to work with the lawyers.

At Mecklenburg that summer, death row had been through another execution. On July 19, Richard Boggs, age twenty-eight, had become the ninth person to die in Virginia's electric chair since Roger Coleman came to the row.

Sharon Paul had returned to school at Rutgers University to seek a degree in wildlife ecology, which she thought would provide a more interesting career than teaching kindergartners. She and Roger had their first argument. He had been concerned when he did not hear from her for more than a week after one of her visits. He was afraid she had been in an accident, and placed a frantic call to her parents. When Sharon found out, she was angry that he had upset her mother and father, and he was angry that she had not contacted him. They promptly made up on the telephone.

—

Chapter 17

September 1990: Back to Grundy

In mid-September the Coleman team began an extensive effort to follow up the information they had developed. On the eleventh, Chris Yukins and Jim McCloskey interviewed Teresa Horn. Teresa repeated the story of her encounter with Donnie Ramey and his confession to the murder of Wanda Fay McCoy. There were no significant discrepancies with the story she had told a month earlier. To McCloskey, who was meeting her for the first time, she seemed honest, sincere and credible. Based on the earlier interview, Yukins had prepared a written statement for Teresa to sign, and when their meeting was over she readily signed it, making one small correction in her own hand. Teresa's mother, Brenda Keene, raised no objection to her daughter putting her charges in writing. McCloskey was greatly relieved. He had learned from bitter experience that it is not uncommon for a witness to provide crucial information but refuse to put it in writing, often at the urging of a frightened relative.

After finishing the interview with Teresa, Jim and Chris drove to Goldie Owens's log cabin, where she repeated for Chris the story she had told McCloskey in 1988 about her son-in-law Roger Matney, the jailhouse informant. However, when Jim asked her to sign an affidavit, Mrs. Owens said she was afraid that Matney would burn down her house if he learned of her charges. Both Jim and Chris told her how important it was that they have a signed statement, and Mrs. Owens said she would think about it overnight. The next day, however, she was still reluctant to sign anything.

The day served up a bigger disappointment than Goldie Owens's failure to put her information in writing. Teresa Horn had provided directions to a trailer where Mark Helton lived, and McCloskey was anxious to locate him and see if he would corroborate Teresa's story about the attempted rape and Donnie Ramey's confessions. Instead, Helton denied Teresa's story in every important detail. While conceding that he, Donnie Ramey and Jeff Chaffles had once taken Teresa to Chaffles's trailer, and that there had been a "fight" between Donnie and Teresa, Helton denied that Donnie had tried to rape her. The fight, he said, had occurred in the kitchen, after which Teresa left. He also said that Teresa was very promiscuous, implying that if anything happened it was consensual. As for Donnie confessing involvement in the McCoy murder, Helton flatly denied it had happened, or that he had ever said such a thing to Teresa Horn.

Jim McCloskey's sense was that Helton was lying, but, lying or not, his story was a huge setback. Not only did Helton deprive the defense of a crucial second witness to Donnie Ramey's attack on Teresa and confession to the McCoy murder but his story cast serious doubt on Teresa Horn's credibility.

The next day Kitty Behan arrived in Grundy. She and McCloskey quickly agreed that in light of Helton's statement, the first thing to do was to find Kenny Clevenger. If Clevenger failed to support Teresa Horn, a serious reevaluation of her story would be required. They located Clevenger at work, waiting for his coal truck to be reloaded, and he agreed to talk to them between runs. Clevenger had a friendly smile and an open, confidence-inspiring face. Kitty was immensely relieved when he said he clearly remembered Teresa coming to his house in the middle of the night and claiming that she had just been attacked by Donnie Ramey. He further confirmed that Teresa had told him about Donnie's reference to "the girl on Slate Creek" and his two subsequent confessions to the murder.

While Clevenger did not have direct knowledge of either the alleged attack on Teresa Horn or Donnie Ramey's confessions, it was hard to imagine why Teresa would have concocted such a story and

Wanda at age 15. (Mike McCoy)

Brad and Wanda at Brad's high-school prom. (Mike McCoy)

Roger Coleman and Trish in 1980. (friends of Roger Coleman)

Close-up of the Miner's Statue at the Grundy Courthouse. (John Tucker)

The murder house from the front, taken in 1992. The Ramey house is just above and to the right of it. (John Tucker)

Kitty Behan. (Kathleen A. Behan)

Tom Scott, one of Coleman's prosecutors, later organized a campaign seeking to persuade Virginia's governor not to interfere with his execution. (Tom Scott)

Robert White. (Robert White)

Jim McCloskey. (P.T.S. Photo Services/Krystin Granberg)

Roger Coleman and Sharon Paul, contact visit, April 1992. (Sharon Paul)

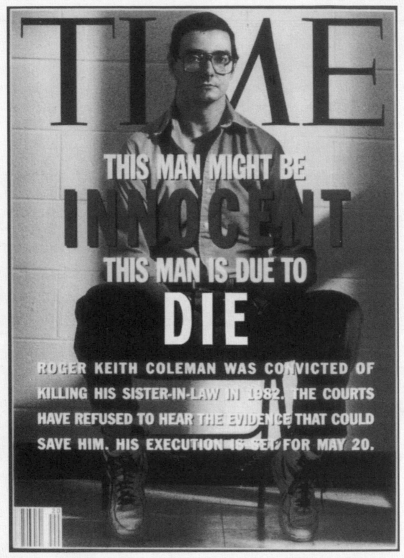

"This man might be innocent; this man is due to die." Cover of *Time* magazine, May 19, 1992. (© 1992 Time Inc. Reprinted by permission.)

awakened Kenny in the middle of the night to tell him about it if it were not true. Clevenger's information might not be admissible in court, but it went a long way toward restoring Kitty and Jim's confidence in Teresa Horn and her story.

Moreover, Kenny Clevenger claimed he had direct knowledge of another incident involving Donnie Ramey that Teresa had described. Reluctantly, he told them about the events that had led to his calling Donnie Ramey "The Hand." According to Kenny, he and a friend, Greg Daniels, were driving home from work along Slate Creek when they picked up a young woman named Jamie Sword who was walking along the side of the road. According to Kenny, Jamie somehow indicated she wanted to have sex with Greg. The three of them went to Donnie Ramey's trailer, where Jamie and Greg went into a bedroom. Kenny and Donnie were in the living room. When Greg came out of the bedroom, Donnie went in. Jamie began yelling and screaming, and then emerged from the bedroom and ran out of the house. When Kenny asked what happened, Donnie said he had shoved his hand into Jamie's "pussy." Jamie still lived in the area, Kenny said, and was now known as Jamie Sword Ross.

Kitty and Jim went back to Roger Lee Coleman's trailer, where they had established a minioffice, and typed out a statement of what Kenny Clevenger had told them. Late that afternoon they carried the statement back to Clevenger and he signed it.

Early the next morning, Kitty and Jim set out to find Jamie Sword Ross. At a country store close to where Kenny said Jamie Ross lived, they learned she had recently moved to an apartment above another country store, in Hurley, a small town near the Kentucky border. That afternoon they found her there. An attractive woman of twenty-three, with long blond hair, Jamie's shy demeanor seemed to belie Kenny Clevenger's story of her youthful sexual escapades. When Kitty told her she was representing Roger Coleman, Jamie said she had heard of him, but didn't know him, and had no knowledge of the murder. Kitty explained that what they were interested in was an incident involving her and Donnie Ramey, in the presence of Greg Daniels and Kenny Clevenger. "Oh," she said, and with little urging agreed to tell her story. She remembered the incident clearly and thought the date was March 17, 1983, when she was sixteen. She had fought with her husband and walked out on him. As she walked along the road beside

Slate Creek, Kenny Clevenger stopped his coal truck and offered her a ride. She knew Kenny and accepted the offer. In the truck was another man she didn't know, but who was introduced as Greg Daniels, also known as "Trigger."

According to Jamie, the three of them went to Ramey's trailer. After they had been there a while, Donnie sexually attacked her in a back bedroom. (She did not volunteer, and was not asked, how or why she was in the bedroom.)

> He climbed on top of me and held me down with his arms and legs and inserted one leg between my legs, using his foot to push down my pants. He was very strong.
>
> To the best of my recollection, I yelled, "Get this mother-fucking son of a bitch off me" and became very scared when Kenny and Greg did not come to my aid. I was surprised and shocked. I cried over and over for them to do something because he was hurting me. I also told Donnie to leave me alone because I had my period, but he said he had "fucked women on the rag before."
>
> Using one hand to hold me down and the other to molest me, Donnie reached his hand into my vagina and pulled out my tampon. It hurt a lot. When he raised himself to throw the tampon aside, I escaped and ran out of the room. I was yelling and swearing and attempting to put my clothes back on when Donnie came into the living room and attacked me again. He shoved me onto the couch and jumped on me again. This time I hit him in the groin and it must have hurt him, because he said, "Goddamn you," and got up. I then ran out of the house.

Just as he had denied assaulting Teresa Horn, Donnie Ramey would later deny under oath that he had sexually assaulted Jamie Sword Ross. Kitty Behan assumed he would do so, but listening to Jamie she felt the story was true. For one thing, there was no apparent reason for Jamie Ross to lie. For another, Kitty realized that Jamie's description of Ramey's behavior was strikingly similar to Teresa Horn's description of his alleged attack on her.

That afternoon Kitty and Jim returned to Teresa Horn's mother's trailer and told Teresa about Mark Helton denying her story. Teresa emphatically repeated her charges and said that Mark must be covering up for his friend Donnie.

It was true that Mark had reason to protect Donnie Ramey, and to Kitty, Teresa again seemed honest and convincing, but she wanted to meet Mark Helton herself so she could make her own judgment of his credibility. There was even a chance he would change his story.

It was 7:00 P.M. when Jim and Kitty arrived at Mark Helton's trailer. Mark emerged wearing only a pair of shorts. His shotgun and shells lay on a table by the door, and a pit bull lounged by the porch.

While Kitty kept a wary eye on the dog, who in truth seemed more lazy than fierce, McCloskey questioned Helton again about the night at Jeff Chaffles's trailer. He pointed out inconsistencies between Helton's story and the story Teresa Horn had told them. Slumped in a chair pulled up to a cluttered table, Mark mostly grunted and inspected his shoes. "Teresa told Kenny Clevenger about the attack right after it happened," Jim said. "Uh," Mark responded. "She's not mad at you, you know. She says after Donnie attacked her you came into the bedroom and rescued her." "Uh," Mark repeated. "Did he take her in the bedroom, Mark? Maybe after the argument in the kitchen you told me about?" "Naw," Helton replied, shaking his head while continuing to look at the floor. McCloskey put the question again, and this time there was a long silence. Finally Mark Helton looked up and mumbled something to the effect that if anything happened, he must have been asleep.

Jim pressed Helton again about whether Donnie had ever said he was involved in the McCoy murder, but Helton continued to shake his head and say no. Finally, when Jim asked if he had heard anything about Donnie molesting other women, Helton described a version of the "hand" incident similar to what they had been told by Kenny Clevenger.

McCloskey ended the interview by asking Helton to call if he remembered anything more about the incident between Donnie Ramey and Teresa Horn. Helton hung his head again and mumbled something noncommittal. Carefully sidestepping the now sleeping dog, Jim and Kitty left. Once she had satisfied herself that the pit bull was no threat, Kitty had watched Helton carefully throughout Jim's questioning. If there was a hearing, the state's lawyers would have to use Helton as a witness, but Kitty didn't think they would be very happy about it.

The next morning Kitty and Jim drove to the Rameys' house overlooking the site of the murder. Climbing the stairs for the first time since learning of Teresa Horn's accusations, Jim McCloskey observed the relationship between the McCoy house and the stairs with new interest. You could practically touch the back of the house from the Rameys' stairs, and the window in Brad and Wanda's bedroom was just around the corner, on the side of the house facing the Rameys but shielded from the street. Kitty wondered whether that window had really been locked on the night Wanda died.

Jim and Kitty had agreed that they would not question the Rameys in a hostile way or reveal their suspicions about Donnie. Rather, Jim would remind the Rameys of his prior visit and ask them to repeat what they knew for Kitty, whom he would introduce as Roger Coleman's lawyer.

Mr. and Mrs. Ramey were home and invited them into the house, where they all gathered around the kitchen table. Helen Ramey remembered Jim, and after some small talk she began to recite her story of the night Wanda McCoy was murdered. Bobby Ramey, weak and emaciated from black lung disease, occasionally nodded his agreement with her recitation, but mostly stared out a window that looked down on the McCoy house and most of the other houses in Longbottom. Mrs. Ramey remarked that looking out the window was now her husband's primary occupation.

The night before, Jim and Kitty had gone over the notes of Jim's conversation with the Rameys in 1988, and listening to Mrs. Ramey's rapid, nervous recitation, Jim was struck by how closely her story mirrored what she had told him two years earlier. Her choice of words and the order in which she recited events were almost identical. It sounded memorized. When she reached the point of describing the police visit to her house on the morning after the murder, Kitty interrupted: "Did anyone tell the police about Roger's truck and Michael seeing a lurking figure beside the porch?" Mrs. Ramey hesitated and looked at her husband, who continued to stare out the window. "Of course," she said. "Donnie told them about the truck, and I told them about what Michael said he saw, but they just acted like I wasn't there."

Mrs. Ramey concluded her story with the observation that while she was a light sleeper and often heard Wanda playing music inside her house at night with the windows closed, she had heard no sounds at all on the night of the murder.

Kitty switched the subject to Wanda McCoy. Mrs. Ramey said she really didn't know Wanda, but went on to say in a slightly disapproving tone that Wanda and her sister sometimes sunbathed beside the house in their bikinis.

Mr. Ramey was roused to a rare interjection. "Wanda," he said, "was one of the best-looking girls I've ever seen." Kitty realized that the place where Wanda and Trish sunbathed was just below where they were sitting, in full view of the kitchen window.

Mr. Ramey also said that based on something he had heard from the Johnsons (the McCoys' other closest neighbors), he thought that more than one person had been involved in the murder. He wouldn't say what the Johnsons had told him.

Kitty decided to risk one last question: What was the blood type of the members of the family? Seeming unaware or unconcerned by the implication of Kitty's question, Mrs. Ramey answered that both she and her husband were type A, and that all the children were type A also, except for two of the girls, who were type O, and Donnie and Michael, whose blood types she didn't know. Kitty could not remember whether two type A parents could produce a type B son.

Before leaving, Jim asked if they could see the other rooms in the house, and Mrs. Ramey graciously showed them around. Standing in front of the kitchen window, Kitty Behan felt a chill. From the window she could look directly into the windows of the murder house. She wondered how often Donnie had watched Wanda McCoy through that window, alone in her house, waiting for Brad to come home.

With the exception of now saying that she had told the police about the figure Michael saw lurking under her porch, Mrs. Ramey's description of the night of the murder had not changed from two years earlier. That evening, discussing her story, Kitty and Jim thought they now understood why the Rameys might tell a false tale about seeing Roger Coleman's truck at the crime scene on the night of the murder. If Donnie was involved in the murder and his family knew or suspected it, they might think the best way to discourage Coleman's lawyers from further inquiry was to claim they had information that incriminated Coleman.

If anything, Kitty thought, the fact that the Rameys were telling a story that was inconsistent with both logic and the undisputed trial testimony of other witnesses increased the likelihood that Teresa Horn's accusations were true.

On Monday morning Kitty and Jim set out to try to locate another man Teresa Horn said she had told about Donnie Ramey's attack. His name was Greg Mullins, and Teresa had provided directions to his trailer, which was perched on the top of a mountain near the West Virginia line. Mullins wasn't at home when Kitty and Jim arrived, so they left Teresa's phone number with his sister Linda and asked her to have Greg call Teresa when he returned. Later that day Kitty called Teresa to see if she had heard from Greg Mullins. Teresa reported that Linda Mullins had called to find out why Kitty and Jim wanted to talk to Greg, and when Teresa explained, Linda Mullins said that she too had once been attacked by Donnie Ramey.

Jim and Kitty immediately retraced their way to the Mullinses' trailer, where Linda was waiting for them. She is a slim, vivacious woman with a strong Appalachian accent, and combines an exaggerated air of toughness with an easy laugh. She knew why Kitty and Jim were there and promptly began to describe an encounter she said she had with Donnie Ramey while she was still in high school.

In the summer of 1982 or 1983, Linda Mullins said, she was visiting friends at an apartment in Grundy. Earlier in the evening she had seen Ramey, whom she knew by his nickname Trouble, and he had asked her to take a ride with him. Linda had declined, but as the evening wore on an argument started between her friends and she decided to leave and take up Ramey's invitation. Linda told a friend what she was planning to do, and the friend warned her that Ramey had a bad reputation, but Linda ignored the warning.

Linda Mullins was silent for a moment. She was no longer smiling. "I was, what, sixteen years old or so. I didn't think anything could hurt me." She shook her head and resumed her story.

I met Trouble down by the arcade. We drove to the airstrip in his car and parked. It was about nine or ten P.M. and very dark and desolate, although I think there was a full moon.

We drank some beer, and I wanted to smoke a cigar, so I asked Trouble to give me the matches. Suddenly, he jumped on top of me and held a big knife to my neck. It was a Rambo-style knife with about an eight-inch blade. He held the knife across my neck and began biting me all over the neck. He tried to stick his tongue in my mouth and he started groping me with his other hand, the one not holding the knife.

He was using his knees to try to pry my legs apart but I stuck the heels of my boots into the floor of the car and fought back. And then he stopped trying to kiss me, and he looked at me, and he said, "I could do anything I want to with you. I could kill you and throw you out of the car and nobody would ever know." He was still holding the knife to my neck.

Linda Mullins stopped speaking again, and laughed ruefully. Kitty and Jim remained silent, watching her from across the room, and in a moment Linda began again, speaking very softly.

So I looked at him, and I said, "Trouble, do it if you're that brave, go ahead. My friend knows I'm with you and she'll tell my brother Glen and he'll kill you by this time tomorrow." And all of a sudden he stopped attacking me. He put down the knife and started crying. He tried to give me the knife but I told him I had my own. I was also crying. He said, "You hate me now, you hate me." I told him, "I don't hate you, I despise you. Don't ever speak to me again."

So then we drove back to Grundy without saying a word. He let me out near the Miners and Merchants Bank. I think I went back to my friends' apartment and told them what happened. I had bite marks all over my neck.

Linda stopped and sighed again, and this time Kitty could see that her eyes were moist. "My God," Jim said. "You could have been killed right there." "I know that now," Linda responded, "but I didn't then. I was too stupid. It wasn't until a couple of years later that I realized just how stupid I was."

Linda Mullins was the third woman in three days who had described a sexual attack by a man who lived a stone's throw from the house where Wanda McCoy was raped and murdered. Unlike Teresa Horn, Linda did not say she had heard Ramey admit to Wanda McCoy's murder, but her story about Ramey's attack was consistent with that of the other two women, and included two facts that Jim and

Kitty found especially significant—the knife, and the threat to use it.*

When Kitty Behan first read the transcript of Roger Coleman's trial, she had been surprised to find that she thought it was possible he was innocent. Now she thought it was not only possible but likely. She knew that Donnie would probably deny all the attacks (as he did), and that none of the women had reported them to the police, but the stories of the three women, together with the circumstance of Ramey living so close to Wanda McCoy, was evidence that was too strong to ignore. She thought that an impartial judge would at least agree that the issue required further investigation and a factual hearing.

* As with the other two women, Donnie would later swear that Linda Mullins's story was false.

Chapter 18

A Supreme Surprise

The success of the interviews Kitty Behan and Jim McCloskey conducted in September 1990 had caused Kitty to be more optimistic about the chance of reversing Roger Coleman's conviction. A month later the Supreme Court raised her hopes even higher. The first week of October had come and gone without action on Coleman's petition for a writ of certiorari. Contrary to everyone's expectations, four weeks later the Court agreed to hear the case.

Whatever else it meant, the granting of certiorari assured Roger Coleman at least an additional six months of life. The fast track to an execution date which everyone had expected to begin with a denial of certiorari in October now could not start until the Court ruled, sometime in the spring.

In order for certiorari to be granted, Supreme Court rules require that four of the nine justices vote to hear the case. To get the necessary votes, the first hurdle is to persuade four justices that the case presents an issue worthy of the Supreme Court's attention. That hurdle eliminates the vast majority of cases submitted for consideration, but even if it is surmounted, a justice considering a vote to grant certiorari may want to feel there is a reasonable chance that his tentative position on the merits of the case will command a majority. A justice who disagrees with an important lower-court decision may nevertheless vote against granting certiorari for fear that if the Court hears the case the decision will go against him.

In many cases, the Court grants certiorari because at least four justices believe the lower-court decision was wrong. But sometimes the justices vote to take a case when they agree with the decision below, in order to establish for the entire country a principle on which the circuit courts are split, or where the law is in a state of flux and the majority wants to settle it.

Each of these possibilities and a dozen more were raised, examined, debated and reexamined by Roger Coleman's attorneys in the wake of the Court's decision to review the case. The optimists argued that four justices must have felt that the lower-court decision was wrong, and that they could somehow find a fifth vote for that position. Certainly, they argued, the idea that a man might be executed because his appointed lawyer filed a document one day late was too harsh a rule for any decent person to embrace. Perhaps the Court had taken the case to draw a line—to show that some kinds of procedural defaults were simply too technical, too minor, to justify depriving a prisoner of access to federal habeas corpus. The problem, as others pointed out, was that a majority of the Court had already enforced state procedural rules in other cases that were almost as compelling. Where, they asked, can you find on this Court four justices, much less five, who are not committed to sharply curtailing federal habeas corpus in state death-penalty cases?

Like a degenerate horse player poring over the racing form in search of a sure winner at a good price, the lawyers discussed and analyzed the prior opinions of each of the nine justices, looking for a sign that he or she might support Coleman's position. Justices Rehnquist, Scalia and O'Connor were hopeless. The first two would send their mothers to the gallows, and while O'Connor was less predictably bloodthirsty where, as here, the issue involved honoring a state court procedural rule, she might be the worst of all for Coleman. After years on an Arizona appellate court angrily watching federal courts fail to give sufficient deference to her decisions and those of her fellow state court judges, Sandra Day O'Connor had been busily "correcting" the balance since her elevation to the high court.

On the other side, Justice Thurgood Marshall was a certain vote for reversal, and Justices Blackmun and Stevens were good possibilities. Justice Brennan had been replaced by David Souter, and since little was known about him, the optimists argued that he might have provided a fourth vote for certiorari. The problem was figuring out where the defense could hope to gain the crucial fifth vote to achieve a majority. Both Justices White and Kennedy were predictably progovernment in criminal cases, and White had voted with the majority in the recent cases limiting habeas corpus. While Kennedy's record was less complete, there was nothing in either his limited service on the Supreme Court or his record on the Ninth Circuit Court of Appeals to suggest that he could be considered anything but a reliable vote to affirm the decision of the Fourth Circuit.

As hard as they tried, the Coleman team could not escape the conclusion that the decision in the Supreme Court was likely to go against them, but at least now there was a chance. And if Coleman did win, so that his federal petition for writ of habeas corpus would have to be considered on its merits, everyone thought there was a good chance the petition would be granted and Coleman given a new trial. With experienced trial lawyers and the information they had developed over the past few months, no one doubted that a new trial would end in a verdict of not guilty.

With the immediate action in the Coleman case shifted to the Supreme Court, where it would remain until spring, the lawyers at Arnold & Porter did what lawyers always do under those circumstances—they turned to other matters. Given the probability that the case would be lost in the Supreme Court and that they would then be back in the position of trying to prove Coleman's innocence, there was lots of work to be done. For now, however, the Coleman case was not itching, and no one was going to scratch it. Even Kitty Behan realized that in light of the huge amount of time she had spent on the case since joining the firm in July, it was important to her career that she now devote herself to working for the firm's paying clients.

On death row, the news that the Supreme Court had granted certiorari rescued Roger from an uncharacteristic period of depression. On October 17, the state had executed Wilbert Lee Evans. Governor Wilder had refused to commute Evans's sentence to life in prison despite a well-organized clemency campaign built around the fact that Evans had allegedly saved a prison nurse and several guards from knife-wielding prisoners, at great peril to himself, during the death-row breakout in 1984.

The new governor had now considered two clemency petitions and denied both, including one that everyone on the row, including Evans himself, had believed would be granted. According to the *Virginian-Pilot* newspaper, just before he was strapped into the electric chair in the basement death house in Richmond, Evans had said: "Chaplain, if I'd of known they were really going to kill me down here, I'd never have let them bring me."

Roger Coleman often had nightmares about electrocution in which he saw himself strapped into the chair and felt the electricity course through his body. Between the electrocution of Wilbert Evans and October 29, when the Supreme Court granted his petition for certiorari, he had that dream almost every time he went to sleep.

In December the lawyers at Debevoise & Plimpton completed and filed their brief asking the Supreme Court to reverse the decisions of District Judge Williams and the Fourth Circuit Court of Appeals. Not long thereafter they were informed that the case had been set for argument on February 25, 1991. The state's brief would be filed shortly before that and Coleman's lawyers would have only a few days to file a reply brief. John Hall, who would argue the case, would then begin an intensive period of preparation for the argument, including practice sessions in which other lawyers would try to anticipate the questions that might be asked by the justices. Hall's answers would be discussed by the group and suggestions would be made for improvement. Every lawyer who has an opportunity to appear before the Supreme Court tries to perfect his argument and anticipate every question that might be asked by the justices. Even so, experienced Supreme Court lawyers know that some justice will inevitably ask a question that no one anticipated. It is the ability to provide an immediate and persuasive answer to those questions that distinguishes the brilliant appellate advocate from the merely very good.

February 25, 1991, was a Monday, and the clerk of the Supreme Court had advised John Hall and his associates that *Coleman* v. *Thompson* would be heard that afternoon as the third case of the day. Even so, lawyers arguing cases before the Court are required to sign in at 9:00 A.M. If they are not the first case to be argued in the morning, they wait until the argument of the case before theirs is called, and then move to tables immediately behind the tables used by the lawyers who are arguing. That way, when one argument ends, the lawyers for the next case are ready to move forward and begin arguing as soon as the chief justice announces their case.

John Hall and his two associates, Dan Goldstein and Marianne Consentino, made plans to go down to Washington on Sunday, but Hall's wife was pregnant, and that afternoon she went into labor. Hall told his associates to go ahead; he would take a later plane. The labor dragged on. Soon it would be too late to catch the last plane. Hall decided he would stay with his wife and catch the first shuttle in the morning. It was 5:45 A.M. when Samantha Hall was finally born.

At the Court the next morning, 9:00 came and John Hall was not there. Dan Goldstein was beyond distraught. He had argued the case in the Fourth Circuit, but this was the Supreme Court, and he hadn't prepared. Hours seemed to pass. John Hall finally appeared. It was 9:15.

When the arguments were over, everyone agreed that Hall had done an excellent job, but from the questions asked by the justices, no one could honestly say they expected to win. And while all this was going on, another turn of events had magnified the importance of the Court's decision.

———

Chapter 19

Dr. Blake Reports Back

In the excitement generated by the new evidence coming from Grundy and the grant of certiorari in the Supreme Court, in the fall of 1990 it was almost possible to forget about the DNA testing under way in California. Then, on November 7, Dr. Blake reported his results.

According to his report, Dr. Blake had been able to isolate and identify Wanda McCoy's DNA from the blood on her sweater, and had found enough sperm on the vaginal swab to identify the DNA of the sperm donor, using the PCR method of amplification. Valid PCR analysis requires the complete separation of the DNA of the sperm from the DNA of the victim, which is present in the cells of the vaginal lining and thus is likely to be picked up on a vaginal swab. Failure to accomplish the separation can create false readings, and renders the test invalid. Dr. Blake reported that he had succeeded in this step as well.

Next, Dr. Blake attempted to determine the type of DNA on the sperm sample. In simple terms, the PCR method of testing allows the scientist to identify the type of DNA, or alleles, on a particular gene known as the DQa gene from a very small amount of genetic material by creating a reaction that copies and amplifies the material. Since there are a total of twenty-one possible combinations of alleles, finding a match is statistically far more significant than a match with one of the four blood types, and since the amount of material necessary to do PCR testing is smaller than that necessary for blood typing, most forensic laboratories do not even bother with blood typing anymore.

Dr. Blake reported that he had succeeded in identifying the alleles in the sperm taken from Wanda McCoy:

> The results of this analysis revealed a sperm mixture where sperm from one individual is present in excess of sperm from a second individual. The DQa type of the primary sperm donor was determined to be type 1.3,2. This DQa type occurs in approximately 2% of the Black and Caucasian populations. Roger Coleman is a member of this population group; and therefore he can not be eliminated as the primary sperm donor in this case.

When Dr. Blake's report was read by Donald Curry, the assistant attorney general who had fought against the PCR test, and by the lawyers at Arnold & Porter, who had fought so hard to obtain it, there must have been some wry grins on both sides. At first glance, it was hard to imagine how the report could be worse for Roger Coleman. Not only did Dr. Blake fail to eliminate Coleman as the person whose sperm was in Wanda McCoy's vagina the night she was murdered; the report seemed to make the case against him stronger. Indeed, as Don Curry would later argue, if blood type and DQa type are independent of one another, the people who would have both type B blood and the 1.3,2 alleles would include only about one quarter of one percent of the population.

Jim McCloskey first heard about Blake's report in Lancaster, Pennsylvania, where he was searching for a witness in another case. He learned that he had a message from Kitty, and called her from a street-corner pay phone: "So I got hold of Kitty, and she told me about the results of the test. And I was stunned, I'll be quite honest, I was just stunned. I thought, Holy Geeze, it looks like he could very well be guilty. Ah, which shocked me. I don't think I said that to Kitty, but I was shaken by it."

At first, Kitty Behan was as disturbed by Dr. Blake's report as Jim. It took only a slightly more careful reading of the report, however, to see what she had missed at first. Dr. Blake had referred to a "sperm mixture" and "sperm from a second individual." Reading further, the reason for this language was revealed—Dr. Blake had identified three alleles in the sperm sample, and no individual has more than two. The third allele, which was identified later in the report as type 4, meant there were at least two separate donors of the sperm found on the vaginal swab studied by Dr. Blake. To Kitty and Jim that meant the report actually confirmed Coleman's innocence. If there were two or more men involved in the murder, as they had long suspected, Roger could not have been one of them. The undisputed evidence from all the trial witnesses was that Coleman was alone the night of the murder up to and including the time of his visit to Boyd's Trailer Park. Moreover, on his first visit to Grundy, McCloskey had located another witness who had seen Coleman at Boyd's Trailer Park on the night of the murder and confirmed that he was alone. She lived right across from the Stiltners, and saw Coleman when he arrived and when he left. It was simply inconceivable that within a few minutes of leaving the Stiltners' trailer, Coleman picked up someone else out of a clear sky and persuaded that person to help rape and murder his sister-in-law. It made no sense.

Kitty realized the state might argue that the second sperm donor was Wanda's husband, but fortunately, in order to foreclose the possibility that a jury might think the sperm found in Wanda was from her husband rather than a rapist, the state had proved that Brad and Wanda had not had intercourse for several days before the murder, and that Wanda had begun her menstrual period in the meantime.

From her scientific background, Kitty had another question about the Blake report. She had no particular knowledge of the PCR technique, but she did know that in other kinds of testing it is often difficult to draw positive conclusions about "mixed samples" and wondered if that would not be true of PCR testing as well. Dr. Blake had concluded that the "primary donor" had the 1.3,2 alleles, because those alleles were "present in excess of sperm from a second individual" (the type 4 donor), but was it proper to pair the two alleles in a mixed sample? And why wasn't there a fourth allele, representing the second allele of the second donor? Of course, the second donor's second allele could be the same as one of the alleles already reported, a 1.3 or 2, but wouldn't adding an extra "dose" of one of those alleles also make pairing difficult?

When Kitty checked, other experts said her doubts were well founded—in a mixed sample, they said, it's impossible to say with certainty that any two alleles "go together," both for the reasons Kitty mentioned and also because the process of multiplying the genetic material that is the basis of PCR analysis does not always produce equal amounts of each allele. In other words, even with a single donor, one allele may amplify more than the other, so that it appears to be present in greater volume. If that occurs in a mixed sample, the fact that after amplification some alleles seem to be present in greater volume than others does not mean they are necessarily paired.

The fact that Dr. Blake had found both of the alleles carried by Roger Coleman in his test of the vaginal swab from Wanda McCoy certainly meant Coleman could not be eliminated as one of the sperm donors, thus dashing the hope that the test would prove his innocence. Nevertheless, Kitty Behan concluded that on balance, by showing that more than one man was involved in the crime, Blake's report helped rather than hurt Coleman. It would be a tough sell. Dr. Blake said that he *could* determine which alleles went together, and that the primary sperm donor had the same alleles as Coleman. Any effort by Coleman's lawyers to disparage the report of the expert they had selected and previously lauded was easy to dismiss as sour grapes. As for the third allele, maybe it was Brad. If not, as the state would argue, let Coleman tell us whose it was—*he* was there.

Chapter 20

Back to Work

As the winter of 1991 turned to spring with no decision from the Supreme Court, Kitty Behan began to worry. With only the rarest exceptions, the Supreme Court decides all pending cases before it adjourns at the end of June. If Coleman lost, he would be on the fast track to execution, this time without any hope that the PCR test would solve his problems. Neither Kitty nor Jim McCloskey had done any investigative work since September, and while Arnold & Porter had hired an ex–FBI agent named Robert Craig as an independent investigator, he had not produced much.

Craig did have contacts in the local law-enforcement community, and had been able to interview Jack Davidson about the murder investigation and confront him with some of the facts that Kitty and Jim had uncovered. According to Craig's report of the interview, Davidson had conceded that the theory that the killer was someone Wanda voluntarily admitted to the house was central to his investigation and the state's case against Coleman.

Davidson explained the pry mark to Craig by saying that it wasn't really a pry mark but a mere impression—probably caused by someone hitting the doorjamb with a piece of furniture while moving it into the house. Davidson went on to say that after twenty-two years as an investigator, he knew what a pry mark looked like and this was not one. Kitty hoped she could get Davidson to repeat that remark on the witness stand, since it was Davidson himself who had written that the marking on Wanda McCoy's door "appears to be a pry mark."

According to Craig, Davidson had also said that when Brad McCoy arrived home the night of the murder, he looked around the outside of the house to see if the garbage had been put out, thus indicating that it had been up to Wanda to put out the garbage after Brad went to work. Because of the dirt on her hands and sweater, Jim had previously speculated that Wanda might have been assaulted outside the house, and Craig's report gave new support to that theory. It could not be proved, but, like the pry mark, it was an alternative to the state's theory that the murderer had to be someone Wanda would admit.

Later, Jack Davidson would deny making the statement about Wanda taking out the garbage, and his assertion that Craig had not quoted him accurately was given credence by several apparent errors in Craig's report of other parts of the interview.

Kitty's concern about the lack of progress in the Coleman investigation was exacerbated in early 1991 when two older lawyers who had been working on the case both announced that they were leaving the firm. It had been clear for some time that the firm was relying on Kitty to do the lion's share of the work, and she had long since become the lawyer Roger Coleman relied on when he had a question or suggestion about his case. But, as self-confident as she was, Kitty knew she needed help from a more experienced lawyer. Phil Horton, a young partner, agreed to be available for advice and review, and Stephanie Williams, a paralegal, and two younger associates were assigned to the case, but saving Roger Coleman would primarily be up to Kitty Behan. Her growing belief that Coleman was innocent made that a frightening burden.

In early April 1991, Kitty convened a meeting of the Coleman team at Arnold & Porter to plan a strategy for the coming months. One of the new lawyers would concentrate on developing a clemency petition in case that became necessary; the other would work on identifying documents and information in the hands of the state that might be helpful, and attempt to obtain that material through freedom-of-information requests or other means.

Kitty assigned herself to continue investigating Wanda McCoy's

murder. She knew that if the Supreme Court case was lost, the only
chance for relief in the courts lay in developing a convincing case of
innocence, and she had been advised by Marie Deans that innocence
was also the only feasible basis for obtaining clemency from Governor
Wilder. Marie said rehabilitation and good works would not be
enough, and the wisdom of that advice had been shown by the execution of Wilbert Evans the previous fall.

At Mecklenburg, with his case in the Supreme Court, no execution
date and spring in the air, Roger Coleman's life was as good as life can
be on death row. His relationship with Sharon Paul was flourishing, as
was his youth program. From the time he was in high school Roger
had wanted to improve himself. Now, ironically, he felt he had grown
tremendously, primarily because of the love and friendship of people
he would never have met had he not been sent to death row.

Roger had always loved to read, and he had developed a routine
that gave him more time to do so. It was too noisy to concentrate during the day, so he would stay up reading all night and go to sleep after
breakfast. He found that by tuning his radio to a station that produced
only static, he could drown out the daytime noises. Once he got used
to the static he could sleep right through it.

Roger would copy poems he had read and send them to Sharon.
Sometimes he wrote them himself. One poem he sent her in the spring
of 1991 was called "I Am." Sharon wasn't sure if he had copied it or
composed it.

> ## I AM
> *I am a prisoner*
> *I am not a number*
> *I am a convict*
> *I am not an animal*
> *I am locked up.*
> *I am not without hope,*
> *I am a man!*

At night Roger sometimes stood on his bunk so that he could look
out the window of his cell. One night, he told his friend Robert White,
he stood for hours watching two kittens playing in a parking lot. He
told White that with the clear prospect of an early death had come a

diminished concern for "large" issues and a greater appreciation of small things like watching kittens play.

Later, when Robert White developed a medical condition that his doctor said could be fatal, Roger said that from that point on Robert would be able to see the world the way Roger did—and Robert found he was right. He stopped worrying about faculty politics and began rising before dawn to sit on his front porch watching the clouds in the dark sky and the birds and squirrels beginning to move through the trees as dawn approached. When Robert White mentioned how much Roger had taught him about the richness of life, Roger was amused and pleased. He thought it was surprising that a college professor would say he was learning about life from an uneducated coal miner on death row.

Coleman's dreams about execution had become less frequent since the Supreme Court took his case, but they were replaced by other dreams that were, in a way, more painful. He dreamed that he was free, roaming the hills of his childhood, or eating a pizza, or kissing Sharon, and the sight or taste or touch in his dreams seemed as real as life. Then he would wake up and hear the static from his radio and smell the stale odors of death row and slowly realize where he was, and he would be devastated.

Despite the sense of urgency that was building in Kitty Behan, with the case still in the Supreme Court and plenty of paying work to be done, progress on the Coleman case at Arnold & Porter was slow. It was May before document requests were sent to the Division of Forensic Science, the Bureau of Criminal Investigation and the Grundy Department of Police. And it was early June before anyone went back to Grundy.

On Tuesday June 11, 1991, Kitty Behan and Jim McCloskey resumed their investigation. Kitty had brought two Arnold & Porter paralegals with her, and that morning they headed for the Buchanan County Courthouse to look for records of any criminal charges brought against Roger Matney. It was a fruitful search. With the assistance of a clerk who showed them how to locate and trace the relevant records, the paralegals discovered that in October 1981, while Matney was in the Buchanan County Jail, a fellow inmate named Randy Blackburn had claimed that Matney had forced him to "suck him off" by threatening to put him in the hospital if he didn't. Matney had been charged with fellation, a serious felony. The charge, however, remained dormant and Matney had been released from jail in February 1982, shortly before the start of Coleman's trial. Ironically, the order entered on February 3, which had reduced Matney's prison sentence, recited that Matney "has lately conducted himself while incarcerated in an exemplary manner . . ." The order had been agreed to by Mickey McGlothlin. Then, a month later, Matney testified against Roger Coleman. In July, after Coleman's trial was over, Matney was finally indicted on the fellation charge, but the case was continued until July 1983, when, with the approval of McGlothlin, the charge was reduced to assault and battery. Matney pled guilty and was sentenced to thirty days in jail to be served on weekends.

Although the fellation charge against Roger Matney did not arise until after Matney claimed he had heard Coleman confess, the way it was handled again suggested that Matney had received favorable treatment in return for his testimony. If Coleman's trial lawyers knew about the pending charge at the time of trial, the transcript does not reveal any effort to bring it to the attention of the jury.

Kitty and Jim began the day by trying to find Donnie Ramey. Kitty wanted to obtain a sworn statement from Ramey about the night of the murder, which could be used if Ramey later tried to change his story.

When they arrived at Donnie's trailer, there were two trucks in the driveway and they could hear the television playing inside, but no one came to the door. Returning later in the day, one of the trucks was gone and again there was no answer to their knocks. Later in the week they learned that Donnie's parents were also gone, and began to suspect that the Rameys were avoiding them. Although Donnie had not been named in anything Kitty had yet filed, there were plenty of rumors around town about the investigation, and it was certainly possible that the Rameys had gotten wind of the fact that Coleman's lawyers now considered Donnie a suspect.

In the afternoon, Kitty and Jim again called on Goldie Owens, Roger Matney's mother–in–law, who had twice before declined to give them a written statement about her claim that Matney had disavowed his testimony that Coleman had made a jailhouse confession. When they arrived at her log cabin home, Goldie was outside pushing an old rotor lawn mower through her yard in her bare feet. Despite her labors, her long, simple one-piece dress was immaculate. Goldie greeted them warmly and invited them into her house, but she was still afraid her son–in–law would retaliate if she gave them a written statement.

This time, however, Jim had come prepared. When Goldie agreed that the affidavit Kitty showed her was accurate, but declined to sign it, Jim looked at her sternly. "If we're going to obtain justice for Roger Coleman," he said, "we have to have your help. You know, Goldie, the Bible says the first thing the Lord tells us is to do justice."

"Where does it say that?" Goldie asked, looking doubtful.

"Micah 6:8," Jim responded. He walked over to where Goldie's Bible was displayed near her front door and found the passage he had cited in the Old Testament. Goldie joined him and examined the verse. Returning to the kitchen table where Kitty was sitting, she signed the affidavit.

On Wednesday, Kitty met with Jackie Stump in an effort to enlist his support for a potential clemency plea. Stump was both president of the United Mineworkers local and the area's representative in the state legislature. He and his legislative assistant listened carefully to Kitty's presentation and agreed to study the evidence of Coleman's innocence and help with the governor if they became convinced that a miscarriage of justice had occurred.

While Kitty was politicking, Jim McCloskey followed up two leads. The first had come from Roger Coleman. With the emergence of the claims about Donnie Ramey, Roger said he now recalled that after the murder, Wanda's sister Peggy Stiltner said she had received an anonymous phone call saying Trouble Ramey was scratched on the day after the murder and had been arrested. McCloskey was able to persuade one of Peggy's friends to ask her about it, but Peggy said she did not remember such a call.

In a recently discovered copy of the letter Roger wrote to Peggy Stiltner in December 1981, however, Roger asks: "Whatever happened to Trouble Ramey, I thought his face was all scratched up and he had been arrested?"

The second lead was a rumor that yet another woman had been the victim of a sexual assault by Ramey. McCloskey found the woman, and when he told her the reason for his visit, she agreed to tell him the story. She said that seven years earlier, when she was thirteen years old, her older sister was dating Ramey. One day Ramey picked up the younger sister in Grundy, ostensibly to drive with him to pick up her sister at work. Instead, the woman claimed, Ramey drove to a secluded road, where he parked and asked her to have sexual intercourse with him. When she refused, he exposed his penis, and, holding her with his right hand, masturbated with the left.

However, the woman refused to sign a written statement about the incident, saying she did not want to revive old and painful memories. Despite many efforts, Jim McCloskey never did obtain a written statement from the woman. Instead, McCloskey had to tell the story in his own affidavit, and later Ramey denied the incident under oath.

The balance of Kitty and Jim's time in Grundy was devoted to minor witnesses and blind alleys until the day they planned to leave. On Thursday, June 13, before leaving for the airport, they met briefly with Tom Scott, the lawyer who had helped Mickey McGlothlin prosecute Roger Coleman. Scott had sent word that he would like to talk to them about the case, and might be willing to help. He was currently defending a man accused of capital murder who he believed was innocent, and he told Kitty and Jim that while he had once favored the death penalty, his experience in his current case had changed his mind. Scott said he still thought Roger Coleman was guilty, but if they could convince him to the contrary, he would "go public" for Coleman.

Without naming Ramey, Kitty and Jim told Scott what they had uncovered, including the fact that they had a new suspect who had committed similar acts, and that the PCR test had suggested the presence of two rapists. Scott seemed interested, and agreed that Coleman had been poorly represented, especially in attacking the forensic evidence. On the way to the airport, Kitty and Jim decided they would continue to send material to Scott, but avoid disclosing information that could be used to hurt them, in case his professed interest was a subterfuge.

A week after Kitty returned from Grundy, an anonymous letter arrived at Arnold & Porter. The letter was typed, and appeared to have been written by a reasonably well–educated person. It seemed to provide independent confirmation that someone in the Ramey family may have been involved in the crime:

> Welcome to Grundy, Virginia . . . one of the most crooked towns in the State of Virginia and the Nation for that matter.

You certainly have your work cut out for you.

The Ramey Family that lived directly behind the McCoy girl, were having a family fight the night of the girls murder. Looking into the whereabouts of the Ramey sons and Father might be interesting. The Father was drunk that night.

You have already found that people are afraid to come forward for fear that the authorities will later remember them and move to destroy them or their families.

Despite repeated efforts, it would not be until the morning Roger Coleman was scheduled to die that Jim and Kitty would find out who wrote the letter, what the author knew and how she knew it.

Chapter 21

A Case About
Federalism

On the day the anonymous letter about the Rameys arrived at Arnold & Porter, the Supreme Court ended the next to last week of its term without issuing a decision in the Coleman case. Only a handful of cases remained undecided, and as usual they included the most controversial and difficult issues on the Court's docket for the October 1990 term. All of them would be decided in the week ahead.

For the Coleman case to be included in the group of late decided cases was itself a surprise to those who had predicted a quick affirmance of the lower-court decision, and over the weekend the lawyers once again consulted their tea leaves and tarot cards, trying to construct theories of why the delay was a sign of potential victory.

On Monday morning, June 24, the Court ended their speculations. In a six-to-three decision written by Justice O'Connor, the Court held that the mistake made by Coleman's lawyers in filing a document one day late created a procedural default that prevented consideration of his federal petition for a writ of habeas corpus. In doing so, the Court finally buried the remains of *Fay* v. *Noia*, the 1963 decision holding that the law could not justify punishing a person whose conviction was obtained in violation of the Constitution simply because his lawyer made a procedural mistake.

Coleman's petition had alleged that his conviction was obtained from a biased jury, that his appointed trial lawyers had failed to defend him adequately and that the state had withheld exculpatory evidence and presented testimony that it knew or should have known was false, all constitutional violations if true. To Justice O'Connor and the other justices who comprised the majority, however, the truth of those claims was inconsequential, even though Coleman had been sentenced to death. "This," Justice O'Connor announced in the first words of her opinion, "is a case about federalism."

To Justice O'Connor and the *Coleman* majority, allowing a federal court to consider the constitutionality of Coleman's conviction and death sentence when his lawyer had missed the state deadline would give inadequate weight to "the respect that federal courts owe the States and the States' procedural rules. . . ."

As Justice Blackmun observed in dissent, "One searches the majority's opinion in vain for any mention of . . . Coleman's right to a criminal proceeding free from constitutional defect or his interest in finding a forum for his constitutional challenge to his conviction and sentence of death."

————

Chapter 22

Keeping On

Whatever Kitty Behan thought of the Supreme Court's concept of justice, which wasn't much, the Court had spoken, and there was no higher court to go to. A petition for rehearing would be filed, but it was certain to be denied when the Court returned to work in the fall. Soon thereafter Kitty would have to file a second state petition for habeas corpus. At the state level, procedural rules, including one that barred consideration of newly discovered evidence more than twenty-one days after a judgment of conviction, made it likely the petition would fail no matter what evidence was presented.

Privately, Kitty believed that despite the twenty-one-day rule, Judge Persin would have found a way to save Coleman if the DNA evidence had excluded him as the sperm donor, and she thought that he would do the same even now if she could persuade him of Coleman's innocence. She also knew, however, that finding anything as persuasive as a DNA exclusion would be almost impossible. This was not television.

The strongest link in the state's case against Coleman was the forensic evidence, and Kitty knew she needed her own forensic experts to review the reports and testimony of the state's witnesses.

Dr. William McCormick, a forensic pathologist, agreed to review the autopsy report and Elmer Gist's blood tests. Morris Clark, who had been chief of the FBI unit that deals with hair analysis and later chief of the FBI Crime Lab, reviewed the hair evidence; and Dr. Bruce Kovacs, an internationally known geneticist, became Kitty's DNA expert. None of them could declare from the evidence that Roger Coleman was innocent, but each agreed that additional tests and information were necessary to arrive at a scientifically valid opinion on the forensic issues.

Another addition to the Coleman team was Roger Mullins, a respected southwest Virginia trial lawyer who would now act as local counsel. After reading the trial transcript and other materials supplied by Arnold & Porter, Mullins said he could think of a dozen criminal defense lawyers in the area who would have won Coleman's case hands down if they had defended him at trial.

Kitty also followed up on her earlier discussion with Tom Scott by sending him a packet of information Arnold & Porter had developed for interested journalists. In mid-July Scott wrote back that if Brad McCoy could be tested and eliminated as the supplier of the third allele reported by Dr. Blake, he would consider helping the defense on the grounds that if two people were involved, the state had failed to prove which of them had struck the fatal blow. Such proof is required for a death sentence under Virginia law. Scott said he would contact McCoy and ask him to agree to a test if Kitty wished.

It was not an attractive suggestion. There was no guarantee that having Tom Scott say the state had failed to prove Roger was the "trigger man" would save his life, and to focus on that argument would detract from what Kitty believed was the truth—that Roger Coleman was not guilty of anything. Moreover, she knew that the type 4 allele is very common, so there was a good chance Brad would have it, and while she was convinced that he was not the person responsible for its presence in the sperm sample, she also knew that if Brad did have the type 4 allele, a court might assume that the mystery of the second sperm donor was solved. Kitty and Jim agreed that, at least for now, trying to persuade Brad McCoy to provide blood for a DNA test did not make sense.

On death row, following the Supreme Court decision, Roger Coleman's dreams again turned to scenes of the electric chair. On December 13, 1990, Buddy Earl Justus became the last man to be executed in the basement of the state penitentiary in Richmond. For years the city had been anxious to be rid of the ominous gray stone fortress that occupied some of its most valuable riverfront property. The state had finally agreed to build a new maximum-security prison and home for the electric chair about an hour south of Richmond in Greensville County, near the town of Jarratt. It was nearing completion when Justus died.

Then, on July 24, 1991, Albert Clozza became the first man to be killed in the new death house at Greensville Penitentiary. A month later, on August 22, Derrick Peterson became the second. Now, unless something changed, Roger Coleman really was next in line. To make matters worse, the state had botched Peterson's execution in the new facility. After waiting for Peterson's body to cool off after he was electrocuted, a doctor placed a stethoscope to his chest, stepped back and announced, "This man has not expired." At first the warden did not know what to do, but after hurried consultations, Peterson was electrocuted a second time, eleven minutes later. This time he was dead.

In mid-September, Kitty and Jim returned to Grundy. Their first mission was one more effort to see the Rameys. While they were in the Longbottom neighborhood, they also planned to search for the author of the anonymous letter that had been received in June. Kitty assumed the letter had been written by someone who lived close enough to the Rameys to see or hear the family fight that it mentioned.

Kitty and Jim's effort to visit the Rameys dispelled any remaining doubt that the family was now avoiding them. When they approached the Ramey home, there were lights on and smoke was coming from the chimney, but as Jim and Kitty walked up the long stairs behind the murder house, the lights went off and no one answered the door. Later, as Kitty and Jim canvassed the neighborhood for the anonymous letter writer, Mrs. Ramey emerged from her house and started down the stairs. At that moment Jim and Kitty came around the corner and they spotted each other. Jim raised his hand in greeting, but Mrs. Ramey turned and ran back up the stairs into her house. There was no point in following.

None of the neighbors claimed responsibility for the anonymous letter. The Johnson family seemed to be avoiding them, and Mrs. Johnson remained their prime suspect as the letter writer because of the location of her house immediately across from the McCoys'.

One of the neighbors they talked to reported rumors that Brad McCoy had been involved with drugs, and that the murder was ordered by someone in the drug trade in North Carolina but carried out by someone from Grundy. The rumor about drugs was inconsistent with everything Kitty knew about Brad, and while she thought it was necessary to investigate the claim, she never developed any evidence to support it.

Every time she was in the area, Kitty had tried unsuccessfully to locate and interview Keester Shortridge, the man who had reported finding a garbage bag containing sheets and a pair of scissors shortly after the murder. In May 1991, Shortridge and his wife, Nell, had been divorced, and by chance Keester had moved to a large brick home situated on a hill above the motel where Jim and Kitty always stayed. On Friday night, after a long day of fruitless investigation, Jim and Kitty returned to the motel and noticed that the lights were on at Keester Shortridge's house. They immediately climbed the hill and rang the doorbell. Keester was at home. He was a stout, friendly man of about fifty-five, with sandy hair and a ruddy complexion.

After introductions and some small talk, Kitty turned the conversation to the garbage bag. Mr. Shortridge said he recalled the incident well, and remembered telling Chris Yukins about it the year before. There was something he had not told Yukins, however, that accounted for the fact that he and Nell believed the bag and its contents were related to the murder—the sheets in the bag had been covered with fresh blood.

Kitty and Jim were thunderstruck. Neither Keester nor Nell Shortridge had previously said anything about blood. A story that had seemed merely curious was suddenly explosive. They asked Shortridge to start from scratch and tell them what had happened. The story he told was essentially identical to what he had told Yukins the previous fall, except for the blood. Keester thought the bag also contained some bloodstained pillowcases.

Did he remember where he threw the bag, Kitty asked, and would he be willing to show them the place the next morning? To both questions, Keester Shortridge said yes, although he warned them that the bag had probably been covered over with dirt. A culvert had been placed in the ravine where he threw the bag and a bulldozer had pushed dirt on top of the culvert to create a road used to haul coal from Keester's mine. Whether the bag of bloody sheets was now under the road or alongside it in the ravine, Keester could not say.

After agreeing to meet Shortridge at nine o'clock the next morning, Kitty and Jim returned to the motel to review the events of the day, of which Keester Shortridge's revelation was by far the most interesting. It was almost impossible to doubt that the bag of bloody sheets was related to Wanda McCoy's murder. The amount of blood Keester described had to have come from a major wound, and its discovery within sight of the murder house right after the murder was not likely to be a coincidence. Could the scissors that were also in the bag have been the murder weapon? The flashlight Shortridge had mentioned also made sense if someone had been prowling around at night and was afraid the light might have gotten blood on it. The presence of a clock in the bag was harder to explain. Why would the murderer carry away and dispose of a clock?

There was also a discrepancy between the contents of the bag as described by Keester and by Nell, who had made the original anonymous call a year earlier. Keester and Nell agreed on the sheets and scissors, but Nell had also mentioned shirts, but not the flashlight or clock.

Kitty and Jim decided it was not surprising that both Keester and Nell recalled the two items that caused them to associate the bag with the McCoy murder—the bloody sheets and the scissors—but that each of them had forgotten other items, or perhaps not even seen them.

There were a couple of other mysteries about Keester Shortridge's find that could not be solved that night, if ever. Why would the killers think they could dispose of evidence by putting it in the back of someone's pickup truck? Didn't that suggest that whoever did it knew the Shortridge family's routine for disposing of trash? Why, if Mrs. Shortridge reported the find to Sheriff Ratliff, was there no follow-up? And, most important, how could they be sure this evidence, if they recovered it, would help rather than hurt Roger Coleman? Keester Shortridge's house on Slate Creek was, after all, on the route Roger Coleman might have taken if, as the state had argued, he left his truck across the creek and made his way back to it from the McCoy house, dumping the evidence in Keester Shortridge's truck as he passed by. What if they found the bag and its contents could somehow be traced to Roger Coleman?

The answer, Kitty and Jim agreed, was simple. They both firmly believed Roger was innocent. Unless they could prove it, he was almost certainly going to die. Keester Shortridge's bag of bloody sheets might provide the proof they needed. If they were wrong—if Roger was guilty—he was going to die anyway. If the bloody sheets proved his guilt, so be it, there was really nothing to lose.

On Saturday, September 21, 1991, Jim and Kitty met Keester Shortridge for breakfast and rode with him into Grundy, where Keester picked up a woman he had been dating since his divorce. At breakfast, before Keester arrived, Kitty told Jim that when she talked to her boyfriend the evening before, he had urged her not to go off into the mountains with Keester. It might be a trap, he said, a ruse to get Jim and her alone in a secluded place and end their investigation by killing them. Kitty was half convinced, but Jim quickly persuaded her that she was just suffering from paranoia, the occupational disease that was the result of all such investigations. Kitty laughed at herself, but even so, picking up Keester's friend was something of a relief— she was a friendly middle-aged woman who clearly did not fit into a murder plot.

From town, Keester drove out the Slate Creek road to Upper Mill Branch and up the branch to an abandoned mining road. Where the mining road crossed one of a number of steep ravines on its way up the mountainside, he stopped. He was pretty sure, he said, that this was the place he had dumped the bag of bloody sheets ten years earlier. On either side of the road the ravine was grown up in briars, bushes and small trees, but Jim and Kitty plunged down the hill, searching for some sign of a plastic garbage bag. While they were scrambling around in the underbrush, Sue Farris, the owner of the land, walked up the road to see what was going on. Farris, it turned out, had read one of Kitty's press packets and was quite convinced that Roger Coleman had not gotten a fair trial and might be innocent.

Kitty and Jim's search was fruitless, and Keester Shortridge said his bet was that the bag had been covered over when the road was built. Sue Farris quickly agreed to Kitty's request to come back and excavate the site. She warned, however, that before any excavation would be allowed, permission had to be obtained from the Mine Reclamation Bureau.

On the way back to the motel, Kitty asked Keester if he would sign an affidavit describing his discovery of the bag of bloody sheets and scissors. He agreed, and, not wanting to take a chance on catching up with him again, Kitty wrote out an affidavit in longhand, which Keester Shortridge read and signed.

Shortridge had told Kitty and Jim that his son Tim was working with him when he found and disposed of the bag of bloody sheets, and that Tim might be able to add his own recollections of what was in the bag. That afternoon they found Tim at home and told him about their contacts with his father. When they asked him about the bag of bloody sheets, Tim Shortridge denied knowing anything about it. However, he then volunteered that if there was anyone they should talk to about the murder, it was the Ramey family. When Kitty asked why, Tim Shortridge said he didn't know—probably just because they lived so close to the McCoy house.

On their way back to the Roanoke airport the next day, Kitty and Jim agreed that, whatever else might happen, the story of the bloody sheets added another element of mystery to Wanda McCoy's murder, and enough mystery might be almost as good as the proof of innocence they were seeking.

Although Kitty Behan was working on a number of other cases and had to fulfill her commitments to those matters, by mid-September 1991 it was clear that the Coleman case was going to require essentially full-time attention until it was resolved one way or the other. Kitty solved the problem the only way she could—by working twelve to sixteen hours a day, often seven days a week.

When she returned from Grundy on Sunday, September 22, Kitty began working on a final draft of the state habeas corpus petition she would have to file after the Supreme Court denied rehearing. It was a good thing. The Court denied rehearing on September 24.

Working day and night, Kitty had her petition completed and filed in the Circuit Court of Buchanan County on October 14. In addition to the petition itself, she filed motions for discovery and for an evidentiary hearing, supported by an extensive legal brief and a volume of twenty-five exhibits. The primary thrust of Kitty's argument was that newly discovered evidence showed Coleman was innocent of the murder of Wanda McCoy, that the real killer was probably Donnie Ramey and that the state had deprived Coleman of the opportunity to prove his innocence at trial by failing to disclose crucial exculpatory evidence.

The exhibits Kitty filed to support these claims included the statements of Teresa Horn, Kenny Clevenger, Jamie Sword Ross and Linda Mullins regarding Ramey's alleged attacks on other women and confession to Teresa; the anonymous letter, which also pointed to the Ramey family; Robert Craig's report of his conversation with Jack Davidson; Keester Shortridge's affidavit about the bag of bloody sheets; Goldie Owens's affidavit that Roger Matney had told her Coleman had not really confessed; the records relating to the fellation charge against Matney, which had been pending when he testified; the police reports relating to the pry mark and the interviews with Scott and Sandy Stiltner; and an affidavit from Dr. Bruce Kovacs challenging Dr. Blake's claim that he could identify a primary sperm donor from a mixed sperm sample and pointing out that Blake's test showed at least two sperm donors. In addition, an affidavit by Dr. McCormick, the forensic pathologist, explained the tests that Gist had not performed on the sperm and blood samples received from the autopsy. Both McCormick and Morris Clark, the hair expert, spelled out the need for discovery and a hearing to resolve the discrepancies they had found in the testimony and reports of the state's expert witnesses. Especially important, they said, was discovery of the contemporaneous notes made by Gist and Oxley when they performed the autopsy and forensic testing. No one connected with the defense had ever seen them.

While convinced that her petition raised serious doubts about Coleman's guilt, Kitty knew that it did not conclusively prove he was innocent, and that the state would probably respond with affidavits contradicting some of the evidence. Therefore, Kitty emphasized the need for discovery and an evidentiary hearing. If the state were required to open its files, she felt sure that additional useful information would be disclosed, and if Donnie Ramey denied the charges laid against him by Teresa Horn, Jamie Ross and Linda Mullins, Kitty was quite content to let Judge Persin determine who was telling the truth after hearing their testimony.

From the time she returned from Grundy on September 22 until the petition for habeas corpus was completed, Kitty had arrived at her office before sunrise almost every morning, and seldom returned home before midnight. When the documents were finally ready to be shipped off to Grundy for filing, Kitty went home and collapsed for the weekend. She and her boyfriend, another lawyer named Mark Masling, were now living together. It was just about the first time she had a conversation with him about anything but Roger Coleman for more than a month.

With the filing of Coleman's petition, the rumor mill in Grundy began to grind at full speed. One of Coleman's supporters called with a batch of stories she said were "running through Grundy like fire in the mountains." They included the assertion that someone in jail in Grundy on another charge had confessed to the murder; that a man named Randy "Pegleg" Wolford in Pikeville, Kentucky, knew who did it and it was related to a drug ring; and that some powerful people in the area were involved. Most of the rumors were ridiculous on their face. Those that seemed to have a remote possibility of being true and had a name attached would be investigated as time permitted.

Kitty had planned to return to Grundy while waiting for the state's response to the habeas petition, but her main objective was to find the bloody sheets, and obtaining permission from the reclamation authorities took longer than expected, so the trip was postponed. The postponement would allow Kitty to investigate anything new the state might come up with in their response. Perhaps, Kitty dared to hope, the attorney general's office would simply move to dismiss the petition without responding to its factual allegations, relying on the strength of their legal position. She doubted Judge Persin would dismiss a petition that contained uncontroverted allegations that her closest neighbor had admitted to killing Wanda McCoy.

Chapter 23

The State Responds

Donald Curry had no intention of letting Coleman's second state petition for habeas corpus delay his execution any longer than necessary. He had thirty days to respond to the petition and was determined to do it without asking for an extension of time. Gathering up the pertinent legal authorities would be no problem—defending against state and federal habeas corpus petitions in death cases was almost all Curry did. He knew most of the recent cases on the subject by heart. Whenever a new decision came down anywhere in the country, it was on his desk within a day or two, and most of the time he would have read it by the next morning.

Curry intended to use all the procedural and technical reasons available to seek dismissal of Coleman's petition without a hearing, and they were substantial. Nothing that had been raised and decided in prior proceedings could be raised again. Moreover, nothing that Coleman knew or could have known before any prior petition was filed could now be raised for the first time. The most helpful, and perverse, rule was articulated in some of the cases interpreting that principle. In essence, they said that if a fact "existed" before a prior petition, it could have been discovered by the defendant, and thus could not be raised, even if the defendant did not actually know about it and had no real chance of discovering it. For example, Donnie Ramey's alleged statements to Teresa Horn about involvement in Wanda McCoy's murder had supposedly occurred in 1987, before Coleman's first federal habeas corpus petition was filed in 1988. Under the rule as some courts interpreted it, knowledge of those allegations could be attributed to Coleman, and his failure to include them in the 1988 petition would prevent considering them now, even though Coleman did not actually know of them until Teresa Horn responded to Arnold & Porter's newspaper ad in 1990.

Curry also asserted that as a matter of law, evidence of innocence is not a basis for granting habeas corpus, which deals only with constitutional errors. Put in its bluntest terms, the argument is that the conviction and even the execution of an innocent man does not violate the Constitution if he was afforded due process. A petition for writ of habeas corpus is not a motion for a new trial based on newly discovered evidence—and if it was, Curry had an answer to that as well: the Virginia rule that newly discovered evidence must be raised within twenty-one days of the judgement of conviction. In other words, at least in theory, the last time Coleman could have sought a new trial based on newly discovered evidence was in the spring of 1981.

For all the strength of his legal position, however, Donald Curry was too good a lawyer to rely on those principles alone and let the case go to Judge Persin for decision of his motion to dismiss without also challenging Coleman's claim of innocence. As soon as he finished reading Kitty Behan's papers, Curry called Grundy and mobilized the law-enforcement authorities there to refute as much of Coleman's "newly discovered evidence" as possible. By the time Curry finished his response and motion to dismiss the habeas petition, he had affidavits of his own to file.

First came an attack on Teresa Horn's story and her credibility. Donnie Ramey and Mark Helton both filed affidavits denying that Donnie had attempted to rape Teresa Horn. Donnie admitted he had taken Teresa into a bedroom to have sex, but said that as soon as Teresa indicated she wanted him to leave her alone, he "did so, and left the room." Needless to say, Ramey also denied having had anything to do with the murder of Wanda McCoy, and denied ever telling Teresa Horn or anyone else that he had. By way of attacking Teresa's overall reputation and credibility, Donnie went on to claim that about a month later, he met Teresa at a party and she told him she would like to have sex with him. Afterward, Ramey claimed, the two of them went to an isolated place and had intercourse. Ramey even claimed that Teresa had lived with him for a few days. Donnie Ramey's affidavit made no mention of the charges made by Jamie Sword Ross or Linda Mullins.

Mark Helton supported Ramey both with respect to the attack on Teresa and by denying that Ramey had ever told him he had killed Wanda McCoy. He also denied that he had ever told Teresa that Donnie had said such a thing. Helton's affidavit went on to assert that Teresa had a reputation as an alcohol and drug abuser, a whore and a liar, and concluded with an attack on Jim McCloskey, claiming that he had "attempted to put words in my mouth . . . and get me to say that Donnie Ramey told me he killed a girl on Slate Creek."

As a further attack on Teresa Horn, the current Commonwealth's Attorney filed an affidavit saying that Teresa had once accused her uncle of trying to rape her, but later said she didn't want to prosecute. The Commonwealth's Attorney said this caused him to believe Teresa's charges were unfounded.

To refute the claim that Ramey had been a suspect whose identity should have been disclosed to Coleman's defense lawyers, Jack Davidson, Randy Jackson and another policeman who had interviewed the Rameys the morning after the murder all gave affidavits denying that Donnie Ramey was a suspect or that they had any information about him that would have been helpful to Coleman.

Perhaps the most significant information about Donnie Ramey, however, was the last paragraph of his own affidavit. There Ramey asserted that he was blood type A. To support his claim he had attached an employment card identifying his blood type, which, he said, had been given to him by his employer in 1981.

Kitty had always realized that if Donnie Ramey was not blood type B, that fact would be used to refute her charge that Ramey was the killer, but there had been no way to find out Donnie's type. There were other explanations for Donnie being a blood type different from that identified by Gist from the sperm on the vaginal swab, not the least of which was that the PCR test had shown that the swab included the sperm of at least two men. Donnie could be the second sperm donor of the vaginal sperm, or he could be the person whose sperm Gist found on the anal swab but could not identify by type, or he could have been there but not participated in the rape. Still, the assertion that Donnie Ramey was blood type A was harmful, and Kitty knew it.

Regarding the bloody sheets, Jack Davidson said there were no sheets missing from the McCoy house. Keester Shortridge provided an affidavit claiming he found the bag of sheets about three days after the murder, although he gave no explanation of why he had previously signed an affidavit saying it was the following morning. Shortridge also said that he normally dumped any garbage from his truck each morning, so the bag must not have been placed there until several days after the murder, and that although his wife told him she was going to call Sheriff Ratliff, he didn't know if she actually did so.

As far as Kitty was concerned, the important thing was that Keester did not change his story about what was in the garbage bag. Indeed, he confirmed it. Whether it was one day or three days after the murder, a bag containing bloody sheets and scissors found so close to the murder site had to be significant. The real problem was turning the scissors and bloody sheets into evidence that Roger was innocent—a gap that Kitty was well aware she had not yet closed.

Regarding Goldie Owens's claim that Roger Matney had admitted to lying about Coleman's jailhouse confession, Matney and his wife both denied he had said such a thing and attributed Goldie's statements to her opposition to her daughter's marriage to Matney.

Without referring to the pry mark mentioned in his crime-scene report, Jack Davidson denied there was any sign of forcible entry into the McCoy house, denied telling investigator Craig that Brad had said he looked to see if Wanda had put out the garbage and claimed the police had carefully inspected the area around the outside of the house and found no sign of any struggle or other evidence that Wanda might have been seized there. Davidson also denied telling Craig that he didn't believe Matney, although he conceded saying that Matney was not a credible person.

Donald Curry also dealt with the questions the defense had raised about the scientific evidence. Affidavits from Dr. McDonald and Dr. Oxley said they had no reason to believe that more than one person was involved in the murder.

Oxley also said that he did not think Wanda's wounds could have been caused by scissors, and that he had seen no gross evidence that

Wanda was menstruating—a fact that the state apparently brought out to allow for the argument that the third allele found by Dr. Blake came from Brad McCoy, despite the fact that Brad himself had testified at trial that his wife had begun menstruating since they last had sex, and the safety pin in her panties seemed to confirm it.

Elmer Gist provided an affidavit saying that he had performed the blood-typing test on the vaginal sperm sample twice because the B reaction the first time was "weak," and that he saw no indication of any blood type other than B. Gist also said the reason he had not done a PGM test on the sperm swab was because after doing the ABO typing twice, there wasn't enough of the sample left for the additional test. (He did not explain how he had made that determination, or why he had not done any additional tests on the type O blood found on Roger's blue jeans.)

As Kitty had expected, Curry presented the Blake report as his trump card. Continuing his attack on the good faith of Coleman's defenders, Curry wrote:

> When [Dr. Blake] reported . . . that Coleman's "genotype" was identical to that derived from sperm found in the victim's vagina—in effect reconfirming that Coleman was the person who had raped and murdered Wanda McCoy in 1981—neither the Commonwealth nor this Court could have ever reasonably imagined that Coleman would have the effrontery to come back before this Court proclaiming his "innocence."

Supported by affidavits from his own experts, Curry argued that only two tenths of one percent of the population could have the combination of alleles and blood type found by Blake and Gist and shared by Roger Coleman, and that the third allele could be Brad's even if Wanda had menstruated since they last had sex.

For Coleman, it was a devastating analysis. If Edward Blake was right that he could pair alleles in a mixed sample and conclude that someone with the same alleles as Roger was the primary sperm donor, it greatly enhanced the power of the state's circumstantial case against Coleman. And, as Curry repeatedly reminded the court, Dr. Blake was the expert Coleman's own lawyers had chosen to do the PCR testing.

Chapter 24

—

Digging Deeper

Not much could be done about the state's strongest points. There was no practical way to challenge their claim that Donnie Ramey was blood type A short of obtaining a court order requiring Ramey to be tested, which was highly unlikely. Besides, there was no real reason to doubt the accuracy of the employment card the state had submitted. Kitty Behan contacted the coal company, but they declined to search through twelve-year-old records to see if they could tell if the card was authentic. Kitty would have to point out the many reasons why Ramey could be type A and still be involved in the murder.

As for the more troublesome issue of Dr. Blake's analysis of the PCR test, Kitty had already filed Dr. Kovacs's affidavit challenging Blake's ability to identify a specific sperm donor in a mixed sample, and now she obtained a second affidavit that made the same point in stronger language.

What Kitty *could* do was go back to Grundy to look for additional evidence to support the innocence claim, and obtain a response to the attacks leveled by the state against Teresa Horn and the other witnesses. Jim McCloskey was unavailable, so on November 19 Kitty headed back to Grundy, accompanied by Eric Hermanson, the newest member of the Coleman team at Arnold & Porter.

The first order of business was to try to locate the bloody sheets Keester Shortridge had thrown away almost eleven years earlier. Kitty, Eric, Roger Lee Coleman and Roger's father made their way up the old mine road about a mile to the culvert Keester Shortridge had pointed out in September. Charlie Frank, a local backhoe operator, and Sue Farris, the owner of the property, had already arrived. Frank excavated a trench about thirty feet long without turning up anything of interest.

Sue Farris thought that the culvert they were excavating had been put in by a different mining operation, and that a smaller culvert a little farther up the hill was the one Keester Shortridge had built. A large rock consistent with Keester's description of the site tended to support her belief.

The backhoe was moved to the new site and a second excavation was made on one side of the culvert without success. After a few minutes of digging on the other side of the culvert, however, some old trash was uncovered, and a few minutes later the backhoe turned up a dirty torn piece of fabric. Everyone agreed that it appeared to be a piece of sheet that had been torn from a larger piece of material. It was about two feet square and perforated by four small slash marks made by a sharp instrument. The material was marked by several dark-brown stains.

Kitty Behan felt sure they had found a piece of the bloody sheets. The questions now were whether the dark stains could be analyzed and identified as blood; if so, whose blood; and whether the material would somehow lead to Wanda McCoy's killer. It was a long shot, but one that had to be taken. Photographs were made of the piece of material, after which Kitty placed it in a plastic bag for delivery to a leading expert in blood and fabric identification.

A few days later Sue Farris reported to Kitty that Jack Davidson had come to her house. He had heard about the excavation and asked Sue if she didn't think that the material could have been a towel or something other than a sheet, but she had insisted that it could only be a piece of a sheet or pillowcase.

After their excavation efforts were over, Kitty and Eric drove back through Grundy and out the Dismal Creek road to Brenda Keene's trailer, where they had an appointment with Teresa Horn to obtain her response to the state's claim that she had voluntarily slept with

Donnie Ramey after she claimed he had attacked her, and that she had falsely accused her uncle of attempted rape.

Teresa had not yet arrived at her mother's when Kitty and Eric got there. After introducing Eric to Mrs. Keene, Kitty removed the state's filing from her briefcase and read to Mrs. Keene the affidavits asserting that Teresa's charge against her uncle was false. Mrs. Keene was furious. Rising from her chair, she paced the room, indignantly denouncing the state and describing the incident between Teresa and her uncle in detail. In addition to Teresa herself, Mrs. Keene said, two other men had seen her uncle try to molest Teresa. Her daughter had dropped the charge only because it was tearing up the family.

When Teresa Horn arrived, she confirmed her mother's story about the incident with her uncle and vehemently denied Donnie Ramey's claim that she had voluntary sex with him and lived with him for several days.

Kitty prepared written statements reflecting what Brenda Keene and Teresa Horn had just told her and repeating Teresa's charge that Donnie Ramey had tried to rape her and had twice admitted to the murder of Wanda McCoy. The state's brief had suggested that Donnie Ramey's denials were entitled to more weight than Teresa's charges because Donnie's affidavit had been sworn to before a notary public while Teresa's original statement had not been. For that reason Kitty had arranged for a notary public to accompany her from Grundy, and now she asked Eric to bring the notary in from the car, where she was waiting.

As Eric and the four women stood in the crowded kitchen of Brenda Keene's trailer, Teresa Horn and her mother raised their hands and swore to God that their statements were true. Watching the ceremony, Kitty believed Teresa Horn would be a convincing witness if only a judge would agree to listen to her. Teresa was a tough, hard woman who had done her share of sleeping around, but her words rang true.

That night, reflecting on events, Kitty thought the long day that had begun with a backhoe digging up the side of a mountain and ended with the ritual signing of an oath had been fruitful indeed.

When she returned to Washington two days later, Kitty turned the piece of sheet over to Jim Starrs, a forensic scientist at George Washington University, and then spent the weekend at her office preparing a response to the state's motion to dismiss the petition for habeas corpus.

Around noon on Sunday, Brenda Keene called and told Kitty that a man had visited Teresa the night before and said he had been at the Acapulco Club and heard two men there saying that if Teresa kept talking, they were going to set her up to be hurt. There was nothing Kitty could say, except that Teresa should be careful and call the police if anyone directly threatened her.

On Sunday night, Kitty phoned Keester Shortridge's ex-wife, Nell. Auburn Ratliff, the former sheriff, had given the state an affidavit saying he didn't recall receiving a call from Nell about the bag of sheets, but Nell said she had definitely told Ratliff about the sheets and could even remember how Ratliff had responded. "He said, `My office isn't handling that, the town police are. Call Randy Jackson.' I told him to go to hell, and hung up." She had not called Jackson.

Nell Shortridge also repeated her assertion that there were two shirts in the bag her husband had found, and said that there was blood on the shirts as well as the sheets. The presence of two bloody shirts in the bag fit the defense theory that it was related to the murder, and that at least two people had been involved.

It was late Sunday night when Kitty finished her work. Arnold & Porter's night typing pool would turn out the final version, Kitty would read the documents one last time in the morning to make sure no major mistake had crept into them overnight and they would be sent off by messenger for filing. All in all she was pleased with her work, and hopeful. She was under no illusion that the evidence was sufficient yet to prove Coleman's innocence, but she thought there was enough to raise serious questions in the mind of any objective observer—questions that could be resolved only by granting her request for discovery of the state's records and holding an evidentiary hearing where the witnesses would be required to testify under oath.

Of course, all of this assumed that the procedural issues the state had raised would be found against them, or at least put aside until after an evidentiary hearing was held. Based on what Judge Persin had done on the DNA issue, and his apparent reluctance to sentence Coleman to death in the first place, she had reason to hope he would not go ahead with an execution without at least listening to the witnesses who had come forward. In any event, she thought, it was unlikely she could find a judge she would prefer to have make that decision.

As for herself, as Kitty relaxed at home for the first time in weeks and reflected on the case, she understood that something had changed. After her first trip to Grundy she had decided it was likely Roger Coleman was innocent. That had been frightening enough, but this was worse. Now, she thought, she was sure of it.

In the beginning I was very skeptical about Roger's innocence. It had nothing to do with him, per se, but with my general attitude—how did this guy get convicted if he was innocent? What started to change that was the way the attorney-client relationship developed between Roger and me. When I started on the case, if he wanted to talk to someone at Arnold & Porter he'd call one of the older lawyers on the case, and if that person wasn't there, he'd call someone else down the line, until sometimes he got to me. And then, after a while, I became his choice, he just called me first. I guess it was because I was doing most of the investigation, and also I asked him questions about the case, and what happened, and how he could explain this or that piece of evidence, instead of just answering his questions. I think that pleased him. And when I would ask him for an explanation of something, he had an incredibly clear recollection of things going all the way back to childhood, and he would set forth exactly what happened, which was really helpful in doing the investigation, because he was such a good source of information, and if he said he knew something for sure and it was something that could be checked out, it always turned out to be true.

So there was this basic lack of deceptiveness on his part in talking about his case that was very important to me. I could ask him anything, and he would answer. When he talked about what happened the night of the murder, where he was and so on, he was very intense. It wasn't just like, this is my story, but *this is what happened!* It was like he just couldn't believe that anyone would doubt that what he said was true, because it *was* true. And Philip VanDyke, when I interviewed him the first time, was the same way. Like Roger, he just couldn't believe that anyone would think he was lying about meeting Roger that night, or about what time he thought it was when they parted.

And then there were the Teresa Horn interviews. I was deeply, deeply troubled by the Teresa Horn interviews because she truly seemed to me to be telling the truth. When you meet somebody like that and you see what kind of sacrifice they've made to tell you, it is very troublesome. You've got to explain it away, and I could not. So after that, and with all the other people coming forward saying bad things about Donnie Ramey, and things like the anonymous letter that was completely independent of Teresa Horn, by the time our work on the state habeas was done I would have said I was convinced Roger was innocent.

The oral argument before Judge Persin on the state's motion to dismiss the petition for habeas corpus was scheduled for 10:00 A.M. on December 4 at the courthouse in Grundy. Kitty had spent the previous two days preparing her argument, and while waiting outside the courtroom for the hearing to begin, she nervously repeated the argument in her mind while chatting with Roger Mullins, her local counsel, and trying to appear calm.

At Mecklenburg, Roger Coleman was also nervous. He, Kitty and his uncle Roger Lee had arranged that after the hearing Kitty would spend a few minutes telling Roger Lee how she thought it had gone. Roger could then call his uncle in the evening and get a report. He tried to appear unconcerned, but throughout the day before the hearing the only thing Roger could think about was hoping the hearing went well. He believed his life depended on it.

That evening Roger Lee reported that the hearing had lasted longer than anticipated and that Kitty had rushed off to catch her plane without having the conversation they had planned. As far as Roger Lee was concerned, he said, it had gone well. He particularly noted that at one point in the argument the judge had interrupted Donald Curry and asked if he understood that the case against Roger was only circumstantial.

Kitty herself thought the hearing had gone better than expected. In fact, the more she thought about it, she believed it couldn't have gone any better. The judge had said that as he read the law, if there were any material factual disputes, he was required to grant an evidentiary hearing. That was the position Kitty had taken, and if the judge stuck to his statement, she couldn't see how there could be any doubt that a

hearing was needed. Curry had claimed there had never been an evidentiary hearing on a second state habeas petition in Virginia, and
made it clear that if Judge Persin ordered one, he would appeal to the
Virginia Supreme Court. Kitty thought Judge Persin was singularly
unimpressed with the threat, and when Curry asserted that Judge
Persin had no jurisdiction to grant a hearing, she thought she saw the
judge roll his eyes.

The next day, when Roger reached Kitty on the phone, she tried not
to sound too optimistic. The longer they talked, however, the harder it
was to hold back her true feelings, and finally she told Roger that she
was excited as hell about it, and had slept well for the first time in
months.

Judge Persin had told the lawyers he expected to reach a decision
within a few days, but as the days passed, they heard nothing. Roger
called Kitty every afternoon to see if anything had happened. He told
himself that one of the best things that had happened to him in prison
was gaining patience. On death row, life is full of waiting, and he had
learned that he might as well wait patiently.

It was probably true that Roger was more patient than when he
was a young man in Grundy, but it was also true that as he waited for
Judge Persin's decision, he could think of almost nothing else. By
Friday, December 14, ten days had passed and Kitty had still heard
nothing. The next afternoon Roger called his uncle, who informed
him that the local newspapers reported that the judge had reached a
decision on Friday and mailed it to the lawyers, but would not release
it to the public until the lawyers had seen it. Roger called Kitty,
although he knew that if the newspapers were right, she would not
receive the order until Monday. Kitty was not in her office. Then he
thought of Roger Mullins in Tazewell. A letter mailed from Grundy
on Friday might have reached Tazewell on Saturday. Mullins was in,
and had the order. Judge Persin had granted the state's motion to dismiss.

Later in the day, when Roger finally reached Kitty in her office, she
had just heard the news. To Roger she sounded deeply upset, as if she
were in a state of shock. After a short, mumbled conversation, Kitty
said she would talk to Roger again on Monday when she had read the
actual decision. Roger spent most of the rest of his day calling other
people who needed to know—his family, Marie, Robert White and

Sharon. Sharon was the hardest. She was terribly upset, and broke down crying for the first time ever. Roger told a friend that he felt awful—it was his fault for not doing a better job of keeping her from getting too optimistic.

Chapter 25

——

Setting a Date

With the dismissal of his state petition, the tempo of Coleman's march toward a final life-or-death resolution of his case accelerated. There was another perfunctory step in the state case—an appeal to the Virginia Supreme Court—but that would move quickly and the likelihood of success was nil. While delay in the past had worked to Roger's benefit, once Judge Persin set an execution date, time would begin to work against him. As a practical matter, there were only two more chances to prevent his execution—a second federal petition for habeas corpus, and, if that failed, a petition for executive clemency. If the judge assigned to hear the federal habeas petition could be persuaded to hold an evidentiary hearing, he might stay the execution to accommodate it, but otherwise the courts would probably leave in place any execution date established by Judge Persin.

Similarly, it was unlikely that Governor Wilder would stay the execution to consider executive clemency. Once the case reached the point where it appeared that an execution date would be kept, Wilder would make his decision, probably close to the last minute. Kitty Behan could no longer move one step at a time. Completion of the appeal from Judge Persin's decision, preparation of the federal habeas corpus petition, preparation of a petition for executive clemency and the development of further evidence of Roger's innocence would have to proceed simultaneously, and as rapidly as possible. Her bitter disappointment at Judge Persin's decision had slowed Kitty down for a few days, but she was soon back to speed. There was no choice.

The campaign for public support, which was crucial to any chance of obtaining clemency, was dormant except for distributing information in the Grundy area as part of the effort to uncover additional evidence. Now, along with everything else, Kitty knew she had to broaden and invigorate media interest in Roger's story.

The Supreme Court decision in June had resulted in a few editorials and Op-Ed pieces decrying the idea that someone could be executed because his lawyer had filed a document one day late. Kitty had a clipping file of those articles and a list of inquiries about the case from other writers and publications. A new press statement was prepared concentrating on the evidence concerning Donnie Ramey and flatly declaring that Coleman was innocent and Ramey was the real killer. Contacts were made with publications and broadcast media that might be interested in the story. Virginia, they were told, had just ruled that Roger Coleman had no right to a hearing on his claim of innocence. Unless something were done by a federal court or the governor, an innocent man would be executed.

It was a story that had been presented many times before on behalf of condemned men, and it was greeted with understandable cynicism. If someone took the time to study it, however, the presentation was impressive. An alleged confession by a next-door neighbor with a history of alleged attacks on women, buried bloody sheets, the aura of poverty and violence in Buchanan County, and the involvement of the relatively new forensic use of DNA technology were enough to create considerable interest. And if the interest was sufficient to send a reporter out to talk to Kitty Behan, the reporter's initial cynicism was often dispelled. They didn't necessarily come away from a conversation with Kitty believing Roger Coleman was innocent, but they certainly could tell that she believed it, and that it was a story worth looking into. Jim McCloskey also used his substantial credibility with the media to promote Roger's innocence, and his credibility was enhanced that spring when he obtained the release of two men who had been in prison for seventeen years on a murder conviction obtained through the false testimony of a jailhouse informant. Before

Kitty and Jim were done, Roger Coleman's story would be known throughout the world.

Meanwhile, Kitty could no longer fend off the state's effort to have Judge Persin set an execution date. On February 12, 1992, he rejected both Donald Curry's request for an execution date in March and Kitty's plea that no date be set until after a final petition for federal habeas corpus could be heard and decided. Unless the governor or another court intervened, Judge Persin ruled that Roger Coleman would be executed on Wednesday, May 20, 1992.

Following Judge Persin's dismissal of the state habeas petition, Kitty continued to receive reports from Grundy about the McCoy murder. One story that kept resurfacing was that the murder was somehow drug-related. Jim was less dismissive of the idea than Kitty due to his belief that the crime-scene photographs showed crosses cut into Wanda's hands. Several sources now claimed to have heard that Randy "Pegleg" Wolford in Kentucky knew about a drug ring that supposedly delivered drugs to Brad McCoy for distribution in Grundy.* In addition, an anonymous caller had told Roger Lee Coleman that another man, named James Wolford, was a sheriff's deputy in Pike County, Kentucky, and claimed to know about the crosses on Wanda's hands, which were supposedly a sign of a drug killing. In December, Kitty located Randy Wolford in Kentucky and talked to him on the telephone. He denied any knowledge of the murder.

While Kitty didn't think much of the drug theory, her conversation with Wolford left her with an unsettled feeling that he had lied to her, although she had no idea why. She resolved to try to interview him in person.

One of the most interesting rumors Kitty heard was that Donnie Ramey had told his Social Security worker that he had recurring nightmares about committing a horrible crime. Ramey was now supposedly threatening to sue the Social Security Administration for leaking his file, since he thought that was how Roger's lawyers "got on to him."

---

* It should be emphasized that the rumor about Brad McCoy was and is entirely unsubstantiated. No one who knows Brad, including the author, believes he was ever a drug dealer.

Kitty doubted she would get any information, but in February she called the Social Security office and asked for someone with information about disability claims. She explained her problem and asked if Donnie Ramey's file could be examined to determine whether in fact it contained information suggesting he might have murdered Wanda McCoy. If there was such information, Kitty explained, it could save an innocent man from execution. After a moment of silence, the person Kitty had contacted said that to get the file she would have to make a formal request, but that they would let Kitty know if there was anything in the file that was worth pursuing. A few days later Kitty answered her telephone and a person who did not provide a name, but whose voice she recognized, said that while Ramey's file did not say anything about the McCoy murder, it described a psychiatric interview in which Ramey allegedly said that he had beaten his girlfriend, that he had recurring nightmares and that he was afraid he might seriously hurt someone. On February 18, Kitty wrote to the Social Security Administration asking that Ramey's files be released.

While Kitty devoted most of her time in late January and February to working on the federal habeas corpus and clemency petitions, two collateral events occurred that were bound to have an impact on the Coleman case. On January 23, 1992, hours before Herbert Bassette was scheduled to die in Virginia's electric chair, Governor Wilder commuted his sentence to life in prison.

Of the seven men whose execution dates had previously arrived since Wilder was elected, six had been denied clemency and gone to their deaths, including Wilbert Evans, the black man who had put his life on the line to protect a prison nurse and guards during the 1984 death-row escape. Then, in February 1990, Wilder had reduced Joe Giarratano's death sentence to life in prison on the basis of a claim of innocence. He would not release Giarratano, he said, because he was not absolutely certain he was innocent, but there was enough doubt that Giarratano should not be executed. Almost no one had been happy with the decision, including some of the governor's African-American supporters, who asked why Wilder had spared Giarratano, a white man, when he had denied clemency to Evans.

Bassette, like Giarratano, was claiming innocence. And like Wilbert Evans, he was black. Cynics said Bassette provided Wilder with the perfect opportunity to make up for not commuting Evans and to regain the affection of his black supporters without offending any but the most avid proponents of capital punishment.

To some of Roger Coleman's supporters, Wilder's action in commuting Bassette came as a huge boost. They believed the doubts about Coleman's guilt were at least as strong as those in Bassette's case. Surely the governor would also commute Coleman, and one day the evidence of Coleman's innocence would be so overwhelming that Wilder or some successor would release him altogether.

Others were not so optimistic. Public support for the death penalty was getting stronger by the day, and Wilder was adopting more and more stringent anticrime positions. In the old days in Virginia it was essential that a politician not be outdone in opposing integration. Now it was essential not to be outdone in supporting the death penalty. Wilder had evened the racial score, and pessimists thought it would be a long time before he exercised his clemency power again.

The second "outside" event involved a death-penalty case from Texas, where lawyers for Leonel Herrera were fighting for his life. The lawyers had filed a federal petition for writ of habeas corpus containing substantial evidence of Herrera's innocence, and on February 16, 1992, three days before he was to be executed, a federal judge granted a stay of execution in order to conduct an evidentiary hearing on the claim. Texas immediately appealed, and the day before Herrera's execution date, the Fifth Circuit Court of Appeals vacated the stay, holding, as Texas had argued, that even assuming Leonel Herrera was innocent, innocence was no basis for granting a writ of habeas corpus. In other words, the court held, nothing in the United States Constitution prohibits a state from executing an innocent man as long as his constitutional right to due process was not violated in the course of his trial.

If the decision of the Fifth Circuit seemed bizarre to most Americans, what occurred next was equally strange. The next day— the day Herrera was to be executed—his lawyers filed a petition for writ of certiorari and an emergency motion to stay the execution in the Supreme Court. Hours before the execution was to take place, the Court ruled. The required four justices agreed to review the decision of the Fifth Circuit, so certiorari was granted. However, in a move so arrogant that at first those who learned of it could not believe what they were hearing, none of the five justices who opposed certiorari would agree to Herrera's request for a stay of execution. Since such a motion is decided by majority vote, it was denied, five to four. No matter that four of their colleagues had agreed that the stark question of whether the Constitution permits the execution of an innocent man should be reviewed by the nation's highest court—innocent or not, Leonel Herrera would die that night.

When Herrera's lawyers recovered from their shock, they began placing emergency calls to Texas judges at their homes, trying to find someone who would stay the execution. Minutes before Herrera would have been executed, the Texas Court of Criminal Appeals entered a stay.

In one respect, the grant of certiorari in the Herrera case was good news for Roger Coleman. Virginia, like Texas, was sure to argue that proof of innocence is not a constitutional issue to be determined in federal habeas corpus. With the issue now before the Supreme Court, there was a chance that a court would grant a stay of execution in Coleman's case to await the decision in *Herrera*, and a stay would provide more time to prove Coleman's innocence. On the other hand, the action of the five justices who had refused to stay Herrera's execution even after their colleagues had granted certiorari was a frightening measure of the Court majority's determination to limit the scope of habeas corpus and carry out the death penalty quicker, and more often. Herrera's case might prolong Coleman's life, but it seemed unlikely that the final decision in the case would be helpful.

Chapter 26

March 1992: Teresa

With the setting of an execution date, the probability that Roger Coleman was going to die in the electric chair had greatly increased, and Roger knew it. For the most part he tried to maintain a façade of confidence in dealing with Sharon, Marie, Roger Lee and Kitty, but in truth he thought it was quite likely he would be dead before summer, and from time to time he would admit it. His state of mind may have been reflected in another poem he sent to Sharon:

> *Time Means Nothing . . .*
> *. . . because love is forever*

> *Do not stand at my grave and weep;*
> *I am not there. I do not sleep.*
> *I am a thousand winds that blow;*
> *I am the diamond glints on snow.*
> *I am the gentle autumn's rain.*
> *When you awake in the morning's hush,*
> *I am the swift uplifting rush*
> *Of quiet birds in circled flight*

I am the soft star that shines at night
Do not stand at my grave and cry.

In early March the Social Security Administration denied Kitty's request for Donnie Ramey's file, as she expected. Rather than take valuable time filing a separate and probably unsuccessful case under the Freedom of Information Act, Kitty decided she would try to obtain an order for the production of the file from the judge who would hear the federal habeas corpus petition. Without compromising her source, she could reveal enough for the judge to understand that the file might contain important information.

Also in early March, Kitty decided to make a quick trip to Grundy to obtain affidavits from two minor witnesses and provide moral support for Teresa Horn, who had decided to grant an interview to a television station in which she would repeat her charges against Donnie Ramey. Teresa was nervous about appearing on television, and somewhat fearful that doing so would increase the possibility of retribution. Kitty had tried not to influence her one way or the other when Teresa told her about the station's request for an interview, but she was glad Teresa had decided to do it. It could only improve the climate of local opinion, and might stimulate someone else to come forward with helpful information.

The interview was scheduled for Thursday, March 5, at Teresa's mother's trailer. At the last minute Linda Mullins had agreed to participate in the interview, and when Kitty arrived, Linda and Teresa were waiting. Teresa was suffering from chronic back pain from an automobile accident and had taken a heavy dose of prescription pain medicine that morning. The medicine made her seem woozy and slurred her speech, but she insisted on going ahead with the interview. The reporter who was conducting the interview soon arrived with a mobile camera crew, and after the usual preliminaries the interviews proceeded. If Teresa's condition made her less persuasive than Kitty had hoped, she nevertheless told her story with obvious emotion. Linda Mullins added her own allegations about her encounter with Ramey at the Grundy airstrip. All in all, Kitty felt, it had gone well.

Back in Washington on Friday night, Kitty was exhausted, and the next morning she slept later than usual. When she arrived at her office there was a message from Roger Lee Coleman in Grundy. Teresa Horn had been found unconscious in her home sometime the previous evening and was transported to a hospital by ambulance. At 9:00 P.M. on Friday, March 6, the emergency room physician had declared Teresa Horn dead on arrival.

There was no question in Kitty Behan's mind that Teresa Horn had been murdered, and that it was because of the accusations she had made about Donnie Ramey. Kitty was distraught:

> When I got the message I couldn't believe it. It was a bad dream, or a sick joke. I knew it wasn't a dream. Who would play such a sick joke? Maybe Donnie Ramey himself. He could easily call my office and leave such a message. I called Roger Lee. It was no joke.
>
> As soon as I found out it was true, I knew it was me who killed her. I had killed her as surely as whoever did whatever they did. I started killing her when I got her to sign an affidavit to file in court, and I finished her off when she did the television interview. I didn't tell her to do it, but she could see I wanted her to. She knew I thought it might help, so she did it even though she was scared, just like she signed the affidavit even though she was scared. She did it despite the guy who told her straight out that someone was threatening to get her, and that she should keep her mouth shut, and despite the hang-up calls she had been getting. She came forward on her own, and then kept on coming step by step when I asked her, and now she was dead, and I killed her.
>
> I called her mother. I thought she wouldn't talk to me, or if she did she would curse me. But she didn't curse me. She cried, and I cried too, and I said it was all my fault, but Brenda said "No, it wasn't you, you didn't do anything wrong. Teresa was proud of coming forward and proud she was doing the right thing even if she was scared, so don't blame yourself, just get the bastard that killed her."
>
> So I asked how Teresa was killed, and Brenda said the police were saying it looked like a drug overdose, but she didn't believe it because there was no way Teresa deliberately killed herself and she knew too much to take an overdose, so it was either poison or if it was drugs someone forced her to take them or injected them or something. And I agreed with her.

If Kitty Behan's first reaction to the death of Teresa Horn was guilt and grief for Teresa, it did not take long for her to realize that when Teresa was lowered into her grave, she was probably taking Roger

Coleman with her. With Teresa dead, there was no admissible evidence to support the claim that it was Donnie Ramey, not Roger Coleman, who had killed Wanda McCoy.

When Kitty recovered from her initial shock, she tried to arrange for Dr. McCormick, her forensic pathologist, to attend Teresa's autopsy, but it had already been performed on Saturday morning by Dr. Oxley, the same man who had autopsied Wanda McCoy eleven years earlier. Oxley said Teresa's death was the result of edema, or swelling, of the brain and heart, probably caused by the ingestion of multiple drugs. Preliminary tests indicated the presence of a variety of drugs, but a final diagnosis would have to await the report of a toxicologist. It was a month before the toxicology analysis and report were completed.

Teresa Horn was buried on March 9, 1992. It was a beautiful spring day, the first really warm day of the year, sunny and in the seventies. When Brenda Keene and the other mourners looked at her in the open casket, they saw large bruises on her left wrist and the back of her hand, which seemed to surround puncture wounds. To Brenda Keene it was obvious that someone had held Teresa very tightly and injected something into her veins with a hypodermic needle. Teresa, her mother knew, was not an intravenous-drug user.

Over the next several weeks, rumors swirled about Teresa's death. Kitty and Brenda Keene demanded that the police investigate the death as a possible homicide, with special attention to her role in the Coleman case and her charges against Donnie Ramey. Given her level of confidence in the local police, Kitty also asked the United States attorney's office and the FBI to investigate, on the grounds that Teresa's death might have been designed to obstruct justice.

Donney Ramey denied any knowledge of Teresa's death. The police reported that he had an alibi for the afternoon of the sixth, and that it had checked out. Later, Ramey said he also took and passed a lie-detector test about Teresa Horn's death. The lie test apparently did not cover the murder of Wanda McCoy.

According to the medical examiner's office, the bruises and punctures Brenda Keene observed were the result of intravenous punctures made by the paramedics during efforts to resuscitate Teresa. Brenda was not convinced, but Kitty's pathologist said it was a reasonable explanation. Brenda reported that she had found a slip of paper indicating that on Wednesday, March 4, Teresa had obtained and filled a prescription for methadone, and that on Thursday, the day of the TV interview, she was taking Fiorinal for her back pain from a prescription she had apparently filled that day or the day before. Teresa had no history of heroin addiction, and Brenda could not understand how or why she would have obtained methadone.

There were also reports about various people who had been seen in the vicinity of the trailer where Teresa and her boyfriend were living on the day Teresa died, some of them allegedly friends of the Rameys. Another rumor was that there was a delay in calling the paramedics and getting her to a hospital. The autopsy report itself showed that two hours elapsed between the time the police were informed that Teresa had been found unconscious and the time she was reported DOA at the hospital, which seemed excessive.

In the end, however, all the speculation about how and why Teresa Horn died the day after she had repeated her charges against Donnie Ramey on television would come to naught. The final toxicology report showed significant amounts of methadone and butalbital in her blood, a combination that, the report asserted, would act synergistically to cause an overdose, which in turn could have caused her death. No one has ever discovered how or why Teresa Horn obtained a prescription for methadone, or how she happened to take the fatal combination of drugs together—knowingly or unknowingly, voluntarily or otherwise.

In any event, Teresa was dead. For Kitty and Roger, it was a huge setback.

Chapter 27

—

Four Interviews

On the day of Teresa Horn's funeral I arrived in Grundy for the first time, seeking information and local color for a magazine article on the Coleman case. Monday was spent visiting the murder scene and getting acquainted with the area and some of the witnesses.

Tuesday, March 10, was the eleventh anniversary of Wanda McCoy's murder. The weather remained sunny and even warmer. Since I had already interviewed Kitty Behan and Jim McCloskey, I was anxious to talk to people on the "other side." I had directions to Donnie Ramey's trailer, but several efforts to find him failed. Over the next two days, however, I did interview a number of participants in the case, including Mickey McGlothlin, the prosecutor; Terry Jordan, the defense lawyer; and both Brad McCoy and, briefly on the telephone, Trish Thompson, Roger's ex-wife and Wanda McCoy's sister.

Mickey McGlothlin professed little recollection of the details of the case beyond what was in the transcript. Roger Coleman, he assured me, was guilty, and if the evidence in the murder case left me doubtful, I should consider his prior conviction for attempted rape and the claim that just two months before the McCoy murder he had exposed himself and masturbated in the library. Coleman is a dangerous sexual psychopath, McGlothlin declared, and if there had been only one woman in the library that night he probably would have killed her as well, just as he probably would have killed Sandy Stiltner instead of Wanda McCoy if Sandy's husband hadn't been home. As for Donnie Ramey, McGlothlin said, he knew little about him except that his nickname "Trouble" was apparently earned. McGlothlin said he had no reason to believe Ramey was involved in the murder, but if he was, or if there was some other second person there, the one man who knows who that person is, and should say so, is Roger Coleman.

I had learned before my trip to Grundy that Trish Thompson had a short, unsuccessful marriage to another man after her divorce from Roger Coleman and was now living with a brother on Home Creek. Phone calls to the house found her out, but late one afternoon I learned she was attending classes at a community college after work and would be at a friend's house that evening. I obtained the phone number and called, asking for Patricia Thompson.

When Trish came to the phone, she had no idea who I was or why I was calling, and when she found out she said she didn't want to talk—but for a few minutes she did. Like almost everyone in Grundy, she was too polite to just hang up. Did you suspect Roger from the beginning? I asked. "No, I didn't think he had anything to do with it. But then they brought me the proof." What proof? "The blood tests, the hair." Did he ever tell you he did it? "No, he always denied it—but they brought me the proof. You have to believe what's down on paper, no matter what people are telling you."

Patricia Thompson's soft voice began to waver. "They should have got it over with a long time ago. . . . It's hard on Mamma and Daddy when it keeps coming up." Her voice wavered more. "It's hard on me."

I found Brad McCoy at his job at United Coal Shop No. 1 at the end of the work day, and he agreed, albeit reluctantly, to sit and talk for a few minutes in my car. The day had turned from sunny to cloudy and it was now raining hard.

The interview itself was not as interesting as my impression of Brad. Since first reading the trial transcript I had wondered why the police were so quickly persuaded that he was not involved. True, when Davidson interviewed him he had no scratches or apparent blood on his clothes—but still, the timing was suspicious, he could have changed his clothes, and when a wife is killed the husband is always a prime suspect unless he has an airtight alibi. Even then the question persists of whether he may have found someone else to do it for him. True, Brad took and passed a lie test several weeks later, but the record suggested that the test was a mere formality, a checking off of what had to be done—virtually all the police attention from the day after the murder was on Roger, not Brad.

It did not take long for me to answer my own question. Quiet, soft-spoken, shy in a way not unlike the reputation of his murdered wife, Brad McCoy simply couldn't have done it. At least that's what I concluded, and what I suspect Jack Davidson concluded when he interviewed him after the murder. He didn't seem as if he could be a murderer, or a drug dealer either.

Like Trish, Brad said he did not suspect Roger at first. In fact, even after the issue was raised, he didn't think Roger had anything to do with it. They were friends. He was family. But then came the blood types, the pubic hair—and of course, there was the prior record. He thought Roger was strong enough to have done it alone. He thought at the time that the black substance on Wanda was coal dust—and he's still not sure it wasn't. Now he just wanted it to be over.

Brad confirmed that there had been a falling out with Danny Ray Stiltner. He was not sure exactly what time he got home the night of the murder, but he did punch out from his job, and the police got the time card and found out when it was.

Brad McCoy remarried on February 18, 1983, and has a son, Matthew, born in 1988, and a daughter, Kaitlin, born after my interview. He said he has a wonderful wife, and with her help, and God's, most of the time he doesn't think about that night. Most of the time—but he doubts he will ever be able to wipe it out completely.

By the next morning the weather had changed dramatically. Overnight the temperature had dropped into the low thirties and the rain had turned to heavy snow. The tops of the mountains were white, and the roads slushy and slippery. From my motel, the thirty-mile trip to Grundy was slow and, it seemed to me, very dangerous. Big, heavily loaded coal trucks were out in force and ignoring the storm, barreling down the mountains and around the icy curves on Route 460 as though they could stop on a dime. Maybe they could, but I doubted it, and wherever possible I stayed in the right lane and watched the rearview mirror, ready to hit the shoulder if I saw a truck coming too fast behind me.

After several tries earlier in the week, I finally caught up with Terry Jordan in his office. He told me about his effort to avoid being appointed in the case because of his inexperience, and also because he was just getting his practice going and thought representing Coleman was unlikely to endear him to potential clients. Judge Persin, however, wouldn't take no for an answer, and Jordan figured he couldn't afford to piss off the local judge.

Jordan said Roger had always insisted he was innocent, but Jordan wasn't sure. He thought the state had a strong case, and although Roger had a good alibi, it wasn't perfect. It was Jordan who revealed that after the jury retired to consider its verdict, the state offered a life sentence in return for a guilty plea. He and Arey advised Roger to take it, but Roger refused.

One reason I was anxious to talk to Jordan was to show him the police report about the pry mark on the front door of the murder house. I wanted to know whether Jordan had known about it. Despite the answers he had given at the first state habeas hearing about having had access to the prosecutor's file, it seemed unlikely to me that even lawyers as inexperienced as Jordan and Steve Arey could have known about the pry mark and failed to use it.

When I pulled out Jack Davidson's report and asked Jordan if he had seen it and known about the pry mark, Jordan said he didn't think so, but, given the passage of more than ten years, he could not be certain. I asked if he would have used the pry mark at trial if he had known about it, and Jordan said, in substance, "Yes, which is why I don't think I saw this report." I next showed him the page of the crime-scene diagram where the location of the pry mark was featured. Jordan stared at the paper and appeared upset. After a minute he threw the diagram down on the table and declared emphatically, "I can't be sure about the report you showed me, but I *know* I never saw this."

I knew Kitty Behan had been trying, without success, to reach Jordan by telephone to ask the same questions, so when I returned from Grundy I told her of Jordan's answers. My report would result in yet another strange twist in the tortuous trail of her effort to save Roger Coleman.

Chapter 28

Contact

Different states have different rules and practices regarding visits to death-row prisoners, ranging from regular conjugal visits to complete physical isolation, and those rules and practices change with changes in prison administrations, governors and public sentiment.

Virginia in 1992 was close to the strict isolation model, but there were some exceptions. Although visiting family and friends were usually limited to the telephone cubicles in the visitors' room, once the prisoner was moved to deathwatch, where there were enough guards to provide constant surveillance, the prisoner would be allowed one or more "contact" visits with someone he could designate. A contact visit meant that after the visitor went through a complete strip search, he or she would be locked in a visiting room with the prisoner, under the constant watch of a guard. The visitor and prisoner were permitted to hold hands, and even to hug and kiss at the beginning and end of the visit.

It was, one supposes, a kind of reward, given in gratitude for the prisoner finally approaching the point where the prison system would soon be rid of him. And if the prisoner had behaved, Virginia even provided the possibility of an extra, earlier contact visit at Mecklenburg to celebrate the setting of a final execution date.

Thus Roger Coleman had greeted the setting of his execution date with mixed emotions. It meant that a date had been set when he was likely to die, but it also meant that, after nine years, he might finally be permitted to touch and hold Sharon Paul.

Roger and Sharon settled on Friday, March 20, as the date they would request for a contact visit. When the warden received Roger's request, he sent word that he would consider it, but doubted he would approve it. Mothers were considered more appropriate and less troublesome visitors than girlfriends. However, on February 22, Roger was notified that his request had been granted. He called Sharon with the news. He sounded as excited as when he learned the Supreme Court had agreed to consider his case.

When March 20 arrived, Sharon was searched and taken into a visiting room, where Roger was soon brought to join her. There was a table in the room with a chair on either side. They had been sternly instructed that they could hug and kiss each other briefly across the table, and hold hands as long as their hands remained in sight of the guard, but that the table had to remain between them at all times. Any violation of the rule would bring the visit to an immediate end.

After an awkward hug and kiss across the table, Roger and Sharon held hands, talked, gazed into each other's eyes and spoke of love for the next hour. At the end of the hour Sergeant Williams, the guard assigned to monitor the visit, allowed them to hold each other again, this time without the interference of the table, and Williams took several pictures of them with a Polaroid camera kept in the unit for that purpose. Then Sharon was required to leave, although she was allowed to go to the regular, noncontact visiting room, where she and Roger spent another hour talking on the telephone, separated by the glass partition.

The only words Sharon could find to describe the experience were that it was "amazing—from the moment we first touched I felt we had been holding each other all my life." In his diary, Roger went on for pages. It was like a dream. It was the happiest hour of his life. He *had* to find a way to prove his innocence so that he could be with her for the rest of his life.

By Sunday, Roger was deeply depressed. The pressure of his approaching execution date had been building up for weeks, but the anticipation of his contact visit with Sharon had kept it at bay. Now reality was crashing down on him.

A phone call to Sharon helped to cheer him up, and the next day a draft of Kitty's federal habeas corpus petition and several letters from troubled teenagers arrived in the mail. All required his attention, and he was soon back to normal.

Chapter 29

—

The Experts

As Roger Coleman's execution date drew closer, Kitty Behan's efforts to stimulate media support began to succeed. Newspapers in Virginia were covering the Coleman story and publicizing his claim of innocence. Then, in late March, a writer for *Newsweek* called Kitty with the news that the evidence she had supplied, together with Teresa Horn's suspicious death and his own investigation in Grundy, had persuaded him and his editors that Coleman was probably innocent. *Newsweek* would print an article suggesting that the case should be reopened.

The *Newsweek* story appeared on March 31 and ran for two and a half pages. It featured a large photograph of Roger in handcuffs and leg chains, staring at the viewer with a sad but appealing expression. The headline read, HUNG ON A TECHNICALITY—A VIRGINIA MURDER CASE SHOWS HOW NEW COURT RULES MIGHT LEAD TO A FATAL ERROR. The text of the article all but declared Roger innocent, and a sidebar focused on Jim McCloskey, including his recent success in freeing two men in California from false murder convictions.

In close order, major articles favorable to Coleman appeared in *The Washington Post*, *The New York Times* and *The New Republic*. Kitty knew the articles would unleash a stream of mail to Governor Wilder asking that he grant clemency, and the publicity began to help in other ways as well. People in Buchanan County began to feel more comfortable about coming forward with information, especially about Donnie Ramey, now that *Newsweek* had printed the story and named him.

The attention, however, was far from welcomed by the Buchanan County establishment. The *Newsweek* article, in particular, had belittled Grundy as a "small, sooted town of central Appalachia" and suggested that during Coleman's trial, "The courthouse should have had a big top." It also suggested that evidence favorable to Coleman had been suppressed by the prosecution.

Tom Scott was incensed. On April 3 he faxed an impassioned letter to *Newsweek*'s editor denouncing the story, and began organizing local support for proceeding with Coleman's execution. His effort to reverse the tide of stories favorable to Coleman succeeded with a few regional newspapers, but for the most part the media continued to ask why a man should be executed without at least exploring what appeared to be serious evidence of innocence.

For Kitty, the media campaign was succeeding beyond expectations. She was excited by the experience of seeing "her case," and often her name, in the national press, and buoyed by the attention and favorable comments of her friends and older lawyers at Arnold & Porter. But she was not deluded. *The New York Times* and *Newsweek* could not give Roger Coleman a hearing or commute his sentence of death. Kitty was already working night and day on the federal habeas corpus petition, and in conversation with Phil Horton and Jim McCloskey everyone agreed that it had to be filed soon or run the risk of being dismissed out of hand as a desperate last-minute ploy.

They also knew they had to try to strengthen their evidence of innocence. Kitty had the names of a half dozen people who said they either had heard Donnie Ramey admit participation in the murder or knew someone who had heard it. With the death of Teresa Horn, Kitty no longer had such a witness. Jim McCloskey had to go back to Grundy to search for a new Teresa Horn, and as hard as it was to leave the task of preparing the petition, Kitty felt she had to go with him, at least for long enough to interview some of the women who had provided information to her on the telephone.

Besides, Kitty also wanted to talk to the pathologist, Dr. Oxley, and to Elmer Gist, the state's blood and hair expert. She had some questions about the work they had done in 1981, which, depending on their answers, could be extremely important to Roger's claim of innocence. Although she didn't realize it until later, she had some doubts of another kind as well.

On April 6, Jim and Kitty again headed for southwestern Virginia. Jim went directly to Grundy, while Kitty stopped in Roanoke to try to talk to Oxley and Gist. She had considered asking the state to arrange the interviews, but decided that Don Curry would probably refuse and tell the men not to talk to her. She was also afraid that if she called them to set up an appointment, they would turn around and call Curry, with the same result. She decided to hope she would find them in their offices and could walk in on them without notice.

Arriving at the institutional-looking brick building that houses the western regional offices of both the Division of Forensic Science and the medical examiner, Kitty was surprised to find that admission was subject to tight security. A uniformed officer at the public entrance asked what her business was and said he would have to contact the man she wanted to see and obtain clearance for her to proceed to his office.

Kitty guessed that Dr. Oxley was less likely to be secretive about his work than Gist, and decided to try him first. After explaining who she was and why she wanted to see Oxley, Kitty waited anxiously as the guard dialed a number and spoke into the telephone. Replacing the phone in its cradle, he looked at Kitty and announced "He says to come up." Provided with a visitor's pass, Kitty was directed to Oxley's office, where she found a friendly middle-aged man dressed in casual clothes sitting behind a desk that looked almost as disorganized as her own.

After introductions and some small talk, Kitty pulled a lined yellow pad and two copies of Oxley's autopsy report from her briefcase. She gave Oxley a copy of the report, glanced at the questions she had written on the pad during her flight from Washington and decided to begin with the issue that was most responsible for her desire to question him.

"Your report says you took a rectal swab from Wanda McCoy's body, and Elmer Gist reports finding sperm heads on that swab. Someone says the sperm may have just run down from her vagina. Is that possible, or does finding sperm on the rectal swab mean she was sodomized?"

Oxley looked slightly annoyed. "Whoever said that doesn't know what they're talking about. The way I took the rectal swab—the way any competent forensic pathologist would take one—you only get sperm on the swab if there was penetration. Otherwise you could never be sure if there was sodomy, which is the point of taking the swab."

Kitty Behan tried to conceal her relief as she rephrased the question. "So, there was definitely anal penetration and ejaculation?"

"Yes," Oxley replied, "there was."

Then there wasn't time, Kitty thought. *I don't care what kind of man Roger Coleman is, there just wasn't time for him to do all that happened to Wanda. Not even if the state is right about when he was at Boyd's Trailer Park.*

Kitty was so pleased, she almost thanked Oxley and left without asking the rest of her questions, but she caught herself, remembering the cuts on Wanda McCoy's hands, which Jim thought were X's, but which Oxley hadn't even mentioned in his report.

When Kitty asked about the cuts, Oxley examined his report and laughed. There weren't any cuts on her hands, he said. If there were cuts, I would have reported them.

Kitty looked at Dr. Oxley and tried to decide whether to challenge him. From examining the crime-scene photographs she felt certain there *were* cuts on Wanda McCoy's hands, and Jack Davidson himself had referred to them as "defensive wounds." She decided not to press the issue. She had other questions, and there was no point in taking the risk of offending Oxley and perhaps losing the chance to talk to Gist. Since Oxley hadn't reported the cuts at all, he certainly wasn't now going to say they were in the form of X's, and from looking at the photographs Kitty herself had doubts.

Kitty's final questions had to do with why Oxley had made no effort to preserve any material that was trapped under Wanda McCoy's broken fingernails. Oxley uttered a sigh. "It's a common myth," he said, "that you can find something of forensic value under broken fingernails. This was before DNA. Nowadays, with DNA testing, sometimes you can get something, but before DNA testing it was very rare. As I said in my report, I could see there wasn't any appreciable quantity of material beneath the nails."

Kitty thought Oxley appeared annoyed by her questions about

material under Wanda's broken fingernails. His answer seemed defensive—and not very convincing. Still, there was nothing to gain by pursuing the matter—Oxley had done what he did, and there was no way to change it now. Kitty steered the conversation back to some pleasantries and then asked how she could find her way to Elmer Gist's office. Oxley graciously offered to escort her.

Elmer Gist was as waspish and abrupt as Oxley had been friendly. With an air of impatience, he made it clear that Kitty was an unwelcome intruder. Even so, he said he recalled the case, examined the copy of his report that Kitty tendered and responded to her initial questions.

With Gist, Kitty was primarily interested in finding out why he had characterized the result of his analysis of the anal sperm as inconclusive. Kitty had long ago realized that "inconclusive" seemed to mean something different from the notations that appeared elsewhere in his report that a sample was "insufficient" to obtain a result, but Gist's report contained no explanation. Why, if there was sufficient sperm to obtain a result, was no blood type reported? One possibility was that the donor was not a secretor, which would prove that he was not Roger Coleman just as certainly as if Gist had found a different blood type. Another possibility was that Gist had obtained a tentative result, which for some reason he was reluctant to report.

Kitty began her questions as though she had not noticed the difference between *inconclusive* and *insufficient*. Did his report on the anal sperm mean there wasn't enough material to test, she asked. "No," Gist snapped, "if there wasn't enough to test, I'd have said *insufficient*." "Then what does *inconclusive* mean?" Kitty asked. "It means I thought the results of the test were too unreliable to report." "Why?"

Gist said there could be lots of reasons—contamination, problems with the controls and so forth. When Kitty asked what the reason was in this particular case, Gist said he didn't recall, he'd have to look at his notes. But when Kitty asked if he could do so, Gist said he could, but he wouldn't. They were in a different file. The interview was over.

Riding down in the elevator from Elmer Gist's office, Kitty was frustrated, and furious. Elmer Gist was supposed to be a scientist, not a prosecutor. Besides, a man's life was at stake. If Gist's test had suggested that the donor of the anal sperm might have been a nonsecretor, or some blood type other than B, it would be further evidence that

he was someone other than Roger Coleman. Surely even a prosecutor would agree that was evidence that should be considered before Roger was executed. Why would Elmer Gist refuse to reveal what he had found and recorded in his notes?

In her car, now headed for Grundy, Kitty had gone only a short distance when she realized that while Gist had said he didn't recall why he called the test inconclusive, she had not asked him a direct question about whether he had seen any evidence of another blood type. If Gist really didn't recall, which she doubted, she bet that by now he had dug out his notes and looked.

Kitty stopped her car the next time she saw a public telephone. Gist answered. "Listen," Kitty said, "I need to know one thing. I understand that the result of your test on the anal sperm wasn't reliable enough to report—but could you just tell me if your notes contain any indication of a blood type other than B?"

"All I can tell you," Gist said, "is that if there was an indication of any other blood type, I had a good scientific basis for not reporting it."

"So, you're saying there *was* some indication of another blood type?" Kitty asked. "No," Gist replied sharply. "I've said what I'm saying." He would say no more.

When Kitty regained her composure, she decided the day had gone as well as she could have expected—maybe better. Oxley's emphatic assertion that Wanda McCoy had indeed been raped anally spoke for itself on the question of whether Roger had time to commit the crime, and it seemed unimaginable that a court would fail to order that Elmer Gist produce his notes and explain the "inconclusive" result of his test on the anal swab. Kitty doubted the explanation would be helpful to the state, or Gist would have given it to her.

It was sometime later that Kitty realized her interviews with Oxley and Gist had been important for another reason:

Long before I talked to Oxley and Gist I thought I was convinced Roger was innocent, but I realized later that because of the forensic evidence I still had some skepticism. I thought it was damaging—the hair evidence, for example—but I really didn't understand the scientific problems. I understood about the DNA because I had some background and I talked at length to the experts, but the other stuff I guess I just kind of accepted at face value, until I went down there and talked to those two guys. They seemed to be qualified to do what they were doing, but frankly they didn't seem very credible to me. There's no question that when I came out of those interviews my thought was, the evidence, if anything, pointed away from the state's theory about how this happened, and they should have known that. Also, Gist seemed evasive about the possible presence of other blood types, and from then on I just disregarded that forensic testimony.

And that's when I really became totally convinced of Roger's innocence, in terms of losing all of my skepticism, which is not necessarily good, because skepticism is a healthy thing to have as a lawyer.

Chapter 30

Roller Coaster

If her interviews with Oxley and Gist had strengthened her belief that Roger Coleman was innocent, when Kitty finally checked into Mullins Motel that evening, the clerk handed her a message that was certain to complicate her ability to convince others.

In late March Tom Scott had persuaded Brad McCoy to have his blood tested to see if he carried the type 4 allele that Dr. Blake had reported. On April 7 Scott faxed Kitty's office that Brad's alleles had been found to be 1.1,4. Kitty knew the state would now claim it had accounted for the extra allele and destroyed her argument that Blake's test proved that more than one person was involved in the rape and murder of Wanda McCoy. Newspapers soon reported that the state was saying just that.

Kitty saw at once that since Brad also had the 1.1 allele, which Dr.Blake had not found in the vaginal sperm, the most reasonable interpretation of this new information was that Brad was *not* the second sperm donor. Thus, the test that Scott was presenting as the final proof of Coleman's guilt might really be the strongest evidence yet of his innocence.

Kitty did not delude herself, however, that arcane arguments about the DNA results were likely to carry the day. Ultimately a court might conduct an evidentiary hearing to sort out the conflicting scientific claims, but, if possible, Kitty needed additional evidence of a more conventional nature to support Coleman's claim that he had not murdered Wanda McCoy. With that objective, Kitty Behan and Jim McCloskey once again scoured the hills and hollows of Buchanan County and beyond, searching for the elusive witness who might help to convince a cynical judge or politically sensitive governor that Roger Coleman was innocent.

Chasing from rumor to rumor's cousin to cousin's friend, calling telephones that never answered and searching for houses where no one was home, running into walls of fear and silence and starting over in another direction, Jim and Kitty nevertheless found and interviewed forty-one potential witnesses in twelve days.

There were dozens of disappointments and a few minor successes, but in the end the significance of the trip depended on their efforts to verify information about four new witnesses who had supposedly heard Donnie Ramey admit he had participated in Wanda McCoy's murder.

Apparently as a result of stories in the press, two women had called Kitty in March to report that a friend had said she heard Ramey admit involvement in the crime. Kitty gave the information to Jim McCloskey, who would be in Grundy two days ahead of her, and by the time Kitty arrived he had located and interviewed both informants.

Sitting in his motel room, Jim filled Kitty in on the interviews. One of the women, Betty Smith, had said a friend named Tammy Lee claimed she had heard Donnie Ramey admit that he and his brother Michael had killed Wanda. Smith had agreed to repeat her story in an affidavit. Next, McCloskey had met with Tammy Lee. Tammy said she was a friend of Donnie's live-in girlfriend, Cookie Helton, and had seen bruises around Helton's neck, which Cookie had said were from Donnie beating and choking her.

However, when Jim asked if it was true that Tammy had heard Donnie say he and his brother had killed Wanda McCoy, Tammy hesitated and said she didn't want to say anything more.

Jim's contact with Betty Hurley produced similar results. Hurley reported that Cookie Helton herself had said that Donnie once threatened her by saying "I'll do you like I did Wanda McCoy." Hurley was willing to provide an affidavit about what Cookie had told her, but she doubted that Cookie Helton would talk about it with Jim.

Kitty thought Tammy Lee might be more willing to tell her story to a woman, so Jim arranged another meeting with her. Despite Kitty's pleas, Tammy still refused to say whether Donnie had talked to her about the murder.

As Betty Hurley had predicted, Cookie Helton wouldn't agree to talk to them at all. One day Kitty and Jim saw her talking with a friend across the road from her trailer. They approached, but as soon as Cookie realized who they were, she fled back home.

Kitty Behan also had a report that a woman named Jennifer Lester had heard Donnie admit he was involved in the murder. When Jim located Lester, she denied it, but directed him to another of Cookie Helton's friends, a woman named Angie Tester. According to Jennifer, Angie said she had obtained a copy of the Arnold & Porter press packet and delivered it to Ramey's trailer. Angie had remained while Cookie Helton began reading the packet to Donnie. She came to the part where Brad McCoy described what he saw when he returned home on the night of the murder: "He peered through the peep hole in the door and noticed the afghan spread laying on the . . ."

Cookie stopped. Her photocopy of the press packet was apparently smudged and she could not make out the next words. As she hesitated, Donnie impatiently blurted out, "sofa." (The text actually read "seat of the couch.") There was a moment of silence as Angie Tester stared at Donnie. "I've got to go now," she said, and quickly left. According to Jennifer, Angie said she thought the only way Donnie could have known what he blurted out was if he had been there.

Kitty knew there were other ways Donnie could have known about the afghan on the sofa. Brad McCoy had testified about it at Roger's trial eleven years earlier. Still, it was a good story. Donnie couldn't read, so he didn't learn of it that way, and there was no reason to believe he had attended the trial. Besides, by now Kitty felt almost as sure that Donnie Ramey was in Wanda McCoy's house that night as she was that Roger Coleman was not. So it made sense.

It took Kitty and Jim several missed connections before they were able to talk to Angie Tester, but on April 10 she kept an appointment to meet them at her home, not far from Ramey's trailer. By chance, a writer named Trip Gabriel was in Grundy that day gathering information for an article about the case, and Jim and Kitty had agreed that he could accompany them on their rounds. When Kitty told Angie that Jennifer Lester had repeated her story about Cookie and Donnie and the Arnold & Porter press packet, Angie confirmed the incident and said it had shaken her badly. But when Jim asked if Angie would sign an affidavit recounting the story, Angie recoiled and grew silent. "I don't want my name used," she said. "I didn't think Donnie would have to know."

Jim McCloskey looked at her and spoke softly, urging her to agree. "Look," he said, "there's an innocent man on death row. Unless you help, he's probably going to be executed." Angie Tester did not answer.

Trip Gabriel described the end of the interview in his story in *The New York Times Magazine*: " 'What's going through your mind and heart?' [Jim] asked. `Fear,' the woman replied. `The way Teresa got killed, I believe, was over that.' "

Although Jim returned several more times trying to persuade her, Angie Tester would not repeat her story in writing. On his last visit she backed away from the story altogether.

The day Trip Gabriel accompanied Kitty and Jim to Angie Tester's house was the same day they finally tracked down Harold Smith. They had learned earlier that Smith claimed he had heard Ramey confess to the McCoy murder at a party they both attended in the late eighties.

Smith turned out to be a burly thirty-year-old unemployed maintenance man living in a trailer with his mother, his wife and two small children. The woman who answered the door was Harold's mother. She called for Harold at Jim's request, and when he appeared Jim and Kitty introduced themselves and got right to the point: "We're trying to save Roger Coleman's life, and we think Trouble Ramey was involved in the murder. We've been told you know something about it." Smith stepped out of the trailer, closing the door behind him and motioning for Kitty and Jim to follow him into the yard. "I don't want to talk about it in front of my mother," he said, "but I know at a party I was at some years ago Trouble said he had a hand in it."

Pressed for details, Smith described the circumstances. The party was at the house of a friend. Smith, the owner of the house and a couple of other men were crowded into a bathroom where they were smoking pot. Someone opened the door, but the host wouldn't let him in, saying. it was already too crowded.

According to Smith, the man was Donnie Ramey. When he was refused entrance into the bathroom, he muttered something about being involved in "that incident up on Slate Creek." Harold Smith thought it sounded like something between a threat and a boast. To the best of his recollection, Ramey's exact words were "I helped them."

Did anyone say anything back, Kitty asked? Yeah, Smith responded. Somebody said, "Are you blowing again, or are you telling the truth?" but Ramey never answered.

Kitty Behan looked at Jim McCloskey, and her expression reflected her thoughts as clearly as any words could. Harold Smith's story did not provide as clear an admission of guilt as Teresa Horn's had, but finally they had another witness with firsthand knowledge of Donnie Ramey apparently claiming he was involved in the murder. Now, if Smith would put it in writing, under oath, they would almost be back to where they were before Teresa died.

You ask, Kitty said to Jim with her eyes. Jim did. "Will you sign a statement about what you just told us?" Harold Smith said he didn't see why not. Jim promised to bring it by the next day.

It was Friday, and Kitty could wait no longer to begin finalizing the habeas corpus petition. That afternoon she and Jim drafted Harold Smith's affidavit, and the next morning Kitty flew home. Jim would stay in Grundy to pursue a few more leads and get affidavits signed by Harold Smith and anyone else who came up with helpful information they were willing to swear to.

As Kitty and Jim took stock of the trip, they realized that in some respects their investigation had become focused on Donnie Ramey as narrowly as Jack Davidson's had focused on Roger Coleman eleven years earlier. The difference, they decided, was that they had simply followed the evidence, while Davidson had reached a premature conclusion which had caused him to see the evidence in a different way.

Saturday, when Jim went back to get Harold Smith to sign his statement, Harold's mother answered the door and said he was asleep. Jim agreed to come back on Monday. When Jim arrived at the trailer on Monday morning, Smith again motioned that he wanted to go outside to talk. He took the affidavit from Jim and read it slowly. He looked up at Jim when he was finished and removed his glasses. Sheepishly Smith announced that he had changed his mind. On Saturday, he said, he had received an anonymous phone call. A man asked if anyone had talked to him about the McCoy murder. When Harold Smith responded, "No, why?" the man said, "It's none of your concern" and hung up. Smith took the call as a warning not to talk, and he told Jim he was concerned for the safety of his family, especially because he had small children. He wasn't going to sign a statement. Jim used every argument he could think of to change his mind, but Harold Smith insisted he was not going to do anything that might endanger his family.

That night Jim McCloskey called Kitty at her office. When he told her about Harold Smith, Kitty cursed eloquently. She could not believe it. In just over a week they had identified four people who had allegedly heard Donnie Ramey make an incriminating statement, and not one of them would sign an affidavit. Cookie Helton was understandable, but the others were not. A man's life was at stake. It was simply not believable that they would stand by and let an innocent man be executed when they had information that might save him.

Jim said it was not so unbelievable. He had been through it before:

> We were asking them to do something that I don't even know I would do myself if I were in their positions. I ask an awful lot of people. It's not easy for them to step forward with information that they know will piss off someone who may be a killer. And it's not just that they're scared for themselves. Their loved ones are all telling them, "Don't get involved." And of course, in this case, after Teresa Horn died we had an even worse problem. We were suggesting ourselves that Teresa's death was the result of what she said about Donnie Ramey, and people would say things like "Look what that boy did to Teresa Horn—I'm not going to be another Teresa Horn—I'm not going to help you." So I understood their dilemma. Harold Smith was especially concerned about his kids. He was scared, and he had a right to be scared. I'd say, "I understand, but Harold, we've got an innocent man here, we can't let him be executed." And Harold would say, "I know, but I've got to think of my family first."

Jim decided he would go back and talk to Smith again, this time taping the conversation with a miniature recorder concealed in his breast pocket. He did, and while Smith would still not sign an affidavit, he essentially confirmed what he had originally said about what he had heard at the party as well as the story of the phone call that had persuaded him not to sign Jim's affidavit.

A transcript of the tape recording could be filed, and if necessary Trip Gabriel could confirm what Smith had said on the first visit, but Kitty knew that a judge who wanted to do so could refuse to consider Smith's recorded statement because it was not under oath, and because in any event there was no indication he would agree to testify even if an evidentiary hearing was held.

In the end, Kitty concluded that the trip to Grundy, like her interviews with Oxley and Gist, had turned out pretty well after all. In addition to the Smith transcript and Jim's affidavit reciting what Smith had said on the first visit, they could file the affidavits of Betty Smith and Betty Hurley reciting what they were told by Tammy Lee and Cookie Helton. Jim's affidavit would also recite what Angie Tester had first told them, with the hopeful assertion that he thought Angie would tell the truth if she were subpoenaed and required to testify under oath.

It wasn't as good as sworn statements from willing witnesses, but Kitty thought it was enough to make an objective judge want to get to the bottom of the Ramey issue before allowing the execution of Roger Coleman to proceed.

—

Chapter 31

Back to Court

With little prospect of obtaining further information in the near future, Kitty returned to Washington to put the federal habeas corpus petition in form for filing.

Meanwhile, Roger Coleman sat down in his cell and wrote a letter to Philip Horton, the partner at Arnold & Porter who was "in charge" of the Coleman case. Roger had something he wanted to say, and he knew he might not have much longer to say it:

> Dear Mr. Horton,
> Since you're the partner supervising the handling of my case I wanted to write to you concerning the representation I've received by Kitty Behan. . . .
> In short, in my opinion Kitty is the best damn attorney on the face of this planet! The best thing that's ever happened in this case in the past 11 years was the day Kitty joined my legal team. She's single handedly accomplished more in the past 2 years than <u>all</u> other attorneys combined have done in the last 11 years. The amount of work and effort she's put into this case literally amazes me, all the more amazing because of the toll it's taking on her personally. . . . Yet she continues to tirelessly work to prove my innocence. . .
> I don't know what will happen on May 20th, but if I'm executed it

won't be because of a lack of effort on Kitty's part. . . . I just hope you and the other partners appreciate her abilities. In my book she's the best!

Horton showed Kitty the letter when he received it. She knew it was not the kind of thing someone in Roger's position would usually do. She was pleased, but frightened and worried.

On Friday, April 24, Kitty filed Coleman's petition for writ of habeas corpus, together with a motion to stay his execution pending a decision on the petition. The petition claimed that Coleman was innocent, and that his execution would therefore constitute a "fundamental miscarriage of justice" in violation of the United States Constitution. With the petition Kitty filed a volume of seventy-two exhibits, which, in their totality, spelled out the basis for the claim of innocence. In essence, the claim was based on four propositions:

1. That Coleman could not have committed the crime because he did not have time to do so, as demonstrated by the timecard-supported testimony of Philip Van Dyke that Coleman was with him at Looney Creek until 10:30 P.M., the impeachment of Sandra Stiltner's contrary testimony by Jack Davidson's interview reports, Dr. Oxley's confirmation that Wanda McCoy was sodomized as well as raped and the fact that the killer or killers had completed their terrible work and fled undetected before Brad McCoy arrived home at about 11:05.
2. That Roger could not have been the killer for the additional reason that the timing of the crime, the crime-scene evidence, the evidence of sodomy, Elmer Gist's "inconclusive" test of the anal sperm and Dr. Blake's DNA tests all showed that at least two persons were involved in the crime, while the undisputed testimony of all the trial witnesses showed that at every stage of the evening Roger was by himself.
3. That the central theme of the state's case—that the killer was someone who Wanda would have let into her house—was impeached by the pry mark found on her door, which had apparently not been disclosed to Roger's lawyers, and by the dirt on her hands and sweater, which was found nowhere else in the house.
4. That the victim's next-door neighbor, a man with a history of

alleged sexual assaults on women, had reportedly admitted the crime to several people.

There was no question in the minds of Coleman's lawyers that the evidence they had developed was sufficient to win an acquittal for Coleman if his case could be retried. But that was not the situation they faced. The term *fundamental miscarriage of justice*, which Kitty had used in the petition, was not something she had made up. It was a phrase the Supreme Court had used in describing the rare case in which a federal court could now intervene to overturn a state court conviction in response to a second or "successive" habeas corpus petition, and while the Court had not clearly defined what that meant, most lawyers agreed that it meant the defendant had to prove he did not commit the crime.

No longer was the burden of proof on the state, and no longer did it matter if there were errors, even constitutional errors, in the conduct of the original trial. Rather, Coleman had to prove he was factually innocent, and while the extent of his burden was not clear, it was certainly more than "might be innocent" or "probably innocent." A federal judge had to be persuaded, in effect, that no reasonable, objective person could still believe that Coleman was guilty.

Kitty's evidence was stronger than it had been in state court, but she knew that on its face it was still insufficient to meet that burden. She did believe it justified ordering the state to produce the records and notes of the forensic witnesses and the complete interview reports of the other important witnesses. Thereafter, any judge concerned about executing an innocent man would conduct a hearing where the witnesses could be examined under oath and subject to cross-examination. In such a hearing, Kitty believed, Roger Coleman's innocence would be proved.

Although legally Kitty's petition probably could have been filed in the United States District Court in either Richmond or Roanoke, the decision had been made to file in Roanoke. Judge Williams, who had heard the first petition, was now on senior status, and habeas cases were normally assigned only to the active judges. Moreover, Williams had been ill, and Kitty had heard that even now he was in the hospital. He was the last judge she wanted to hear the case, but under the circumstances it seemed unlikely it would be assigned to him. Kitty believed that the judge who was most likely to be assigned the case was Chief Judge Turk, who had a rare reputation for giving careful consideration to habeas corpus cases. It was the assignment she was hoping for, and when the clerk who accepted the papers for filing stamped the name of a judge on the face of the petition, it was Judge Turk's.

Within hours, Donald Curry notified Arnold & Porter that he was filing a motion to have the case transferred from Judge Turk to Senior Judge Williams "in the interest of judicial efficiency." Because Judge Williams had heard the first federal habeas petition, Curry argued, he was familiar with the case and could better dispose of it promptly and efficiently. By which, of course, he meant dismiss it without a hearing.

The state's motion was not a surprise. Kitty had already done some research in anticipation of it, although in truth research was not of much use to either side—the question was one on which Judge Turk had complete discretion. Kitty's response, urging that the case not be reassigned, was faxed to the court at 2:47 P.M. Shortly thereafter, Kitty learned that Judge Turk had decided to contact Judge Williams to ask what he wanted to do. Within the hour an order had been entered granting the reassignment. Despite his reported illness, Judge Williams had apparently welcomed the case.

The reassignment was a disaster, and Kitty Behan knew it. Through the years she had remained hopeful that somehow Roger Coleman would be saved. Now she began to consider seriously the possibility that he was going to die:

> Roger would tell me all the time, he'd say, "There's a slim-to-none chance, but I'm going to continue to fight." But I was still in denial. Then, when we heard about the reassignment, I think Roger and I both thought it was over. Somehow I heard Judge Turk had already read the petition and pretty much indicated he would give us a hearing, but Judge Williams—well, his ruling on the first habeas certainly didn't bode well for us.
>
> Shortly thereafter, Roger's girlfriend, Sharon, came into town, and I had lunch with her. I had talked to her on the phone before, but this was the first time I'd met her. And while we were having lunch she said something like "Well, I know you'll save him. You're doing a good job; I know you'll save him." She clearly thought he would be saved, and she had total confidence in me, and that made me petri-

fied. . . . I'm the only person that stands between Roger and the electric chair, and Sharon and this great sorrow. And, you know, I'm a
pathetic substitute for Superman, which is the only person who can
save this guy.

I just had phenomenal guilt after that. After that lunch, I think I
had a very hard time not working close to around the clock on the
case. Which is a little extreme, but there was still a lot to do and stuff,
so . . .

So, Kitty worked around the clock. In fact, she had been working
almost around the clock for some time now. The strain had already
caused the symptoms of her lupus to reappear, and she had increased
the dosage of her medication, which in turn had begun to create its
own symptoms and side effects. It did not require a doctor to know
that Kitty needed more rest. She had planned to take the weekend off
after the habeas petition was filed, but with the case reassigned to
Judge Williams, she saw no choice but to spend the time working on
the clemency petition. It seemed increasingly likely that clemency was
Roger's only hope. Kitty worked both Saturday and Sunday, but she
did leave her office in time to have dinner at home on Sunday night
and get to bed at a reasonable hour.

On Monday, Judge Williams's clerk called Phil Horton to say that
the judge wanted to set up a phone conference to establish a schedule
for filing the state's responsive pleadings and any additional motions.
He had already talked to Donald Curry, he said, and was told that the
state would be filing a motion to dismiss the petition without further
proceedings. After Horton checked with Kitty, everyone agreed to a
conference call on Wednesday morning.

During the conference call, Curry suggested that he be given two
weeks to file his motion to dismiss, and that the judge decide the
motions on the papers, without oral argument. Kitty protested, pointing out that with a May 20 execution date it was essential for the judge
to have adequate time to consider the voluminous evidence and arguments they had presented in support of Coleman's petition. The state
should be required to file sooner, and the court should hold oral arguments so that they could answer any questions about the law or the
facts.

To Kitty Behan's surprise, Judge Williams agreed. The state would be required to file all of its papers by 10:00 A.M. on Wednesday, May 6, and oral arguments would be held the same afternoon at 2:30 in the federal courthouse in Richmond. Judge Williams would travel to Richmond to avoid the necessity of the lawyers coming all the way to Abingdon. Moreover, he told Donald Curry, if the state was planning to file any factual material, he wanted it sent to Coleman's lawyers as it was obtained, rather than waiting until the sixth, so that they would have a chance to investigate it and file a reply.

When the conference was over, Kitty felt a surge of hope. Perhaps she had been wrong to assume that Judge Williams would automatically favor the state—he certainly hadn't done so in the scheduling conference. Her enthusiasm did not last, however. Someone pointed out that Glen Williams was a smart, experienced judge who would want to make sure that no appellate court thought he had been unfair to Coleman procedurally, and thus wonder about the fairness of his ruling on the merits. By ruling for Coleman on scheduling, he not only avoided a claim that the schedule was unfair but he demonstrated that he would not automatically rule for the prosecution—at no cost to the state's position other than making Don Curry work longer hours over the next week. Kitty understood. But still . . .

Chapter 32

Russ Ford:
Chaplain to the Dead

At Mecklenburg prison, not long after learning his case had been assigned to Judge Williams, Roger Coleman asked to see Russ Ford, the death-row chaplain.

Russ Ford is six feet two, with an athletic build, sandy hair and an easy smile. His voice is soft and strong at the same time, with little trace of the accent you would expect in a man who was born and raised in Richmond, Virginia. There are strong similarities between the way Russ Ford came to his work on death row and the way Jim McCloskey came to his work with the wrongly imprisoned, although Ford experienced a religious calling at an earlier age. As a seminary student Ford became an intern chaplain in the Virginia prison system. He found the work satisfying, and three years later accepted a full-time position with Chaplain Services, an organization funded by a group of Virginia churches to provide chaplains for the system.

When Virginia reinstated the death penalty, Chaplain Services planned to rotate its chaplains through death row, but it soon became apparent that Ford was the man best able to establish a connection with the inmates. Death row became his parish, the condemned his congregation.

In 1985, Ford accompanied a man named Morris Mason to the electric chair. As they walked to the death chamber, Ford, in time-honored tradition, recited the Twenty-third Psalm. Intellectually, Morris Mason was a child, Russ Ford has said. "My daughter, who was five years old at the time, could think abstractly better than he could. I might as well have been speaking Greek as reading the Twenty-third Psalm."

Russ Ford resolved to do better, and by the spring of 1992 he had learned a lot about ministering to men who are waiting to be killed by the state. He was forty years old, and had walked ten men to the electric chair. In 1990, he had nearly been electrocuted himself. For some unexplained reason, after Ricky Boggs was strapped into the chair and a mask placed over his face, there was a delay in throwing the switch that would send nearly two thousand volts of electricity through his body. Russ Ford stepped back to comfort Boggs, placing one hand on the back of his head and taking his hand with the other. At that instant the warden yelled, "No, Russ!" Turning at the sound, Ford saw that a light on the deathhouse wall had turned green, a signal that the executionèr, in another room, should throw the switch. Russ Ford was less than a step away when the roar of the current began and Boggs's body lurched forward against the restraining straps.

Ford had learned to be sure he was a safe distance away before the warden turned on the green light, but over the years he had learned a great deal more. He had learned that waiting to be electrocuted is not much different from waiting to die of cancer, and he had studied the literature of dying and learned how to help his congregation move through the stages of denial, anger and bargaining to the final stage of acceptance. He is an ordained Baptist minister, but he is as likely to refer his flock to the writings of Carl Jung or Joseph Campbell as he is to the Bible, and he borrows freely from whatever religion or philosophy seems appropriate to a given situation.

When Russ started on death row, the corrections officials operated on the theory that the less the men knew about the procedures that would lead to their death, the better. It was a process that slowly but surely deprived the inmates of their dignity, their mental stability and their sense of self, culminating an hour or so before the execution with the ritual of shaving their heads and placing them in the loose-fitting gowns in which they would be executed. Once we shave them, the guards would say, we have them. It takes away their hearts. After that, they're helpless.

One of the first things Russ Ford learned when he began working on death row was that the men wanted to know what was going to happen to them, in detail, and that by giving them that information he could help them maintain their dignity and sense of worth to the end. As a result, most of them could reach that final sense of peace and acceptance. At first the prison authorities were angry at Ford's intervention, but in time they came to realize that a man who had achieved peace was no more trouble than the men they had broken, and less likely to attempt suicide or have to be dragged into the execution chamber in front of the legally mandated witnesses.

In late April, when Roger Coleman asked to see Russ Ford, it was to talk about the execution procedures he would face if all else failed. Marie Deans was also a source of information, and, like Russ, believed it was best for the men to know as much as possible. But Roger had come to know and love Marie too much to want to talk to her about shaved heads and death warrants. He would rather talk to Russ, whom he didn't know as well.

According to Ford, no one had ever asked about quite so many details, or discussed them so intelligently. One of the first questions almost everyone asked was whether they would feel pain. Russ had always answered, "No, I understand the electricity instantly knocks you out, so you don't feel anything." When he gave Roger Coleman that answer, Coleman was silent for a moment, and then replied: "That's bullshit, Russ. Nobody's ever come back to tell you, so how could you know? Nobody knows." Russ Ford had to agree, and from then on when anybody asked, he gave them Roger Coleman's answer.

———

Chapter 33

End Game

A day or so after the scheduling conference with Judge Williams, Donald Curry sent Kitty some materials he had already collected for the state's response to Coleman's petition.

Dr. Oxley, the pathologist, repeated his claim that a three-inch knife could have caused the four-inch-deep wounds in Wanda McCoy's abdomen and chest, and went on to say that in his conversation with Kitty Behan he had not said that he found any trauma indicating anal penetration but only that the finding of sperm on the rectal swab meant there had been such penetration. (Which was all Kitty had claimed or cared about.) Also included was the report indicating Brad McCoy had the 1.1,4 alleles, as the state had previously revealed.

To that point, nothing in Curry's submission caused Kitty any great concern. There was another document, however, that both disturbed and enraged her. It was an affidavit, signed by Terry Jordan, that contained factual allegations harmful to Coleman. In Kitty's mind the affidavit was worded in a way that suggested she had attempted to suborn perjury by asking Jordan to sign a false affidavit.

For weeks Kitty had been trying to obtain an affidavit from Jordan reflecting his statement to me that he did not believe he knew about the pry mark at the time of Coleman's trial. After several unsuccessful telephone calls she faxed him a draft affidavit. Since the defense had failed to bring out several other facts at trial that would have helped Coleman, Kitty included the assertion that those facts had also not been revealed to Jordan before trial. Along with the affidavit, Kitty sent a letter asking Jordan to sign the affidavit and fax it back, or to call her if he had any questions about it. Kitty heard nothing back. Jordan had neither signed the affidavit nor called to discuss it by the time Kitty decided she could wait no longer to file her petition.

Now Jordan's affidavit for the state suggested that Kitty had asked him to sign an affidavit without regard to its truth, and claimed that before the trial he had been aware of all the facts mentioned in the draft affidavit.

Jordan's affidavit also gave an explanation of why the pry mark and other exculpatory facts were not used by the defense during the trial. It concluded with a statement suggesting that in pretrial interviews with Jordan, Coleman had withheld incriminating information about his whereabouts on the night of the murder. Specifically, Jordan claimed Roger had not told him about going to Boyd's Trailer Park.

Over the course of Kitty Behan's responsibility for the representation—and life—of Roger Coleman, the filings submitted on behalf of the state had become increasingly vituperative and personal in their treatment of the defense. The effort to obtain DNA testing had been characterized as a transparent and meritless attempt to delay the proceedings. In opposition to the second state habeas, the claim that Coleman was innocent was described as unimaginable "effrontery," "an avalanche of contrived claims masquerading as `newly discovered evidence'" and a "flagrant attempt to manipulate the judiciary." And in his reply brief filed the previous December, Curry had characterized Kitty's efforts as a "charade" and the evidence she had gathered as a "fairy tale of `possible suspects.'"

Now, Kitty thought, the attack had gone beyond mere heated rhetoric, inferring that she had deliberately attempted to obtain false testimony. Worse still, her effort to obtain an affidavit from Jordan, which was peripheral to the central objective of persuading the court that Coleman was innocent, had boomeranged into a declaration by his former lawyer that could only be read to suggest that Coleman had lied to him and that the lawyer believed he was guilty.

Less than three years out of law school, exhausted, desperately worried about her ability to save the life of a man she believed was innocent and now accused of ethical misconduct or worse, Kitty Behan broke down. A few weeks earlier, Roger had sent her an "award"—a hand-drawn certificate, complete with seal and ribbons, declaring that Kathleen Behan was the world's best lawyer. Kitty had taped it to her office wall. Other than an abstract expressionist painting that was her own work, Roger's certificate was the only decoration Kitty had hung in her small office. Now, sitting alone, staring at the wall, Roger's token of appreciation seemed a cruel irony. She saw that her career as a lawyer was over before it had really started. Worse, her mistake in sending the affidavit to Jordan and asking him to sign it had injured Roger's case, perhaps fatally. Everything she had done was wrong, and there was no way to fix it. She had never felt such unremitting despair.

Kitty Behan's misery was short-lived. Within the hour she recovered her composure and returned to the task at hand, which for the moment was to figure out what to do about Jordan's affidavit. A phone call elicited my promise to provide an affidavit describing the March meeting in which, contrary to his affidavit, Jordan had said he did not believe he knew about the pry mark at the time of trial and had emphatically denied seeing the crime-scene diagram that showed that the police thought the mark was significant. My affidavit would also question Jordan's claim that he had failed to use the pry mark at trial because he knew it was "just a light pressure mark" that could not have been evidence of a possible forced entry. As I noted, Jordan had previously testified that he had never gone into the McCoy house or inspected its door.

Upon analysis, most of the remaining assertions in Jordan's affidavit were innocuous or easily answered. The assertion that was most dangerous was Jordan's claim that when he interviewed Coleman about his whereabouts on the night of the murder, "he never told me about his visit to Boyd's Trailer Park that night until after I saw Sandra Stiltner's name on the prosecution's witness list for trial. . . . It was only then that Coleman admitted to me that he had been in such close proximity to the victim's home between 10:00 and 11:00 P.M. when the murder occurred." The assertion that Coleman had withheld information from his lawyer undermined the claim of innocence that stood as the last barrier between Coleman and death in the electric chair. Why would Coleman have lied to his lawyer if he was innocent?

Jordan's assertion was probably a simple mistake. Ten years after the fact, he may have recalled the issue surrounding Coleman's alleged failure to tell Jack Davidson about visiting the Stiltners, and forgotten that Roger had always said he went to Boyd's when he left Looney Creek. Coleman had told Davidson about going to Boyd's when he was interviewed the morning after the murder, and there is no conceivable reason he would not have told Arey and Jordan the same thing when they first interviewed him.

Kitty could and did point all this out to the court, but Jordan's suggestion that his client had lied about a crucial issue was likely to create a negative impression that would be hard to erase. In the end, the impact of Jordan's affidavit will never be known. Nor, apparently, will the facts surrounding his decision to provide an affidavit for the state or his change of mind regarding his knowledge of the pry mark. Since his affidavit was filed Jordan has repeatedly refused to answer the author's questions on those or any other subjects having to do with his representation of Roger Coleman.

While Kitty worked on her reply to Donald Curry's filings in the habeas corpus case and prepared for the May 6 hearing before Judge Williams, she was also preparing Coleman's petition for executive clemency. Walter McFarlane, Governor Wilder's chief counsel and point man on clemency issues, had said he would welcome receiving the petition as soon as possible. Thereafter, he would meet with Coleman's lawyers face-to-face so they could answer his questions and make an oral presentation. Kitty planned to hand-deliver the petition to McFarlane's office when she went to Richmond for the habeas corpus hearing.

There had been some discussion among the lawyers about who should argue before Judge Williams. Phil Horton was one possibility, and Roger Mullins, their local counsel, was another. Both were far more experienced than Kitty, and Mullins had the added advantage of knowing, and being known by, Judge Williams. Neither of them, however, had anything close to Kitty's knowledge of the facts or the applicable law. In the end, both agreed that Kitty was the best person to argue the case, but that the final decision should be left to Roger Coleman, who, after all, was the one whose life was at stake. Coleman did not hesitate. Even if the others had recommended to the contrary, he said, he would insist that Kitty make the argument.

It was agreed that Roger Mullins would also attend the hearing to show the flag for southwest Virginia. It might help for Judge Williams to know that a respected lawyer from his own part of the state was involved on behalf of Coleman, not just a bunch of intermeddlers from Washington.

By the end of the day on May 5, everything was ready for filing with Judge Williams and the governor. Kitty Behan stuffed the papers into her briefcase and drove to Richmond, two hours away. The next morning she filed her response to the state's motion to dismiss the habeas petition at the federal courthouse, dropped off a copy in Don Curry's office and delivered the clemency petition to Walter McFarlane in the Virginia capitol, an ornate building in downtown Richmond. McFarlane's office was directly across the hall from Governor Wilder.

Also that morning, Donald Curry filed additional material supporting his motion to dismiss, including several new affidavits. Most of Curry's new documents were expected or relatively innocuous, but three new affidavits were troublesome. The first was from Jack Davidson, who said that he had recently interviewed Harold Smith and that Smith had now "disavowed" hearing Donnie Ramey admit to participating in the McCoy murder. According to Davidson, Smith also said that McCloskey had presented him with an affidavit that was false, which he had refused to sign. Smith's own affidavit said, in substance, that he did not actually see the person who referred to the "incident on Slate Creek" at his friend's party, nor could he identify his voice, which was slurred from drinking alcohol. Smith said he had refused to sign McCloskey's affidavit because it mentioned Wanda McCoy by name, whereas the man had referred only to "Slate Creek," and because "every bit of it" was "untrue."

Smith's affidavit provided no explanation of how these assertions could be squared with the tape recording of his conversation with McCloskey, which showed that he *did* identify Donnie Ramey as the person who said he had a hand in the incident up at Slate Creek, and also showed that the reason he gave for refusing to sign McCloskey's affidavit was not because it was untrue but because he had received an anonymous phone call and was afraid for the safety of his family.

Nor did Smith try to explain the statements he had made about Ramey in his first meeting with McCloskey, which were also heard by Kitty and Trip Gabriel, the writer.

Perhaps Smith's about-face was influenced by the fact, which Jack Davidson was careful to reveal, that when he went to interview Smith, Davidson informed him that there was an outstanding warrant for his arrest on a charge of selling marijuana on school property—a serious felony. Davidson had not arrested Smith, but "advised him to surrender himself the following day."

The impact of the Davidson and Smith affidavits would depend on the frame of mind of the judge who considered them. If he was of a mind to do so, Judge Williams could look upon Smith's affidavit as conclusively refuting his prior unsworn statements to Jim McCloskey and eliminating the only remaining claim of a live witness that he had heard Donnie Ramey admit to participating in the McCoy murder. Or, if he was of a different mind, he could decide from all the circumstances that Smith's initial statements were at least as likely to be true as the affidavit procured by Jack Davidson. Kitty Behan knew that she was not objective, and that Judge Williams might be hostile to her case, but even so, given the life-and-death importance of the issue, it seemed unimaginable that a judge would not try to determine the truth by holding a hearing where Smith could be examined under oath in open court.

The third troublesome affidavit was from Edward Blake, and it was both damaging and infuriating. When Brad McCoy's blood was tested and found to have the alleles 1.1,4, the state had claimed that the mystery of why Blake had found a type 4 allele in the vaginal sperm was solved. The problem with that claim was that Blake had not reported finding a type 1.1 allele. Now Blake reversed himself, saying he *had* found a "faint" trace of the 1.1 allele, but failed to report it because he couldn't be sure it didn't come from Wanda McCoy, whose alleles were 1.1,1.2.

According to the state, Blake's statement explained away the troubling second sperm donor once and for all. To Kitty Behan, Blake's admission that he was not sure where the 1.1 allele had come from meant his entire analysis was questionable. The first task faced by a scientist performing PCR analysis is to separate the cells of the victim from the donor DNA. If that cannot be achieved, the results of the test will be ambiguous. In his initial report, Blake had claimed that he had in fact separated the sperm DNA from Wanda's. Now he was saying, in effect, that perhaps he hadn't.

While Kitty believed that scientifically Blake had now admitted that no valid conclusions could be drawn from his PCR analysis, she knew that to someone looking for answers, and especially to a judge, who by training is anxious to find a reason not to reopen a ten-year-old case, the state's argument could be persuasive.

Since filing the habeas petition, Kitty had acquired important, impartial support for her contentions about the PCR test in the form of a National Science Foundation report entitled "DNA Technology In Forensic Science." The report repeated much of what Kitty's experts had said about the difficulty of pairing alleles in a mixed sperm sample. It also explained the necessity of separating the donor's DNA from that of the victim's. The problem was that it was written in the tentative and arcane language of science. Kitty did her best to summarize its favorable conclusions and attached the full report to her arguments on the PCR test. She could only hope Judge Williams would read it closely enough to see that there was a serious dispute that could be resolved only in an evidentiary hearing.

Late on the morning of May 6 Kitty met with Roger Mullins to discuss the afternoon hearing before Judge Williams. It would be an oral argument on two motions—Coleman's motion for discovery and an evidentiary hearing on the petition for habeas corpus, and the state's motion to dismiss the petition without further proceedings. While there were numerous legal issues presented by the motions, Kitty and Mullins agreed that only one issue mattered, and it could not be resolved by reference to any case or statute. That issue was whether Kitty's argument and the evidence she presented would persuade Judge Williams that Roger Coleman might well be innocent. If so, one had to hope he would deny the motion to dismiss and schedule a hearing so that he could judge firsthand the credibility of the witnesses and the strength of Coleman's claim. If not, he would probably find a procedural basis for dismissing the petition, and neither the Fourth Circuit Court of Appeals nor the United States Supreme Court was likely to reverse him.

In years past, when the government had the money and inclination to construct public buildings in the grand manner, courthouses in particular were built to look important and impregnable, and the court-rooms within were designed to instill a sense of awe in those who entered. The federal courthouse in Richmond, Virginia, is of that era, and the high-ceilinged, wood-paneled courtroom that a local federal judge had loaned to Judge Williams for the hearing was a worthy example of the art. Judge Williams had sent word that the hearing would start a half hour late so he could finish reading the papers that had been filed that morning, and it was exactly 2:30 P.M. when he emerged from chambers and mounted the steps to his bench as the bailiff cried for order. Perched well above the tables and seats provided for lawyers and members of the public, Judge Williams invited Kitty Behan to begin her argument for the petitioner, Roger Keith Coleman.

If there had been any doubt on the subject, it did not take long to see that Kitty faced a steep road. From the start Judge Williams signaled that he was unimpressed with both the legal and factual bases for Kitty's argument that he should conduct an evidentiary hearing. A good lawyer likes nothing better than to have her argument interrupted by questions that provide insight into the judge's thinking and an opportunity to answer problems the judge finds troublesome. But Judge Williams's frequent interruptions, though framed as questions, sounded more like expressions of disbelief. Although Kitty pointed out that the importance of the newly discovered evidence could be understood only when viewed in the context of the evidence as a whole, Judge Williams insisted he was interested in hearing only about "new" evidence.

A more experienced lawyer might have found a way to present a more cohesive argument than Kitty managed in the face of the court's interruptions. Even so, with admirable perseverance for so young an advocate, Kitty maintained her position, answered hostile or rhetorical questions with intelligence and respect and gradually built as strong a case as possible for Coleman's innocence given the judge's stated limitations on the evidence he would consider.

When Kitty was through, Donald Curry delivered a well-organized and workmanlike exposition of the state's position. Like Kitty and Roger Mullins, Curry knew that regardless of the legal issues, the only way he was likely to lose his motion to dismiss was if the judge was persuaded that Coleman was probably innocent. With particular emphasis on the Jordan affidavit and the affidavits from Dr. Blake,

Jack Davidson and Harold Smith, which he had filed that morning, Curry concentrated on refuting, and in some cases ridiculing, Kitty's arguments on the subject of Coleman's innocence. In truth, Curry asserted, as a result of the DNA evidence the case against Roger Coleman was stronger now than it had been when he was found guilty by a jury ten years earlier.

After providing Kitty with the opportunity to present a brief argument in rebuttal, Judge Williams announced he would take the matter under advisement and adjourned court.

Optimism in the face of probable defeat is an essential part of a trial lawyer's nature. When Kitty and Roger Mullins left Judge Williams's courtroom, Mullins congratulated her on her argument, and they agreed that while the odds were long, they had made progress and had a chance of obtaining the discovery and hearing they needed if they were to have any chance of saving Coleman's life through the court system.

If Kitty was more optimistic than objective about her chances before Judge Williams, she was not foolish. The first thing she did after leaving the courtroom was to call Walter McFarlane, the governor's counsel, and ask him to schedule a face-to-face meeting as soon as possible. The sooner she could find out what questions were bothering him, the more likely she could provide answers in time to persuade him that Coleman's life should be spared. Everyone said that unless McFarlane recommended clemency, Governor Wilder was certain to deny it. McFarlane said he expected to finish reviewing the evidence and the clemency petition over the coming weekend, and agreed to meet with Coleman's representatives at 1:00 P.M. on Monday, May 11. Although Kitty did not know it, McFarlane had already scheduled a meeting on Friday with a contingent from Grundy who would be urging that the execution proceed.

Roger Mullins knew Walter McFarlane personally, and said he would come back to Richmond to participate in the meeting. He and Kitty agreed, however, that Jim McCloskey should take the lead in presenting Coleman's position. The minister whose mission was to free the wrongly imprisoned and who had already succeeded in proving the innocence of more than a dozen erroneously convicted men and women was likely to have more credibility than lawyers whose duty it was to represent Coleman regardless of their belief in his guilt or innocence.

Kitty's next call was to Roger Coleman to tell him about the hearing. On May 1, Coleman had been transferred from his death-row cell at Mecklenburg to Greensville Penitentiary to begin deathwatch in a cell located a few steps from the electric chair.

Roger had not been told when he would be moved to Greensville until 8:20 on the morning of his move, but he had known it was coming, and when the word came he had already packed most of the things he wanted to take with him. While he finished packing, all the other men on death row came by and said their good-byes. Roger described the scene in his diary:

> It's pretty much a ritual. I've taken part in it myself when guys have been taken for death watch. But this time it was different. I was the one leaving. I was the one everyone was looking at differently, afraid to meet my eyes for very long. Feeling helpless and not wanting me to go. Bunch, Jones and Stout were the ones most visibly shaken. When they came to get me and told everyone to lock up [return to their cells], Bunch wouldn't go to his cell until he gave me a hug. He has the most sensitive nature of anyone there. I can imagine the scene there after I left. Everyone talking about how it won't be the same without me, just like I've said every time someone leaves. But they'll quickly adjust to my absence, just as I adjusted to the absence of all those who left before me. Life goes on. At least for the living.

Chapter 34

Back in Grundy: Jim McCloskey

Since their trip to Grundy in April, Kitty and Jim had received a few more leads that seemed worth checking on, so while Kitty was in Richmond for the hearing before Judge Williams, Jim McCloskey returned to Buchanan County.

Beginning on Monday, May 4, and continuing for the next five days, McCloskey again scoured the hills and valleys surrounding Grundy, searching for some new witness or piece of evidence that would help prove Roger Coleman's innocence. With only two weeks until Roger's date with the electric chair, the investigation took on a new sense of urgency and surrealism:

> As the time got closer, it was like some kind of out-of-body experience. When I was in Vietnam I was shot at. And when I realized what was happening I thought, "Say, these people are trying to kill me. I don't believe it." It seemed like a movie. You weren't scared because it wasn't real—and that's the way I felt in May. You're working incredibly hard, your adrenaline is pumping, you're looking for that golden nugget, but you're almost floating through it, like, Is this thing really going to happen? Are they really going to execute Roger Coleman? And you kind of know they are—but you don't accept it.

> You know he's innocent and the evidence to save him is out there—
> and you want to believe you'll find it in time. "Lord, I believe. Help
> my unbelief."

If Jim did not find the golden nugget, he found enough to help his
unbelief. After reading *Newsweek,* a woman named Debbie Vanover
had written Kitty saying she had information about Donnie Ramey.
Jim found her in the Bristol City Jail serving a short sentence for writing bad checks. She became the fourth woman to sign an affidavit saying Donnie Ramey had sexually assaulted her—and the fourth woman
he would later deny assaulting.

Jim also located a man named Danny Bussler near Kingsport,
Tennessee. According to Bussler, shortly after getting off work on the
night of the murder he had driven down the Slate Creek road past
Longbottom. It was a little after 11:00 P.M. Across the creek from
Longbottom he saw a car parked on the shoulder with one man sitting
in the backseat, one in the passenger seat, and a third just getting into
the driver's seat. He thought it was peculiar that a car would be
parked there at that hour, and mentioned it to his wife when he got
home.

When he learned of Wanda McCoy's murder the next day, Bussler
had wondered if there was any connection with the men in the car, but
had done nothing about it. Now that he had seen all the recent news
reports about the case and learned that the defense thought there was
more than one man involved in the murder, he had decided to come
forward. He thought that the car was a brown Plymouth Valiant, and
that the driver was about five feet ten with dark hair. He gave Jim an
affidavit of what he had seen.

After four years of searching, Jim also found someone who could
tell him where Danny Ray Stiltner lived. Danny's former girlfriend
directed him to a relative of Danny's, who in turn referred him to
another relative in Pikeville, Kentucky, who said Danny had moved to
Ohio. He now lived in the country not far from Cincinnati.

Both the ex-girlfriend and one of Danny's relatives told Jim that
although they didn't think he had anything to do with Wanda
McCoy's death, they had heard him say he disliked Wanda and held
her responsible for his breakup with her sister Peggy. Jim thought that
if he could find Danny and talk to him, he would be able to sense

whether he had anything to do with the murder. Personally, Jim thought he already knew who the real killer was, but Danny Stiltner had been the Thompson family's first suspect. Now that Jim had a lead on where he was, it would be foolish not to try to find him and check him out.

On Saturday, May 9, a press conference and rally were to be held for Roger in Richmond as part of the clemency effort. Jim would fly in Friday night to participate in the rally, and remain in Richmond preparing for the meeting with Walter McFarlane on Monday. After that he would fly to Cincinnati and look for Danny Stiltner.

—

Chapter 35

Grundy Comes to Richmond

After the hearing before Judge Williams, Donald Curry felt confident that there was little chance the courts would interfere with Roger Coleman's date with death. He was less confident about the governor. Both Curry and Tom Scott in Grundy were angry and worried about the massive media attention that was being given to the case. It was ludicrous, they thought, that anyone could doubt Coleman's guilt, and yet every day some new newspaper, magazine or television program suggested he was innocent. Curry knew that the volume of mail and phone calls to the governor's office was beginning to get heavy, and that virtually all of it was urging clemency. He had received help from Scott in obtaining the affidavits he had filed with Judge Williams, and with Curry's encouragement Scott also put together a "team" of Grundy residents to meet with McFarlane to urge that the execution be allowed to go forward. It is not clear whose idea it was, but someone seized on the strategy of emphasizing Coleman's "prior crimes" in presenting the case to McFarlane. It was persuasive, easy to understand and virtually impossible for the Coleman team to answer. Curry, of course, would present all the state's arguments and evidence relating to the murder of Wanda McCoy, and Scott would supplement that material with his own arguments and bring Brad McCoy with him to

Richmond to plead for "justice" for the family. But a major thrust of the presentation would have nothing to do with the Wanda McCoy murder. Instead, it would emphasize the library incident and the attempted rape conviction.

Once Tom Scott decided to go all out to fight for Coleman's execution, he contacted Brenda (Rife) Ratliff, the victim in the attempted-rape case, and Pat Hatfield, who had identified Roger as the man who entered the library and exposed himself a few months before the McCoy murder. Both agreed to accompany Scott to Richmond and join in the effort to see that Roger Coleman died in the electric chair. Scott even dug out records showing that when he was thirteen years old Coleman had admitted to making dirty phone calls to two of his schoolmates.

On Thursday, May 7, Scott, Mickey McGlothlin, Brad McCoy, Pat Hatfield and Brenda Ratliff made the long drive to Richmond for their Friday appointment with Walter McFarlane. That night they had dinner at the Tobacco Company, a popular Richmond restaurant located in a converted tobacco warehouse. Sitting at the bar waiting to be seated, Scott realized that the program showing on a television set above the bar was a *PrimeTime Live* segment on the Coleman case. Scott and Hatfield had been interviewed for the show, and Scott tried without success to persuade the bartender to turn up the sound. Although they couldn't hear much, they were disappointed to see that the focus of the program was on Jim McCloskey, who was surely once again proclaiming Coleman's innocence. Pat Hatfield in particular was angry because the show's producer had said that she thought Coleman was guilty, and would have been found guilty by a jury anywhere in the country. Hatfield had been deeply offended by the "hick town" portrayal of Grundy in the *Newsweek* article and the suggestion that Coleman's conviction was the result of prejudice and redneck stupidity. In her mind the producer had promised that the show would refute that portrait and reflect the view that Coleman was guilty. Instead, it seemed to be taking the opposite position. When she returned home, Hatfield wrote the producer an angry letter.

The next day the men and women from Grundy kept their appointment with McFarlane and presented their case, with particular emphasis on the "other crimes." According to Pat Hatfield, near the end of the meeting with McFarlane he looked at Pat and Brenda Ratliff and said, "Do you realize that the two of you and Wanda McCoy look almost exactly alike?" It was a stretch—but all three did have "big" blond hair. If McFarlane said it, it was a good sign that the other-crimes argument had hit home. Tom Scott was still worried about the publicity, but the Grundy contingent left McFarlane's office feeling a good deal better than they had when they entered. He had listened carefully, and he certainly didn't seem to be some kind of knee-jerk anti–death penalty liberal. In fact, they learned, he had spent most of his own career in the attorney general's office, and was born and raised in southwest Virginia, not far from Grundy.

—

Chapter 36

Saved?

When Kitty Behan returned to Washington after the hearing before Judge Williams, there was still a mountain of work on her desk. The meeting with McFarlane had to be carefully planned so that she could be as sure as possible that every question he might pose could be answered at once. When the meeting was over there would be only nine days left before Roger's execution date. Not enough time to tell McFarlane, "We'll find out and get back to you," and then start looking for the answer.

For the same reason, Kitty knew she had to prepare for the evidentiary hearing she had requested from Judge Williams, even though there was no guarantee it would be granted. Unfair as it might seem, if Judge Williams did grant a hearing, he would probably try to conduct it before May 20 in order to avoid postponing Roger Coleman's execution date. From the Supreme Court down, the mood among judges was to accelerate executions, not delay them, and there was no reason to believe Judge Williams dissented from that view.

In addition, in just the few days Kitty had shut herself off from everything to prepare for the arguments before Judge Williams, an enormous pile of unreturned phone calls had accumulated. The extraordinary publicity the case had already attracted was like a virus that kept reproducing itself into a growing mountain of additional publicity and information.

One pile of calls was from people who claimed to know something about the murder. The vast majority of these were kooks, con men and self-promoters, people who had solved the crime through a voice from God, or who would supply information that conclusively exonerated Coleman promptly upon receipt of a substantial sum of money. Unfortunately, most callers did not reveal their financial demands or the extraterrestrial source of their information in the encouraging messages they left. Each call had to be returned, just in case.

Another pile was calls from the media, seeking information and, in most cases, interviews. With the magazine and newspaper articles and recent segments on the *Today* show and *PrimeTime Live*, the requests had multiplied. In addition to newspapers, radio stations and TV shows across the country, journalists and television producers from England, Germany, Japan and a half dozen other countries had picked up the story of the articulate coal miner who was about to be executed for a crime he steadfastly denied, and which, it was increasingly said, he probably didn't commit.

In the past, Kitty had responded to every call from every media source, but now her time, as well as that of Jim McCloskey and Roger Coleman himself, had to be rationed. Only major national media that had the greatest likelihood of generating information or favorable letters to Governor Wilder could be accommodated, although Kitty and Jim agreed that some of the foreign reporters who were planning to send live crews to Virginia should also be helped. Perhaps a flood of letters to Governor Wilder from Europe and Japan protesting the execution would help, even if they weren't constituents.

One person Kitty was especially anxious to hear from was Julie Johnson of *Time* magazine. Johnson had been interested in the case for some time. She had talked to Kitty at length, examined the relevant transcripts and affidavits and obtained permission from her editors to go down to Grundy and conduct her own investigation, including talking to many of the witnesses who had been uncovered in recent years. While nothing was definite, Johnson had told Kitty that she thought it was an important story, and that she herself had come to believe Coleman was innocent. The story was now in the hands of the writers and editors.

When Kitty returned from Richmond she learned that a *Time* magazine photographer had been sent to Greensville to take photographs of Coleman, and that Johnson thought it was almost certain that the editors would approve a story, probably to be published in the edition dated May 18, which would be on the newsstands May 11. Johnson said she was pushing to have it made the cover story, and thought there was a chance she would succeed, at least if no major news broke in the next few days.

Johnson had always been an optimist, and Kitty did not imagine there was any real chance of a cover story, but the fact that a story favorable to Coleman was under review was good news indeed. Next to *60 Minutes*, Kitty thought a favorable story in *Time*, on top of the one already printed in *Newsweek*, was as good as anyone could do to generate pressure on Governor Wilder, and possibly smoke out additional witnesses. Johnson said she would know the results of her efforts within a few days.

Before Kitty had left for the hearing before Judge Williams, her boyfriend, Mark, had extracted a promise. They had had no social life for months. On Friday night, May 8, he was going to have a small get-together at their apartment for a few close friends—if they had any left. Whatever happened, Kitty had to promise she would come home Friday night. She reluctantly agreed, and for the first time in a long time kept a promise to Mark that she would not work.

It was, as Mark promised, a small, quiet gathering with only good friends. All of them, of course, knew what she had been doing and had read or seen some of the stories about the case. Everyone was genuinely supportive, and Kitty was grateful, especially after having spent the past several weeks being called everything from naïve to self-serving to unethical by Donald Curry.

It was still early evening when Mark answered a phone call and summoned Kitty. They had agreed that Kitty would not take any phone calls that night, but this was Julie Johnson, and she said it was important. When Kitty took the phone, Julie told her that the editors at *Time* had made a final decision about the Coleman story. It would run in the volume coming out on Monday.

The text of the story would emphasize the new evidence that Roger Coleman was innocent, suggest that the denial of a hearing because of the one-day filing delay might well result in the execution of an innocent man unless the governor intervened and question why there should be such a rush to execution when so many questions were left unanswered. And, Julie Johnson said, it would be that week's cover story, with a cover photograph of Roger—looking very innocent. It would be the first time in thirty-two years that *Time* had devoted its cover to a story about a condemned man.

Kitty thanked Julie for the call and the wonderful news. It was a real break, she told Mark and her assembled friends, that might help, especially with Governor Wilder. The theme of the story—that Coleman *might* be innocent and it would therefore be a terrible miscarriage of justice to execute him without resolving the unanswered questions—was just right. It was exactly what she had been saying, both to Judge Williams and in the petition to the governor.

Kitty Behan's friends were stunned. It was not a "real break" that "might help," they told her, it was an extraordinary triumph that left Governor Wilder with no real alternative but to commute the death sentence. The cover of *Time* magazine might no longer occupy the position it once held as the unchallenged pinnacle of fame, but it would be hard to name any exposure that replaced it. Did Kitty really think an elected governor was going to proceed with the execution of a man who had appeared on the cover of *Time* magazine in connection with a story saying that it would be a miscarriage of justice to execute him?

There were no dissenters in Kitty and Mark's apartment. Whatever else happened, in the courts or in some kind of hearings the governor might order, they agreed that, for now, Kitty had saved Roger Coleman's life. Before long, even Kitty was convinced. The quiet, sober gathering soon turned into a victory celebration, with Kitty often on the telephone spreading the news to all concerned. She had planned to go to the office early the next morning, but instead she slept late. She was enjoying a leisurely breakfast with Mark when she suddenly announced that she had to leave. The story on the cover of *Time* magazine might save Roger Coleman's life, but Kitty still had to attend a meeting with Walter McFarlane on Monday, and prepare for the possibility of an evidentiary hearing.

———

Chapter 37

Deathwatch: Roger, Sharon and Russ

Everyone on death row knows about deathwatch. The electric chair had been moved to Greensville from the gloomy gray stone fortress on the edge of downtown Richmond, but the routine of moving the condemned man to the place of execution at least two weeks before his execution date remained the same. There he would remain in isolation, under constant watch by a specially trained team of guards. Then, twenty-four hours before the execution, that team would in turn be replaced by new guards—men who had no prior contact with the condemned man, and thus had developed no emotional ties or antipathy to him— the death squad that would escort him to the electric chair to die.

Well before Roger was moved to Greensville he had decided how he would spend his time under deathwatch. Coleman was an avid reader of science fiction, and especially the work of Robert Heinlein involving the space travels of Lazarus Long. He had accumulated twenty-nine books he wanted to read again before he died, and he had planned to read all of them while waiting to be executed at Greensville. In addition, he asked Russ Ford to negotiate a deal involving his contact visits with Sharon and the media frenzy that was already under way. Under the rules, Roger would have unlimited access to a telephone, and in-person media interviews would also be allowed as long as they were scheduled in advance within certain hours of the day. Also in accordance with the rules, Roger would be allowed one contact visit with the person of his choice on the day he was to be executed. Roger told Russ Ford that he wanted to trade his right to media interviews for more contact visits with Sharon. Phone calls too could be limited to Sharon and Kitty. If Russ could make the deal, Roger would tell his lawyers he would not give any more interviews. If it was necessary to get more visits, he told Russ, he was even thinking of telling his lawyers to drop the rest of his appeals. He was going to die anyway.

Roger did not tell anyone of his plan except Russ and Sharon. Russ quickly talked him out of dropping his appeals, and Sharon angrily rebuked him for the rest. Roger was not going to die, she insisted, and Kitty had said the media attention might help. Sharon would not visit him at all if he gave up now. Roger quickly capitulated. Russ did, however, succeed in negotiating a deal with the warden to allow Roger one extra contact visit on the day of his choice. Sharon had been able to get a one-week vacation and planned to spend it visiting Roger beginning Saturday, May 16. They agreed that the first contact visit would be that Saturday. The second one, they told each other, would probably be canceled along with Roger's execution, but Sharon would be there to help him celebrate.

Roger had arrived at Greensville on May 1, and a week later he received Kitty's call announcing that his story would be on the cover of *Time* magazine. Although he was not as sanguine about the matter as Kitty's friends were, for the first time in a long time Roger Coleman really believed he might survive. If Kitty Behan could get an uneducated coal miner from Grundy, Virginia, on the cover of *Time* magazine, he thought, she could probably save his life, and find a way to get him a new trial and an acquittal as well.

When the *Time* magazine with Roger's picture on the cover became available on Monday, May 11, one of the deathwatch guards brought it to him. The picture occupied the entire cover, and showed Roger sitting in a chair against a cement-block wall, wearing handcuffs and leg irons. Across his torso appeared the caption in large block letters:

THIS MAN MIGHT BE
INNOCENT

THIS MAN IS DUE TO
DIE

The words of the caption were in white letters, except for *innocent* and *die*, which were bright red, in a type size much larger than the rest. The guard who brought the magazine to Roger produced a second copy and asked him to autograph it, which he did. A few days later Roger received another autograph request in the mail from a man who wrote that he had collected more than fifty autographed *Time* covers.

Chapter 38

—

Questions and Answers

The meeting with Walter "Mac" McFarlane was scheduled for 1:30 P.M. on Monday, May 11, the same day the cover story in *Time* magazine reached the newsstands. Kitty, Jim, Phil Horton and Roger Mullins met in Richmond on Monday morning to go over strategy for the meeting, although understandably a good deal of their time was spent talking about the *Time* article, and speculating on its impact, especially on Governor Wilder. All agreed that it was bound to be extremely helpful, if not determinative. They also agreed not to bring it up at the meeting unless McFarlane mentioned it first. There were a few minor factual mistakes in the article that they went over so that they could correct them if called upon, but none of them were harmful, so there was no reason to raise them unless McFarlane did.

Mullins filled Jim and Kitty in on McFarlane's background. He was born in Richlands, a few miles from the motel where Jim and Kitty had spent so much time. At some point his family moved to Roanoke, where he graduated from high school.

After graduating from Emory and Henry College in southwest Virginia in 1962, McFarlane attended law school at the University of Richmond and spent three years in the Air Force Judge Advocate General Corps. When he left the service he obtained a job as an assistant attorney general and quickly rose to the position of deputy attorney general, serving in that position under attorneys general of both parties from 1972 until Governor Wilder selected him to be his chief counsel and administrative assistant. He and Mullins had met when McFarlane was doing highway condemnation work for the state and Mullins was representing landowners whose property was being taken. He was okay, Mullins said. No liberal, probably in favor of capital punishment, but not a zealot either.

When Coleman's entourage entered McFarlane's office, he rose and greeted them in a friendly manner. Immediately, he congratulated them on the story in *Time* while in the same breath insisting that they understand the governor would not be pressured in his decision by *Time* or anyone else, but would decide the case on the facts as he saw them. Kitty was encouraged—that McFarlane would make such a statement suggested to her that Governor Wilder was already feeling the pressure of public opinion against the execution.

Next, Mullins and McFarlane engaged in small talk about their past associations and mutual acquaintances. Finally, the meeting moved to substance, with Jim McCloskey leading the way for Coleman. McFarlane's questioning was thorough, and demonstrated considerable familiarity with the facts of the case and the contentions of both sides. He did not rush them, allowing them to make whatever points they thought important in addition to answering his questions. The only issue the Coleman team felt was not discussed as much as they expected was the DNA testing. McFarlane asked almost no questions about it, and it seemed to Kitty that whenever she or Jim brought it up, his eyes glazed over. Kitty concluded that since both sides were claiming the DNA evidence helped them, McFarlane had decided to call it a toss-up and consider the case on the basis of traditional evidence that was easier to sort out. All things considered, it was a result she could accept.

Early in the meeting, McFarlane commented that he had a few questions for them, and a lot of questions for the attorney general. As the meeting progressed, it seemed to Kitty and the others that McFarlane simply did not believe the state's version of the murder any more than they did. He seemed to have particular trouble with the idea that only one person could have committed the crime, especially in the brief time when the state claimed it was done by Roger

Coleman. The downside was that he seemed especially interested in Roger Matney's testimony, and while recognizing Matney's credibility problems on the one hand, on the other he seemed to think Matney's version of what Roger supposedly told him fit the facts pretty well. Kitty doubted the governor would go out of his way to commute Coleman's sentence on the theory that he was there but may not have committed the murder.

When McFarlane asked about the other crimes, McCloskey mentioned that he and Kitty had talked to Frank Spraker, the high school superintendent, who still said Coleman had been with him and his daughter at the time Brenda Ratliff was attacked. As for the library incident, Jim said that, contrary to what McFarlane had been told, he did not think the librarians identified Coleman until after the murder, and after they learned he was the prime suspect.

But, more important, Jim argued, while Coleman emphatically denied his guilt of those charges, the issue the governor had to focus on was not whether Roger had attempted to rape Brenda Ratliff, but whether he had murdered Wanda McCoy. That was the crime for which he was now facing execution. It would be unfair to expect them to prove his innocence of the other crimes as well—they had neither the time nor the resources. Kitty and Jim thought McFarlane seemed to agree. (Years later Randy Jackson and Jack Davidson would confirm that the librarians had not identified Coleman until after the murder. Moreover, a newspaper photograph of Coleman published after he was arrested for the murder looks nothing like the police drawing of the man in the library. That drawing and one made by one of the librarians do, however, look quite a bit like a photo of Coleman in his high school yearbook.)

At the end of the meeting, McFarlane had one more question. "If we said to you we wouldn't give you clemency without a polygraph, what would be your position?"

It was not a new issue. Several months earlier Coleman told them he had heard about an offer by a society of polygraphers to give a free polygraph examination to anyone on death row. Roger had wanted to take the test.

With rare exceptions, experienced lawyers do not believe in lie-detector tests. Time after time, research has shown them to be highly unreliable, but for some reason the public believes in them. If you take one and fail it, the public assumes you are guilty, and the police are happy to go along with it. But if you pass, and the police still think you're guilty, they will offer all kinds of explanations of how you "fooled" the test. To try to avoid an indictment or persuade someone to reconsider a case once a defendant has been convicted, defense lawyers will sometimes have their client tested privately and, if he passes, provide the results to the police or prosecutor and agree to a second test by a qualified examiner for the state. Regardless of the accuracy of the test, someone who has passed once is quite likely to pass again. But the test Coleman had proposed would not be private— it would be conducted at the prison, observed and shared with the state. If Roger failed, his chances of obtaining clemency would be over, and even though such tests are almost always inadmissible in court, it wouldn't do his chances there any good either. Kitty had talked him out of it. If we ever think it's appropriate to take a lie test, she said, we'll select the examiner and pay for it.

Kitty and Jim McCloskey both told McFarlane that they did not believe lie tests were reliable, and that it would be highly inappropriate to resolve the case on the basis of a polygraph rather than the evidence. Certainly, they said, it would be bad advice to tell their client to take such a test. McFarlane said he understood—but all of them knew that if it really came down to the question he had asked, there would be no choice. He would have to take the test.

All things considered, the consensus after the meeting was that it had gone well. Except for the DNA issue, McFarlane seemed to understand their arguments, and although he gave no sign of what he would recommend (McCloskey told the press that "McFarlane would make a great poker player"), he did not seem hostile. The lie-test issue was troubling, and they agreed that they had better find someone good who would conduct the test if the governor insisted. McCloskey recommended Earl Kane, a former head of the New Jersey State Police polygraph unit, who, he said, was absolutely honest. They agreed Jim should contact him when he got back to New Jersey. They hoped his services wouldn't be necessary.

Heading back to Washington, Kitty could not escape the belief that Governor Wilder would commute Coleman's sentence. The mounting outcry against the execution of a man whom the press and public believed to be innocent made any other result unthinkable.

Now she had to figure out how to *prove* he was innocent and get him out of jail.

Despite the good feeling they had about the prior week's meeting with McFarlane, when Tom Scott and Donald Curry learned about the *Time* magazine cover story, they knew they were in trouble. They had presented all of their evidence to the press, including the prior-crimes argument, and they were still losing—big.

The local press in Grundy was with them, as were some of the regional papers, but the overwhelming majority of the national media had concluded that there was substantial reason to believe that whatever else Roger Coleman may have done, he did not murder Wanda McCoy, and their expression of that belief was generating an outcry that would be difficult for any governor to ignore. To make matters worse, Roger Coleman *looked* innocent, and when he appeared in a television interview and gave an articulate explanation of his side of the case, he sounded innocent as well. Now his innocent-looking face was on the cover of *Time*, and it didn't take a call to the governor's office to know what the effect of *that* would be on the governor's mail. As far as Curry and Scott were concerned, it was all bullshit: McCloskey, Behan, the press—none of them really believed Coleman was innocent; he had simply become, as they put it, the "poster boy" of the bleeding-heart, anti–capital punishment Left. But still, they needed something more to provide Governor Wilder the backbone to do the right thing. On Tuesday, May 12, their prayers were answered.

———

Chapter 39

Judge Williams
Weighs In

Kitty Behan doesn't recall exactly how she heard that Judge Williams had rendered his decision in the habeas corpus case, although she knows she was in her office, and it was Tuesday morning. It may have come from a reporter, or Phil Horton may have gotten a call from the court clerk, or she may have gotten the call herself. However the information reached her, what she learned was that a decision had been rendered, and that it dismissed her petition without discovery or a hearing. It was a blow—but not unexpected. In a way, one could argue that it might even be for the best. By granting the state's motion rather than conducting a hearing and declaring Coleman's proof of innocence inadequate, Judge Williams increased the possibility, however slim, that a higher court might reverse his decision, which in Kitty's view was a misapplication of the law regarding when a hearing is required. And if the governor commuted Coleman's sentence, the appellate process could be allowed to take its full course, rather than having to be dramatically expedited to meet the pending execution date. The pressure not to interfere with execution dates at the last minute had become so intense that lawyers were beginning to think that a legal argument presented by a prisoner facing an imminent date with the executioner was less likely to succeed than if he was simply facing a term of years in prison. The mantra "Death is different," which courts had long used to justify favorable consideration of the arguments of defendants facing the death penalty, had been stood on its head.

Judge Williams had written an opinion, and by early afternoon a copy of it was faxed to Kitty in Washington. Only then did she appreciate the awful blow that had been delivered to her case, and to her client. Williams had upheld all of the state's procedural arguments. Each of Coleman's points, he ruled, had been waived, or previously decided, or did not constitute newly discovered evidence, or for some other reason was not cognizable in a successive habeas corpus petition. But Judge Williams had not stopped there. In an abundance of fairness and caution, he suggested, he had considered each of Coleman's claims on its merits—and determined that none of them was valid. "After a review of the alleged `new evidence,'" Judge Williams declared, "this court finds the case against Coleman as strong or stronger than the evidence adduced at trial."

Without conducting an evidentiary hearing in which the credibility of witnesses could be assessed and the conflicting claims presented in the affidavits filed by the opposing sides could be resolved, Judge Williams had rejected the defense evidence and, in effect, reaffirmed the jury verdict of guilty.

Kitty recognized at once the potential impact of the decision. It was exactly what Tom Scott and Donald Curry needed—a statement from an experienced jurist that he had examined the evidence of innocence and found it unconvincing—or worse. If Governor Wilder wanted to deny clemency—and despite all the mail he was receiving now, in the end that was likely to be the politically popular thing to do in Virginia—he now had a solid platform to stand on. That the platform was built by a judge who had not heard a single witness was not likely to weaken its support. Kitty:

> For a hearing to have been denied and for him to have made factual findings just blew me away because what it said to me was, you know, Judge Williams just did not want this innocence allegation to be reopened. He didn't care about that. He wasn't interested in judging the credibility of these witnesses, and he was disregarding everything they had to say.

And that made it clear to me that he was just trying to make sure that his one-day-late ruling was not disturbed. So I was shocked, and I had a very hard time with it because he just seemed so vindictive.

In one respect Kitty was overreacting. Judge Williams had not, in every case, determined factual disputes against her without a hearing. Rather, he said that most of the "new evidence" was either irrelevant, hearsay or unimportant, and thus not admissible in court. And while that was an extraordinarily narrow reading of the evidence, especially in a case where the defendant's life was at stake, it was not in the strict sense a finding of fact. But in the broader sense, her outrage was fully justified. Without hearing any witnesses, the court had adopted the state's version of the DNA evidence, rejected the evidence regarding the alleged confessions of Donnie Ramey and ignored the evidence that Coleman had no time to commit the crime and that more than one person was involved. Without resolving factual disputes and determining the credibility of witnesses, there was simply no basis for the assertion that "this court finds the case against Coleman as strong or stronger than the evidence adduced at trial." With this assertion, the court could have it both ways: turning down Coleman's petition on technical legal grounds, while at the same time assuring readers of his opinion that they need not worry that the result might be the execution of an innocent man. It was this unjustified assurance that was so harmful, and there is little doubt that Judge Williams knew exactly what he was doing.

On Friday, Kitty had called Roger to say she thought his life was saved. Four days later she called to say it might be lost again.

So I called to tell him, and, you know, I was very blunt about it. And I told him that I was shocked by the factual findings, I really was. I said to him, I've never been involved in anything like this, except for one thing, in which you try over and over again to get people to believe you and just listen. And nobody will. And it was—I don't think I used Kafka, but it felt so Kafkaesque. It felt so much like there was just no way out of this, and you just fight and fight. It's like fighting something that's much bigger than you.

What Kitty Behan was thinking about when she said "except for one thing" was her own experience in trying to get someone to believe

her about her illness before it was finally diagnosed. She had never
told Roger anything about it, but now she did.

I told him that it reminded me a lot of what I had been through,
and a lot of why I felt so strongly about the case, and about him, was
that I could see him fighting constantly. Fighting the skepticism of
everybody, including his own lawyers. And having the hardest time
just to get anybody to believe him. And I had gone through a two-
year diagnosis period where nobody . . . you know, I would go in to
doctor after doctor, and they would say there's nothing wrong with
you. You know, this can't be, or they would diagnose me with something I didn't have. And it took me a very long time. I had neurolog-
ical deficits in my record, and people would say, "Well, what's your
problem? Your IQ is still higher than George Bush's, so why are you
worried?" And, you know, a very condescending and paternalistic
attitude that I had faced in just trying to get diagnosed. And this
seemed unfair.

And it was just like that with Roger. The right answer was so obvious in some ways, and there was this morass of procedures that was
being used against him. Your lawyers filed something one day late,
so there's this agency principle, and yeah, we're going to apply that
to your case. It doesn't matter that you had nothing to do with that
one-day-late filing, we're going to apply it to you. All this bullshit.
Never getting to the truth of the matter.

And it just made me feel, you know, that we had this bond too,
because in both instances what you were fighting was this knowledge that if you didn't get the right answer, you were going to die.
. . . I guess at that point I should have caught on to the fact that he
was more resolved than I was about what was going to happen in the
end. I mean, I think what was happening was that I was realizing he
was going to die.

It's like he had some disease, you know? He had some disease
called habeas-corpus-itis. It was killing him. And he knew it was
killing him. He'd come to terms with it. But I hadn't.

That evening Jim McCloskey called from Cincinnati. He had managed to locate Danny Ray Stiltner in a ramshackle house tucked back
in the hills of southern Ohio. They had talked at length.

Jim thought he might be lying about some of the things they talked
about, but his sense was he was telling the truth about not being

involved in the murder. If he *was* involved, Jim had no idea how they would try to prove it in the time remaining.

Kitty agreed. Then she told him about Judge Williams's decision.

Chapter 40

———

Seven Days: Presto

Wednesday, May 13. Seven days to execution date. Jim McCloskey flies back to Richmond from Cincinnati and spends the day responding to press calls about Judge Williams's decision and what they are going to do next.

The media is reporting the decision, but for the most part the emphasis is on the court once again turning down Coleman's effort to obtain a hearing of his new evidence, and the possibility that an innocent man will be executed. Maybe it isn't as bad as Kitty feared.

Kitty remains in Washington, working on an emergency appeal from Judge Williams's decision. A notice of appeal and petition for a certificate of probable cause to appeal are completed and shipped off to Abingdon. Most of the night and the next day are spent working on the merits of the appeal and a brief in support of an emergency motion to stay the execution pending appeal.

Thursday, May 14. Jim remains in Richmond to participate in a press conference held on the grounds of the capitol, in front of the governor's mansion. Marie Deans also participates, and a phone line is set up so that Roger can call in and speak. The media attend in droves.

At Tom Scott's office in Grundy, a "counter" press conference is held by Brad McCoy, Brenda (Rife) Ratliff and the two librarians. Tom Scott can't make it—he's to appear with McCloskey and Coleman on *Larry King Live* that night. McCloskey and Coleman will appear by remote feed, but Scott has decided to fly to New York to appear in person. The Grundy press conference is also heavily attended, but only by local and regional outlets. Nationwide the media is still overwhelmingly favorable to Coleman, and reports from inside the Wilder administration are that the flood of calls and letters supporting clemency is, if anything, increasing.

A call from Phil Horton to McFarlane to ask if he has everything he needs is really a fishing expedition to see if he says anything about the Williams decision. He doesn't, and sounds friendly. So far so good.

Kitty continues her frantic pace in Washington. Neither she nor anyone else really believes the Fourth Circuit Court of Appeals will reverse Judge Williams, or even stay the execution for long enough to give the issue serious consideration, but every possibility has to be pursued to the fullest. Just maybe some judge will see through the technicalities and decide a hearing is necessary.

That night on *Larry King Live*, Roger appears by remote feed from the death house. Roger is as calm and articulate as ever but Jim McCloskey is unhappy with his own performance. Scott's statements and answers to King's questions are short and very certain, while Jim thinks that his are too long and that he sounds less certain of Roger's innocence than Scott does of his guilt. He lies awake all night agonizing over whether he has hurt Roger's cause.

Friday, May 15. In Richmond, Jim McCloskey rents a car and drives down to Greensville to see Roger for the first time in months. He seems more upbeat than Jim expected, and Jim tries to keep his spirits up by telling him about the outpouring of support he is getting. Hundreds of letters and phone calls to the governor's office. Media requests from all over the world. The Japanese have a film crew in Grundy, and they interviewed Jim in Richmond on Monday. Thursday he was interviewed by England's counterpart to Ted Koppel, and when he returns to Richmond he has a lunch appointment with a French TV crew. Roger has been besieged with interview requests, and is already scheduled for *Nightline*, *Good Morning America* and a second appearance on the *Today* show. Jim says he was unhappy about his performance on *Larry King*; Roger says he thought it was fine. They both wonder if any of this will do any good at all, but neither says so.

They say good-bye—see you soon—and wonder about that as well. Jim drives back to Richmond for his lunch interview, and then flies back to New Jersey.

In Washington, Kitty has been up all night again, finishing papers for the court of appeals, which are shipped off to Richmond for filing. Most important is a motion for stay of execution. Unless that is granted, the rest of it is a waste of time. Either the court will grant the stay in order to have adequate time to give Kitty's arguments serious consideration or it will deny the stay and summarily affirm Judge Williams's decision in the next few days. Simple as that.

In her motion Kitty emphasizes the new evidence that Judge Williams failed to mention in his opinion and the factual disputes that Williams seemed to resolve against Coleman without conducting a hearing. Also attached is a new affidavit from Dr. James Starrs, the eminent forensic scientist who had examined the fragment of sheet dug up from Keester Shortridge's mine site but was unable to determine whether the stain on the long buried sheet was or was not blood. This affidavit, however, deals with Elmer Gist's work. Starrs adds his voice to the other experts who say that the blood evidence is ambiguous and that examination of Elmer Gist's notes and further testing are essential. Depending on your point of view, it is either an urgent and eminently reasonable plea to reexamine scientific evidence before killing someone based on incomplete information, or one more desperate attempt to stall a long overdue execution.

When the papers are sent off to Richmond, Kitty finally goes home to bed.

Saturday, May 16. In Atlanta, Georgia, Kitty Behan's brother is getting married today. Kitty will not attend. She has to stay in Washington to work on additional papers to file next week if the court denies a stay. When she arrives at her office, Kitty first goes through a stack of phone calls that came in after she left on Friday. Most are from reporters (with time running out and so much to do, she no longer returns them), but one is from a woman who has been a source of information in the past. The message reads, "You should talk to George Looney. He saw Donnie Ramey & Harold Williamson had scratches the day after the murder. (They were covered up with make-up.)"

Kitty reaches the woman at home, and she says the information came from another woman whom Looney talked to. Apparently Looney and Ramey and Williamson all worked at the same coal mine. She gives Kitty directions to Looney's house.

In New Jersey, Jim is going through letters and phone calls on other cases that have been piling up for weeks. Kitty calls him at home with the Looney information. Can he go back to Grundy and investigate? Checking the airlines, he reserves flights that will get him to Roanoke on Sunday, and calls Kitty back to say he'll go. It sounds crazy, but who knows?

At Greensville, Sharon Paul has arrived for her contact visit with Roger. He is exhausted from the emotional roller coaster of his case and the almost constant media interviews of the past two weeks, but he has been looking forward to this visit above anything. Then, when he is taken out of his cell to go to the visiting room, he is placed in full restraints—the leg irons and handcuffs linked to a waist chain that are used to transport prisoners to outside locations and which severely restrict any movement. When he gets to the visiting room, the guards refuse to remove them. Orders, they say.

Roger is furious. He can't even put his hands around Sharon's waist, much less hold her in his arms. He was told he would not be in restraints. Two guards are there with nothing to do but watch him at all times. The restraints are stupid, and a breach of faith.

For the first two and a half hours of the visit, Roger can think of nothing but the restraints and his anger about them. His complaints are ignored, but he is finally allowed to call Marie Deans, who calls Kitty, who calls someone—and at about 11:45 a prison officer comes and tells the guards to remove everything. After that, Roger wrote, "it was heaven on earth. . . . For the first time ever I could put my arms around her and hold her close to me. It was the happiest and fastest six hours of my life. . . . We spent nearly the entire time in each other's arms.

There is one somber period during the visit. Roger says they have to plan what to do if he is executed. He has thought of several alternatives for disposing of his body. Sharon cries and doesn't want to talk about it, but Roger insists. They finally agree that if it happens he will be cremated and Sharon will go to Grundy and spread his ashes in the mountains.

Saturday afternoon in Kitty's office, a friend calls and says Governor Wilder was on the news and said something about Coleman. It wasn't a decision on clemency, but she heard Coleman's name mentioned. Kitty tracks it down. In the course of a press conference on another subject, Wilder was asked about Coleman. He responded, in substance, that he hasn't made a decision yet, but he is studying the facts carefully, and will say that the people don't know all the evidence. He mentioned that Judge Williams studied the evidence and turned Coleman down.

Kitty thinks it is very ominous. It sounds like he's laying the groundwork to deny clemency despite the public outcry against the execution.

Robert White and Roger Coleman had an agreement that Robert would not visit Roger once he was transferred to Greensville for deathwatch. Now, late on Saturday afternoon, Robert sits down to write what may be his last letter to Roger. It is a long letter, tracing their relationship and its impact on Robert's life. In conclusion, Robert writes:

> You have brought to me a healing, compassionate side that would not have been possible if the pettinesses of the past were still with me. They are not.
>
> You are my Roger, my friend and my brother, and that will not change. . . . If you live, we will continue to discuss all these things. If you do not, let your spirit guide me in learning to be less selfish and more giving. That is the form my devotion to you will take, and has already taken.

Sunday, May 17. Mark Masling is getting angrier and angrier. Kitty is exhausted, and the more tired she gets, the more medication she has to take to ward off the symptoms of her lupus, which include memory loss and other forms of diminished mental acuity, which God knows she can't afford now. The medicine is highly toxic and contains steroids. Her face is swollen, her hair is falling out and even her gait has become unsteady. Mark tells her that if she keeps working around the clock and taking so much medicine, she's going to kill herself, but

Kitty just snaps at him. What is she supposed to do, go to bed and rest while the state executes an innocent man?

Mark has no answer, but he does persuade Kitty to stay home most of Sunday morning. In the afternoon she does some research and preliminary drafting on a petition for certiorari to the United States Supreme Court, in case it comes to that.

Monday, May 18. In Grundy, Tom Scott, Brad McCoy and the Thompson family have organized a memorial service for Wanda, which is also an effort to gather support for proceeding with the execution. Also in Grundy, Jim McCloskey locates George Looney. As Kitty had reported, Looney lives in a trailer at the head of Looney Creek. He is undoubtedly related to the Looney brothers who settled the area, owned most of the land and provided a name for the creek, but, if so, none of their wealth and prominence has passed down to George's generation or branch of the family. He has mined a lot of coal from under the hills his ancestors settled, but all he seems to have retained is the dust in his lungs.

The story he tells is a little different from what was told to Kitty on Saturday. Looney says he worked with Donnie Ramey and Harold Williamson for the Lane Hollow Coal Company at the time of the murder. Ramey's father, Bob, worked there too. Williamson was the foreman. He was a good friend of Bob Ramey, and the son too. No, he didn't say Donnie was scratched after the murder, but he did see Williamson with scratches on his face. What he said was that Williamson was scratched, and that he and Ramey were friends.

McCloskey heads off to look for Harold Williamson, following directions provided by Looney. He is a little nervous. If Looney's story is true, the man Jim is about to walk in on, unaccompanied and unannounced, may be the murderer.

Jim arrives at Harold Williamson's trailer. He knows there will be no time to obtain an affidavit of whatever Williamson says, nor can he take a chance that Williamson will refuse to sign one. Before knocking, he starts the minicassette recorder concealed in the breast pocket of his suit. Harold's wife, Lois, answers the door. She is a pleasant, energetic, gray-haired lady who, it turns out, is suffering from cancer that will soon kill her. Even so, she is a picture of health compared to her husband, who has recently been released from a hospital stay for heart trouble, and whose oxygen machine for emphysema is a constant companion.

Whatever he was like ten years earlier, Harold Williamson is no danger to anyone now, and it doesn't take Jim long to become convinced that he had nothing to do with Wanda McCoy's rape and murder. His health forced his retirement in 1982. Before that he had worked for many years for the Justus family, who owned a succession of drift mines in the area. Harold was the foreman. He and Lois are obviously devoted to one another.

It's true that Harold knew the Rameys well, and he's not unwilling to believe the talk that Donnie had something to do with the murder.* Lois, on the other hand, feels that Brad McCoy was somehow involved. She doesn't know Brad, but all the McCoys are bad, she says. The Hatfields are all right, but there never was a McCoy who made an honest living.

Harold tells Jim that Trouble Ramey (he uses the nickname) worked for him in the mines for several years. The Williamsons and the senior Rameys had been neighbors and good friends in the sixties, and Bob Ramey worked with him in the Justus mines, so when Donnie got old enough, he went to work there too. Trouble had used drugs since he was a kid, Williamson says, and he "had a time with him" in the mines.

But it is Michael he talks about the most. Michael was a strange-acting fellow. Williamson remembers that he came to the house a night or two before the murder, and when Harold asked him if he had a girlfriend, Michael said, "No, but I've got my eye on one. But there ain't but one trouble. She's married." A day or so after the murder, Michael rode his bike over to Williamson's house. He seemed nervous, and got red in the face when Harold started talking about the murder. When Harold said, "Whoever did it should get fried," Michael got up and left.

After the murder, Harold goes on to say, the senior Rameys started to withdraw from all their friends, including Harold and Lois. Bob wouldn't even talk to him at the mine, and they stopped seeing each

* As discussed below, Harold Williamson told several different stories about what he knew or was told about Donnie Ramey and his brother Michael. In the end, however, because of these changes and Williamson's ill health, not much credence can be afforded to his assertions.

other. It was strange. Later on, Donnie and Michael would sometimes come by to see them, but Bob and Helen never did. The odd thing is that just a week or so ago Donnie stopped by to see Harold for the first time in years. Unfortunately, Lois says, Harold was still in the hospital.

Jim takes a long shot. "Would you consider going over to Donnie's house this afternoon, and just kind of bringing up the murder and all to see what he says?" Harold and Lois look at one another. "Sure, why not," Lois says. "If that other boy didn't do it, I wouldn't want it on my conscience I might have helped save an innocent man." It's agreed they'll go by Donnie's after lunch. Jim will come back in the late afternoon to see what they found out.

The call from the governor's office comes in to Arnold & Porter at about ten o'clock. Following lawyers' protocol, McFarlane asks for Phil Horton, the senior lawyer on the team, although he is well aware that Kitty is really in charge. To his credit, when Horton comes on the line and hears McFarlane say that the governor has made a decision, he stops him. "Before you go any further, let me get Kitty on the line."

With Kitty patched in, McFarlane proceeds. "The governor will be releasing a statement to the press in a few minutes. On the evidence that has been presented, he has decided not to grant clemency at this time. I'm sorry." On the other end of the line there is stunned silence. Finally somebody asks, "What do you mean 'at this time'? The execution's in two days. Do you mean he might change his mind?" "Well, maybe," McFarlane says, "but only if some other evidence comes to light." Kitty tells him about the new lead. McCloskey is in Grundy as they speak, tracking down information that Donnie Ramey may have had scratches on his face the morning after the murder. "Well, if you get something important, fax it to me," McFarlane says, but it doesn't sound like it's the kind of thing he's looking for.

Kitty goes to her office, and after sitting for a moment to compose herself she calls Roger with the news. "The governor just announced he has turned down clemency." There's really nothing else to say.

Roger has been called away from a noncontact visit with Sharon to take Kitty's call.

The hard part was going back in the visiting booth and telling Sharon of his decision. News like that isn't something you want to give to the one you love over the phone while separated by a half inch of bullet proof glass. I wanted to hold her in my arms and let her cry on my shoulder. It's hard to comfort someone over the phone. I wanted to put my arms around her, I wanted to hold her tight and try to comfort her. But instead, I had to watch through the glass as she cried.

Later Kitty and Phil Horton confer. Could McFarlane have been hinting about a lie-detector test? They call him back. "What if Roger takes a lie-detector test and passes it. Would that make a difference?" McFarlane indicates it might. "We'll have to think about it and talk to Roger," Kitty says, "but after your comment last Monday we contacted this guy Earl Kane [she goes on to describe the former New Jersey police polygrapher], and he is willing to do it. Assuming Roger agrees, we can get Kane here this afternoon or tomorrow morning." McFarlane says he too will have to talk further to his client, the governor, and also the attorney general. "Maybe there will have to be two guys, yours and somebody picked by the AG." Kitty and Phil agree to call back as soon as they can talk to Roger and make a decision.

It is an agonizing question, one that has no right answer, and yet only one answer. Both of them realize, instinctively, that even if one believes in lie detectors (which they don't), it is ludicrous to think about giving someone a test a day or two before he is due to be executed. Both of them also realize that they have no choice. In his announcement, which they have now received by fax, Governor Wilder has said nothing about "at this time." He has flat-out denied clemency. Unless Jim comes up with a signed and independently corroborated confession from Donnie Ramey or someone else, Coleman's only hope of clemency is to take and pass a lie-detector test. Why Wilder would put so much stake in it is a mystery, but no matter. It is take the test or die. (Later, the "why" question is answered. A source close to one of the governor's political advisers reveals to Kitty that the lie-detector idea came from F. Lee Bailey, the famous trial lawyer who is a well-known proponent of the polygraph. He called Wilder a week or so earlier to suggest it. Bailey reportedly said that "no innocent person would ever refuse to take one if faced with death," and assured Wilder that in his experience the tests are very reliable. Later, the *Richmond Times-Dispatch* reports that on Sunday, Bailey reinforced his phone call with a faxed letter.)

In a long telephone conversation, Kitty, Roger and Philip Horton agonize over the decision. Roger reminds them that he wanted to take a test months ago, and told them on several occasions that if they were ever going to change their minds and suggest he take one, they should do it before it is so close to the execution date that he will have begun focusing his mind on death. That time has already come, he says. He doesn't know if he can possibly take a test at this point. But, of course, Roger too realizes he has no real choice, and soon he is talking about it excitedly. Wilder cannot very well give him the test and then execute him if he passes. And since he is innocent, he will pass.

Leaving Harold Williamson's house in Grundy, Jim turns on his car radio. Within a few minutes the station interrupts broadcasting to repeat a special bulletin. "Governor Wilder announced this morning that he has denied clemency to Roger Coleman. The governor stated: 'I have exhaustively reviewed the record . . .'" Jim does not hear the rest. He drives immediately to the nearest public phone and calls Kitty, who fills him in on the lie-detector issue. There is no choice. Jim will call Earl Kane in New Jersey at once and have him get on a plane for Richmond.

When Kitty and Phil call McFarlane back to say Roger has agreed to the test and their polygraph expert will be on a plane within hours, McFarlane tells them the attorney general has balked about having anyone give the test but the state's own polygrapher. No one else will be allowed to participate. Coleman's lawyers protest, but to no avail. They will have to go back to Roger. McFarlane understands.

More agonized discussion among themselves and with Roger, but again with no real choice. There is a chance, of course, that public outrage over the execution will force Wilder to change his mind, but there is no sign of it. It will be almost impossible for him to reverse himself without some good explanation, and it seems that passing a lie-detector test is the only explanation he has in mind. They call McFarlane again. Roger will take the test. They want someone he knows, Kitty or Jim, to be present, along with their polygrapher, who will simply observe. McFarlane thinks that sounds reasonable. The test will be tomorrow: he'll get back to them with the time and place, perhaps not until tomorrow morning.

In Grundy, at about 5:00 P.M., Jim McCloskey arrives back at the Williamsons' trailer. Their car is in front. Jim turns on his tape recorder, and once again Lois answers the door and invites him in.

They did go to see the Rameys, and Donnie seemed tickled to see them, Harold reports. After some pleasantries they steered the conversation to the murder, and the accusation that he was involved. They knew he wasn't involved, Harold told him, but in all the stories they never had heard what he did that night.

Donnie said he recalled it well. He and Michael had gone up to their cousin Ralph Ramey's house near the Breaks park the night it happened. At Ramey's they got some acid, and then came home. On their way up the stairs, going past the McCoy's house, they saw two handprints of blood on Wanda's window—all five fingers. Later, it ran through Donnie's mind that Wanda might have put her bloody hands on the window as he and Michael were going by, trying to signal them what was happening to her.

Roger Coleman and his wife had been there that afternoon, Donnie said. His father said he had watched Wanda take out the trash at about 4:00 P.M. and go back into the house.

According to Harold, Donnie went on to say that Michael had seen someone under the porch when they got home, and that he, Donnie, was in bed by about 10:30. Donnie said he was off from work the day after the murder because he was going to Jewel Smokeless Coal Company to take some tests for a job. Harold recalls that he did go to work for Jewel sometime around then.

Donnie also said he had heard that Teresa Horn was offered a lot of money to blame Donnie, and that the reason for the bloody sheets was that a dog belonging to the woman who lived next door to the Shortridges had pups on the bed.

The whole time they talked about the murder, Harold says, Donnie seemed nervous, and talked real fast, like he wanted to get past the whole story as quickly as possible. Donnie said that in a few days Roger will be dead and it will be over. Then he'll have peace. They won't ever be able to pin it on him or Michael.

One thing sure, Williamson concludes, them boys weren't in bed by no ten-thirty after taking acid.

Harold Williamson's story about what Donnie told him is one more strange twist in McCloskey's investigation. Parts of what Donnie supposedly said could well be true, Jim thinks, but other parts are clearly not true. In particular, there is no reference in the police reports to bloody handprints on the windows, as surely there would have been if it were true.

In Jim's mind several facts are especially significant. One is that according to Williamson the Rameys bought, and may have used, LSD that night. The catalog of brutal killings performed by people under the influence of acid begins, but by no means ends, with the Manson murders. Second, according to Williamson Donnie's story means that he and Michael were in fact coming home and moving up the stairs behind Wanda's house at about the time of the murder.

As soon as Jim leaves the Williamsons he calls Kitty with the information, which she puts into an affidavit and faxes back to Jim at the motel. Kitty thinks Williamson's statement, or, rather, Donnie's alleged statement to Williamson, may be helpful—but she soon has something much better. Shortly after she and Jim talk, a phone call comes in from a man named Jon Cooper, who is calling because he read the story in *Time* magazine. Mr. Cooper says he had been living with Sandra Stiltner in Charleston, West Virginia, at the time of Roger Coleman's murder trial. He believes Sandra lied when she testified that she knew exactly when Roger Coleman came to her trailer on the night of the murder.

According to Cooper, Sandra told him she had to go back to Grundy to testify at a trial. When he found out it was a murder case he asked her about it, and she said she was supposed to testify about the precise time when she was the last person to see someone before a murder. From what she said, it was clear to Cooper that Sandra did not know the exact time, but when she returned from the trial she told him she had testified that the time was 10:20. When he brought up the apparent discrepancy with what she had said before, Sandra told him she did "what she had to do" and he should "just drop it."

Kitty can barely contain her excitement. The strongest evidence in the case suggesting Roger had time to commit the murder was Sandy Stiltner's testimony that it was 10:20 when Roger came to her door. Short of a confession by Donnie Ramey, Kitty cannot think of more important evidence.

Kitty asks if Cooper will fax her an affidavit, and the answer is yes. Cooper is with his lawyer, and the two of them and Kitty start to draft the fax. Kitty asks what Sandra had said that made it clear that she didn't know the precise time of Roger's visit. Cooper can't recall her exact words, and his lawyer doesn't want Cooper to try to describe the substance of what she said. What he will say is that from their conversations Cooper felt certain in his own mind that Sandra did not know the exact time.

It's not as strong as she would like, but Kitty has no choice but to agree to the language approved by Cooper's lawyer, and on May 18 at 4:14 P.M. the fax is sent, bearing Jon Cooper's facsimile signature.

That night, Kitty prepares an emergency motion to the court of appeals renewing her request for stay of execution and asking that the case be remanded to the district court so that the Cooper affidavit can be considered. In the alternative, if the court turns her down, she asks for rehearing en banc in the Fourth Circuit. For each of these requests Kitty relies heavily on the Cooper affidavit, hoping that by focusing on it she can lead the courts to understand just how significant the time issue is to the entire case, and how important this new evidence is to Coleman's innocence claim.

Tuesday, May 19. In Grundy, Jim obtains Harold Williamson's signature on the affidavit Kitty faxed him the night before, tries without success to track down a few leads that have been left hanging and catches a plane for Richmond.

Tuesday morning in Washington, Kitty is still waiting for McFarlane's call about the time and place for the lie-detector test while continuing to write legal papers. Motions are sent off to Richmond. The telephones at Arnold & Porter are ringing constantly with calls about the case. They are being answered and screened by a paralegal and another young associate. Horton calls McFarlane, but he is out, or in conference, or just not taking calls. Finally McFarlane calls back. The attorney general's office has reneged on the lie-detector test. They will have nothing to do with it. McFarlane is furious, and says the governor is too. Apparently they were bluffing, thinking Coleman's lawyers would advise against taking the test under the conditions imposed.

Kitty and Horton are on the phone with McFarlane together. This, finally, may be the break they need. Kitty tells McFarlane about the Cooper affidavit, and about Williamson. Maybe now he can see that the AG's office has been playing fast and loose all along. Wilder should grant clemency, or at the very least postpone the execution and find some way to conduct a hearing on all their new evidence so that the truth can come out.

No, McFarlane says, the governor still wants a lie-detector test. If the attorney general won't cooperate, he'll have it done himself. Kitty says, in that case, our expert is here and available. We can have him down at Greensville to do the test within two hours. But out of fairness to Roger, and to try to assure an accurate test, the execution should be postponed for at least a week or ten days so that the test is not given in the shadow of the electric chair. McFarlane will call back.

When he does, he says the governor will not agree to any postponement, and the test has to be done by the Virginia State Police. It's too late to do it today, but they will bring Roger to Richmond to do it first thing in the morning if he agrees.

Kitty is furious. It is insane to ask someone to take a lie-detector test on the very morning he is scheduled to be executed. No one could provide an accurate reading under those circumstances. At least postpone the execution for a few days to take some of the pressure off.

I'm sorry, McFarlane says. Those are the conditions. Of course, if your man doesn't want to take the test, he doesn't have to.

More agonizing and conferences. Kane says they are right—it is terribly prejudicial to test under those circumstances. No result will be trustworthy. But, of course, again there is no real choice. Take the test or die. Probably both. Roger agrees.

Kitty calls McFarlane and capitulates again. Can they at least have Jim and their expert there? McFarlane says yes. Kitty thinks he told her where the test would occur; Jim thinks McFarlane was going to let them know the next morning.

Whatever happens, McFarlane tells her, you did a great job. He goes on to say he received a fax from the Pope that morning asking for clemency. "But the best is, when I answered the phone a while ago it was Mother Teresa! It was incredible. I just answered the phone the way I always do, kind of gruff, and there was this voice on the line, and the voice said, 'Hello, Mr. McFarlane, this is Mother Teresa,' and right away I knew it wasn't some joke. I recognized her voice from television. I felt like I was talking to God!"

"What did she say?" Kitty asks. "She said, 'I'm calling about Roger Coleman. I'm not telling you what to do. Just do what Jesus would do.'" McFarlane laughs ruefully. "Jesus," he says. "Do what Jesus would do!"

Late in the afternoon the Buchanan County sheriff's office locates Sandra Stiltner in West Virginia. She provides an affidavit denying Jon Cooper's claim that she was uncertain of the time Coleman arrived at her trailer. The sheriff faxes it to Curry, who files it with the court.

At the end of the day the governor's office reports that thus far he has received 6,146 messages about the case, more than 95 percent favoring clemency. All but one of those that opposed clemency is from the Grundy area.

Book V

—

Roger

Chapter 41

Wednesday: Polygraph

In Washington, Kitty works all night again on a petition for certiorari to the United States Supreme Court that will have to be filed if the Fourth Circuit denies the motions she filed on Monday and Tuesday. Or, more realistically, *when* they are denied.

Large law firms like Arnold & Porter hire dozens of summer associates every year—law students at the top of their classes at America's best law schools, who spend their summer vacations working for very handsome salaries hoping to get jobs when they graduate. By mid-May most of Arnold & Porter's summer associates have arrived for work, and of course they all know about the Coleman case. Nearly a dozen have volunteered to help Kitty at one time or another, and tonight she puts them to work searching the casebooks for conflicts among the circuit courts on how a claim of innocence should be treated in federal habeas corpus cases. One of the major reasons for the Supreme Court to accept a case for full review is to resolve legal conflicts between the circuits; situations in which the Fourth Circuit, for example, has used a different legal test than one of the other circuits in resolving an important issue. Kitty, of course, has long since thoroughly researched the innocence issue, but new cases are decided on a daily basis all over the country, and on a complex issue like this a good lawyer can almost always find something new or different. Working all night on a petition to the Supreme Court in a case that has just made the cover of *Time* magazine! It's fun and exciting for these fledgling lawyers, and they come up with several useful cases. Once they exhaust that assignment, Kitty asks several of them to stay on to proofread her brief.

Kitty and Roger had finalized the decision to go forward with the lie-detector test at about eight o'clock Tuesday evening. Later, at the death house in Greensville, Marie Deans and Russ Ford come to visit Roger. Physically exhausted from his interview schedule and a painful pulled muscle in his back that has kept him from sleeping, and emotionally exhausted by the extraordinary roller coaster of hope and despair that has marked the past several weeks, Roger Coleman is finally beginning to crack. That night, the guards who have been with him in the death house since his arrival two weeks earlier are replaced with a whole new crew—the men who will walk him to the chair and strap him in: the death squad. Russ Ford and Marie Deans have prepared him for this, but it still upsets him.

Worst of all, he tells Russ and Marie, were the negotiations over the lie-detector test. Each time the state proposed something and he agreed to it, the state reneged. He had wanted to take a test months ago and been talked out of it. He had told all of them at the time that if he was going to take a test it had to be before he began to focus on the execution. Now it's too late—they're going to give him the test on the morning of the day he is to be executed, and all he can think about is dying. The state has planned it. They know he can't pass a test under these circumstances—and if he does pass, they'll lie about it and say he didn't. It was their state police who framed him for the murder, and now their state police are going to give him a phony lie-detector test on the morning they plan to kill him.

Russ and Marie have seen all of this before. Usually it comes much earlier—Roger had amazed them with his focused, calm, purposeful demeanor. What Roger is going through is part of the process of dying, but everyone is different, and Russ had begun to think Roger was going to skip this period of anger and emotional turmoil, but here it is.

To Russ Ford, the most important question now is whether Roger will be able to move on to a state of acceptance and grace. But of course there is also the question of whether there is any way Roger can take and pass a lie-detector test. Russ has taught himself not to even consider the possibility that the last-minute efforts of lawyers for the condemned will actually work. They almost never do, but, in any event, that's lawyers' work. His job is to tend to his charge spiritually and emotionally. Innocent or guilty, Russ does not think Roger can pass a lie-detector test or anything else in his present state. All it will accomplish is to interrupt and perhaps defeat his journey to spiritual peace.

Marie is more attuned to the implications of the test. She believes that if Roger passes the test, the governor will commute the death sentence, although she does not at all discount Roger's fear that with a state police examiner there will be no such thing as passing. She also knows that if Roger does not take the test, Wilder will send him to the chair unless a court intervenes, which is the longest shot of all. But observing and listening to Roger, she also agrees with Russ, and Roger himself, that he cannot pass a lie-detector test, even an honest one, even if you believe they are reliable. She is surer of that than she is that Wilder will go ahead with the execution if he refuses to take it. If he takes the test and fails, not only will he be executed but all the public outrage that has been generated over the possible execution of an innocent man will be dissipated. All the work she and so many others have done to generate that outrage will be for naught, and, as Roger says, at least some of the people who have believed in him will lose their faith. On the other hand, if he refuses the test under these grossly unfair circumstances, maybe Wilder will relent after all, either because of the intense public pressure for commutation or because at the last minute he will realize how unfair it is and at least agree to postpone the execution for long enough to provide a fairer test.

Marie and Russ agree they should call Kitty and advise her that the test should be canceled, and why. They try several times to reach her, but she is in seclusion, working on the brief. Finally, at about 1 A.M., Marie gets through from her home. She tells Kitty of Roger's condition, her conviction that he cannot possibly pass a test and the admittedly desperate hope that Wilder might postpone the execution anyway. Kitty has to call it off, she concludes.

Exhausted herself, Kitty reacts angrily. The decision is made and she isn't going to change it. If she did, she might as well pull the switch on Roger herself. She has talked to McFarlane; Marie hasn't. There is no chance at all that Wilder will postpone the execution if Roger refuses the test—they have been through all that. And no, she will not call Roger. It's one o'clock in the morning. If he is not asleep, he should be, and Kitty is not about to take the chance of waking him up and making things worse. If Roger wakes up in the morning and decides not to take the test, that's his choice. If he wants to call her and talk about it further, she will certainly talk to him, but her advice will not change. There is no alternative.

At 5:30 A.M. the telephone rings in Jim McCloskey's room at the Marriot Hotel in Richmond. Sound asleep, McCloskey reaches for the phone and almost hangs up at once, thinking it's his wake-up call. Before he can do so, he hears a woman's voice speaking his name. He realizes that computerized wake-up calls don't often know your name. McCloskey listens as the woman speaks. Soon he is wide awake. The woman is calling from Grundy. She does not want to give her name because she's scared to death of Donnie Ramey, but she has been unable to sleep for days. She has lain awake all night until finally deciding to make this call. She has information she thinks may be helpful to Roger Coleman.

In June 1991, an anonymous letter had come to Arnold & Porter from Grundy. It came after Jim and Kitty began investigating Donnie Ramey as a result of Teresa Horn's allegations, but before their suspicions were made public. The letter suggested they should look into the whereabouts of the Ramey sons and father on the night of the murder because they "were having a family fight the night of the girls murder," and "The Father was drunk that night."

To Kitty and Jim the letter had seemed an independent source that confirmed the possibility of a Ramey involvement in the murder. It was obviously from someone who knew the family, most likely a neighbor. For the past year they had tried everything they could think of to identify the writer, without success. Now, as Jim listens to the woman on the telephone, he realizes he is talking to the letter writer.

They had been wrong in thinking it was a neighbor. The woman's name is Pat Daniels, although she hopes it won't be necessary to reveal it. She owned a hair salon at the time of the murder. Helen Ramey was her customer and a member of the same church, and the two had become friends. Shortly after the murder Helen Ramey confided to Pat that her sons had a violent fight with their father on the night of the murder. The father was drunk. Mrs. Ramey became so upset at the fight that she went into her bedroom to pray, and when she came out she found her husband passed out and her sons gone. They did not return until about midnight. When she came out of her bedroom she could feel "murder in the air."

With Kitty desperately trying to finish the Supreme Court papers, contacts with McFarlane have been taken over by Phil Horton. Jim persuades Pat Daniels to give him her phone number, and tells her Horton will call her. He reaches Horton at home, Horton calls Daniels and Daniels repeats her story.

Jim and Phil Horton both realize that if Pat Daniels's story is true, it destroys the Ramey family's claim that Michael and Donnie came home before ten and stayed home, with Donnie in bed by ten-thirty. It also brings to mind and fits nicely into Harold Williamson's story of Donnie and Michael buying acid that night, and his comment that if they had taken acid they weren't about to go to bed at ten-thirty. High on acid, a violent fight with their father, and then leaving for several hours—it doesn't prove they committed the murder, but it certainly raises further questions about their possible involvement.

Phil tells Pat Daniels he will try to get someone from the governor's office to call her so she can repeat her story directly to them, and answer any questions. She promises to stay by the phone. As soon as he reaches his office, Horton sends a fax to McFarlane, repeating the story and asking that he or the governor call Daniels so they can judge her credibility for themselves.

According to Pat Daniels, no one ever called. Phil Horton discovers later that the fax lines to the governor's office were so clogged with other calls about the execution that his fax may not have gotten through.

In his cell in the death house, Roger Coleman is awakened at 6:00 A.M. and told to get dressed at once for the ride to Richmond for his lie-detector test. When he finishes dressing he's placed in leg irons and handcuffs attached to a chain around his waist and hustled into a state police car, which, along with a cavalcade of additional police cars, is parked alongside the death house.

The day before, Earl Kane told Kitty it was important that Roger's routine before the lie-detector test remain exactly as it had been in the preceding days. She had asked whether that meant Roger should take the pain medicine for his back that he had been taking for about a week, and Kane said absolutely—everything should be just the same as it has been. In accordance with Kane's advice, Kitty tried without success to get the state to conduct the lie-detector test at the prison, but the state insisted that it be given in Richmond. She did get the warden's office to promise that Roger would be given his medication in the same dosages as he was used to. According to Roger, when he asked for his pain pills that morning they were refused. They told him no drugs before a lie-detector test.

Once in the squad car, Coleman is joined by a state trooper on either side and another in the front seat, who sits looking back at him for the whole trip to Richmond. The driver turns on his siren, and, with state police cars in front and in back, the convoy lurches wildly through an open gate in the tall razor wire-topped fence that surrounds the death house. The convoy heads with ever-increasing speed down the narrow road that leads from the prison to the highway. With each turn and curve Roger is thrown from side to side, his handcuffs and leg irons painfully digging into his flesh. Accompanied by a state police helicopter flying overhead, the caravan reaches Division 1 Headquarters of the state police in a suburb of Richmond at about 8:30 A.M., long before the appointed hour for the test, which is 10:00. Coleman is left to wait in a room empty except for two guards. Occasionally he can see someone come to the door and peer in curiously, as though he were a new exhibit in the zoo.

Finally, a little before 10:00, he is escorted by his guards down a long hall to another room, where the polygraph equipment is set up and the police examiner is waiting. As they walk down the hall a tall state police investigator walking in the opposite direction looks at Coleman and smiles. Pointing a finger at Coleman's chest, he says "bzzzzzt."

Jim McCloskey joins Earl Kane at the Jefferson Hotel in downtown Richmond to await a call from Kitty or Phil Horton telling them where to go for the lie-detector test. By 9:30 they have heard nothing, and Jim begins to get anxious. He calls Arnold & Porter, but neither Kitty nor Phil Horton have heard anything. Kitty holds him on the line while she calls McFarlane, but apparently he isn't in yet. Twice more in the next half hour Kitty repeats the process, calling Jim each time to report that she still has not reached or heard from McFarlane. It is 10:00, the time the test was supposed to begin. Jim say he isn't going to wait any longer. He doesn't believe McFarlane isn't in yet. Jim and Earl are going to go and confront him. If Kitty hears anything in the next few minutes she should leave word with McFarlane's secretary.

At about 10:15 Kitty's phone rings. It's someone who says he is with the state police. He's with Roger Coleman and the polygraph operator. They had been told someone would be appearing on behalf of Coleman. Kitty explains that no one has told them where to go; they have been trying all morning to find out. Where is he? The man says they are at a state police facility on Route 1 in Henrico County, outside Richmond. Kitty says her people are waiting downtown; she will have them there in a few minutes. The man says it will take too long to get there from downtown, and they're already behind schedule. It's too late. They're going ahead.

Jim McCloskey and Earl Kane taxi from the Jefferson to the state capitol complex. Although he has been there only once, Jim remembers the way to McFarlane's office, and the two men half walk, half run there and enter the suite, where a secretary/receptionist's desk bars the way to the inner office. "I've got to see Mr. McFarlane immediately," Jim announces, and before the secretary can respond, he's around the side of her desk and heading for McFarlane's closed door. At that moment the door opens and McFarlane emerges, pulling on his jacket. The two men stare at each other for a second before McCloskey holds out his hand and announces, "Mr. McFarlane, if you don't remember me I'm Jim McCloskey, and this is Earl Kane, our polygraph expert. We're supposed to be wherever Roger Coleman's lie-detector test is going to be conducted, but no one has told us where it is. Where is it?"

Walter McFarlane's secretary is sputtering. She's sorry, Mr. McFarlane, she couldn't stop him, she tried. McFarlane waves off her concern. He takes McCloskey's hand for an instant, and says, "I'm sorry, Mr. McCloskey, I can't tell you. The governor has decided no one should be there except the people guarding Mr. Coleman and the man who will administer the test." As Jim McCloskey protests, McFarlane again murmurs, "I'm sorry, those are my instructions," and, moving past McCloskey, walks out the door and disappears down the hall.

In the polygraph room Roger Coleman is directed to a chair, and when he is seated and secured a technician begins attaching electrodes to his arms and chest. If anyone in the room realizes what must be going on in Roger Coleman's mind, no one gives any sign of it.

Coleman begins shaking and sobbing uncontrollably. A man nods his head to the technician, who removes the electrodes. After a bit, Roger regains his composure. The man asks if he wants to go ahead or go back to Greensville. Roger say's he'll go ahead, so the electrodes are reattached and the polygraph test proceeds.

When it's over, the polygraph operator says he will have to spend some time analyzing his charts before he will have a result. Coleman is escorted back to the caravan of police cars, which have remained parked in front of the building. Someone has leaked news of the test and its location to the press, and as they exit the building a crowd of reporters and cameramen shout questions and flash their cameras. "Are you happy with the result?" someone shouts. "Yes," Coleman responds, and then he is shoved into the backseat of an already running police car. The other officers jump in beside him and the car roars off for the return to Greensville.

Not long after Kitty hears from Jim McCloskey about the events at Walter McFarlane's office, a deputy clerk from the Fourth Circuit Court of Appeals calls. The court has just entered an order denying Kitty's motions for stay of execution, for rehearing en banc and for remand to the district court. Now only the Supreme Court is left. The Supreme Court and maybe Doug Wilder.

It is sometime around noon when Phil Horton calls Kitty to come up to his office. McFarlane called while Phil was on the phone and left a message to call him back. They will make the call together. Kitty:

> So Phil made the call, and McFarlane came on the line, and we all said hello to each other, and then he just came right out and he said, "I'm really sorry. He failed. He was found to be deceptive on the key questions, and, um . . . I'm sorry."
>
> And then, I guess he was trying to make us feel better, he said we had done a good job, and how frustrated he had been with the attorney general, and he talked about the Mother Teresa phone call again and how he had never been so touched by anything. And then I said, "I think he's innocent." And I really do.

He said, "I know you do. I know you do, but this was the last thing we could do."

After we hung up I broke down. I . . . I started crying. And I was angry, and I said, "How could this possibly have happened?" You know, we did everything we could. And I thought—I made the wrong decision. Everything we did was all wrong. And I said, "I just . . . I don't know what to do. I don't know if I can handle this."

And Phil talked me out of it. He said: "You made the right decision. We both were against doing a polygraph from the start, and we knew there wasn't a very high chance of reliability, but we had no choice. It was the right thing to do under the circumstances." And he said something like, "I feel totally comfortable with going public with it and saying, you know, we had no choice." He brought me down. He just made me feel better. Because I was . . . I really thought I had made the wrong decision. But what can you do?

Kitty Behan returns to her office, and a few minutes later Roger calls. It's now several hours after the test, and Kitty assumes he knows the result, but within seconds she realizes he doesn't.

He picked up, and started talking, and I said, "What happened, Roger?" He must have thought I was just asking for a report, that I hadn't gotten the result yet, and that's when he started going into it, telling me what happened, and I could tell from his voice he didn't know. He sounded extremely happy. He told me something about he left at six, and they didn't give him his medications or anything to eat, and how they drove so fast, and then he had to wait two hours, and how he freaked out, but then he calmed down after a while, but then, you know, it went fine after a while, la dee, la dee, la dee, da. He thought he had passed. And I was just totally blown away.

I interrupted him in mid-sentence. I said, "Roger, you don't know what happened, do you?" And then I told him he failed. And he took it the way he took all bad news, which was just, you know, his voice went dead.

Before ending the conversation, Kitty reaches Jim and Earl Kane at their hotel and patches them into the phone call. Kane asks Roger to describe the test. There were some questions about other matters, Roger says, and then they asked him just three questions, the substance being "Did you murder Wanda McCoy?"; "Did you rape

Wanda McCoy?" and something like did he participate or was he present. Kane says asking ultimate questions like that is ridiculous. No one could "pass" a test on such questions, especially on the morning of his execution. They should have asked him a whole bunch of questions about the details of the crime—things only the killer would know, if possible, but if not (and Roger by now probably knew as much about the crime as any other human), then just a bunch of small questions about details mixed in with other matters. Even then, he says, getting a reliable result would be difficult given Roger's emotional distress. Kitty asks Kane if he will hold a press conference to explain what he said, and he agrees. No one expects Wilder to change his mind, but at least the public should be told what bullshit it was.

Next Kitty checks to see that her certiorari petition and brief have been filed, and learns that the brief is still being proofread. She breaks down again, filled with an irrational dread that the members of the Court will leave for the day and never receive the petition. She yells at the summer associates who volunteered to stay up all night to help and are still there doing the proofreading. She finished the brief at 6:00 A.M.—it's taking them longer to proofread it than it took her to write it. Forget the fucking proofreading. Just put it together and file it. After an embarrassed silence, Kitty apologizes and goes into her office. Phil Horton comes in and says he'll see to it the papers are filed, and do whatever else may be necessary. He'll stay at the office until the Supreme Court rules. She should go to Greensville to be with Roger.

Chapter 42

"At 11:00 P.M. on May 20, 1992"

The previous day Mark said that if it came to it, he would drive Kitty down to Greensville and stay with her. At the time the offer angered her and she made no response, but she knows Mark stayed home to support her if she needed him, and now she does need him. First she calls Roger. He had said before that if it looked like the execution was going forward, he didn't want anyone close to him to be there—he didn't want them to go through any more pain—but Kitty didn't really believe him. She says that she's coming, that she needs to be there to wait for the Supreme Court to rule, and he says okay, although they both know that isn't true. She says Mark might come, and asks if that's all right—Mark and Roger have never met, but Mark talked to Roger on the phone several times—and Roger says okay to that too.

When Kitty calls Mark, he already knows. It's already all over radio and television that Roger flunked the lie-detector test. Wilder has made some sort of statement about it. He'll pick her up at the law firm in a few minutes.

It's about one o'clock when Mark and Kitty begin their trip. There is little traffic leaving the city, and soon they're in the Virginia countryside. It is sunny and warm, but not yet hot. Still spring, with the trees and bushes fresh green and patches of mountain laurel blooming in the shade of a roadside woods. Mark drives and Kitty talks quietly, filling him in about the double cross on the location of the lie-detector test, and what Kane said, and how Roger didn't even know about it and thought he had passed. Sometimes she cries. After a bit they both fall silent, and an odd, almost surreal sense of peace surrounds Kitty. She is going to an execution, but for now it feels like a pleasant spring drive. Mark turns on the radio and finds an oldies station. At the half hour the music stops and an announcer says Governor Wilder has revealed that Roger Keith Coleman was given a lie-detector test this morning and failed. Coleman, he explains, is the Virginia convict whose scheduled execution tonight has attracted worldwide attention as a result of his claim of innocence. The announcer cuts to a tape of Wilder at his press conference. He is saying something to the effect that the lie-detector test shows Roger Coleman has been fooling with all of us. Kitty angrily shuts off the radio.

Without traffic, the trip to the little town where the penitentiary is located takes about two and a half hours. It is still warm and sunny when Kitty directs Mark onto the narrow country road that intersects the highway and leads to the long driveway into the prison. Kitty is surprised to see that a roadblock has been set up near the far end of the drive. When they stop, a man with a portable telephone asks their names and business, looks at their ID and phones the prison. After a few seconds he waves them in. Kitty has told him that Mark is one of Roger's lawyers, which in a way he is—he helped her with most of the pleadings and briefs she prepared over the past two years.

As Kitty and Mark enter the parking area of the prison, the sight that greets them is almost beyond their belief. A large portion of the parking lot has been cordoned off with ropes and sawhorses. The space behind the rope is crammed with mobile television trucks from every network, from several local and independent stations and from at least six foreign countries. The Fuji blimp is circling overhead. Scores of radio, TV and print reporters are milling around near the ropes. (According to the next day's paper, there were fourteen satellite trucks and fifty TV cameras in operation.) Just as Mark and Kitty are leaving their car, another car pulls up beside them and Jim McCloskey gets out. Jim and Kitty hug for a moment, and the three of them start for the prison entrance. Someone in the group of reporters recognizes them and a howl of questions rises from the crowd, now straining against the rope and thrusting microphones as far as they can reach. Kitty, Mark and Jim walk silently past them and into the building.

The death house at Greensville is a separate building, quite a distance from the administration building and main prison complex. After entering the administration building, Kitty, Mark and Jim are searched and led through a side door to a golf-cartlike tram that carries them to a gate in the separate fence surrounding the death house. After being escorted through the fence and into the building they are searched again, and then admitted into the corridor that runs in front of the four cells that have been constructed to serve as the last residence of the condemned.

At one end, the corridor turns away from the cells, forming the bottom leg of a backward L, and there sits a guard's table and chair. On the wall above is a clock, placed out of sight of the cells. High on the wall opposite the cells, a television set has been hung for the entertainment of any inmate occupying one of the cells. At the end of the corridor at the top of the backward L is the door to the death chamber.

Although there are four cells in the death house, only three of them are intended to be occupied as living quarters. The fourth cell, closest to the door to the death chamber, is used only to hold the inmate for the last hour or so of his life, after his head has been shaved and he is diapered and dressed in the costume of death.

On May 20, 1992, Roger Coleman is the only inmate of the death house. When Kitty, Mark and Jim are admitted to the corridor in front of the cells, Sharon has just left. Her last visit ended at 4:00 P.M. by decree of the warden, who earlier allowed her a second contact visit with Roger, but rejected Russ Ford's effort to persuade him that there was nothing to lose and perhaps much to be gained by letting her stay into the evening. Marie Deans left with Sharon. At Roger's request, Marie is taking Sharon home with her to wait out the night. Russ Ford has also left for a few minutes on another negotiating mission for Roger, this time with the captain of the death squad.

Roger is sitting alone in his chair in the third cell from the death-house door. To Kitty he looks very small, and very forlorn. And yet he greets them calmly and with warmth, smiling and grasping their hands through the bars of his cell.

Russ Ford recognized the change immediately when he arrived earlier that afternoon. The night before Roger had been distressed, agitated and exhausted. Now he is calm, and looks rested. He seems emotionally centered, with a sense of grace and well being. To Russ Ford the minister, Roger has received the spirit of God. To Russ Ford the student of dying, he has achieved the stage of acceptance, the last stage of the process that dying people achieve if the necessary work has been done along the way. A researcher at the Medical College of Virginia has written that the body actually releases certain healing endorphins, and Russ believes it is true, because he has been present when it has happened. When the endorphins "go off," he says, the effect is immediate. A kind of peaceful glow appears. Even the skin seems to relax and become more rounded in tone. Russ was not present when Roger Coleman achieved this transformation, but he sensed it as soon as he arrived, and as forlorn as Roger appears when Kitty first sees him, she soon senses it as well.

Jim and Kitty sit on the concrete floor immediately in front of Roger's cell. He brings his chair to the front of the cell and sits facing them as they talk quietly. From time to time, Mark joins the conversation, but for the most part he remains discreetly in the background. The guards are watching television and pretending nothing is happening. It is tuned so loud that on several occasions Jim or Kitty has to ask them to turn it down so they can talk.

At some point Kitty and Jim each talk to Roger alone, the other moving away. At those times the talk is personal. They are saying their good-byes, although no one uses the word. The rest of the time they talk together, about how stalwart Sharon has been, and how few of his science fiction books Roger has been able to read, and so on. They laugh about how much better Roger was than Tom Scott when they were both questioned on one of the television interview shows, and about a story Jim heard when he was in Grundy—a Coleman supporter supposedly happened on Scott as he sat in a barbershop having his hair dyed and began to yell at him, whereupon Scott supposedly got up and ran out of the shop with dye running down his neck and staining his shirt. Since Scott looks like he wears a bad toupee, they wonder if the story can be true. Surely you wouldn't go to a barbershop to have your toupee dyed. Maybe Scott's poor performance caused his toupee to turn gray, they laugh.

Russ Ford comes back and joins the conversation, and from time to time Sharon calls on the telephone and Roger goes to the back of his cell and lies on his bunk talking to her. Sometimes, he reports, she cries a little, but most of the time she is calm. She is certain something will happen to prevent the execution. No one comments.

A little before 6:00 P.M. the guards say it is time for Roger's last meal. Sometimes, according to Russ Ford, it is a significant experience, one of the landmarks in the process of moving toward death, a true last meal shared with friends—but Roger's last meal is not like that. He has seen a television ad in which a condemned man orders a Tombstone Pizza for his last meal, and partly because he thinks it would be a good joke to do what the ad suggests and partly because he really does love pizza, he has ordered it for his meal, along with Sprite and fudge-stick cookies. The meal, however, was delivered to the death house in mid-afternoon and has sat on the guards' desk ever since. The pizza is cold, with the cheese hard and yellow, and the Sprite is warm. The guards have not bothered to refrigerate it, or to heat the pizza before serving it.

Kitty is furious at their contemptuous treatment of Roger, and Russ feels it has spoiled any chance that the meal will have any significance, but everyone manages to choke down a slice of the pizza and a swallow of Sprite, except for Roger, who eats half a large pizza with relish, finishes his Sprite and eagerly attacks the cookies. While they are eating, the six o'clock news comes on, and in the middle of the story about Roger a clip of his father is shown. This man, who played almost no role in his life since Roger was four, says, "I just want my son to know I love him." Roger looks up but says nothing, his face impassive. To Kitty, his look says, *Who the fuck are you?*

After the national news, which also includes a segment on the case, *Wheel of Fortune* comes on. The television is facing Roger, and he looks up at it from time to time, but the others cannot see it without turning around. At some point during the show, as he, Kitty and Jim are talking, Roger points up at the set, indicating that they should look. The program is in progress, and the three contestants appear to be about halfway to solving a three-word puzzle. The middle word is *of,* and at first Kitty does not see what the rest spells out and wonders why Roger has called it to her attention. Then, as another letter is called out and shown on the screen, she understands—and exclaims something, probably "Shit." Jim sees it at the same time. Hearing Kitty and seeing that she and Jim are looking at the television screen, the others look up as well, just as one of the contestants offers to solve the puzzle and does so. The phrase is *miscarriage of justice*.

Now a guard tells Roger that in another twenty minutes or so it will be time for his head to be shaved. Kitty and the others will have to leave the cell block while he is taken across the corridor to a shower room for the process. It is the event that guards used to say was the final act in taking away the prisoner's heart, before Russ Ford began preparing his parishioners for each step in the process, and especially steeling them for the shaving ritual, teaching them how to survive it with their humanity and spirit intact.

Russ and Roger have worked well together. Kitty is growing more and more tight, and the talk of the shaving ritual unnerves her, but Roger makes light of it. To Kitty, his whole attitude seems to be "I can handle this, and I'm going to keep my guests happy." It's almost like he's entertaining them, trying to prevent them from getting morbid.

While Kitty and the others are outside, they talk among themselves about why they have not heard from the Supreme Court. Kitty expected to hear at about the time the Court would normally close for the day. Now it is well past that, and no word. She calls Phil at the office, and he confirms he has heard nothing. To be safe, he will call the Court, where the death-penalty clerk remains on duty. He calls back. The clerk says there has been no decision. For the first time since morning, Kitty entertains a glimmer of hope. There must be a fight going on. Actually, it must be a pretty good fight, a close fight, otherwise the decision would have been reached hours ago. Kitty decides not to share that thought with anyone, especially Roger. Now is not the time to raise false hopes. Still, she begins to worry again about what will happen if, like the *Herrera* case, they receive the four votes needed for certiorari, but not the fifth vote needed for a stay of execution. She calls Phil and suggests he track down Judge Persin so they can reach him by telephone in case that situation develops.

When Kitty and the others are allowed back into the corridor outside the death cells, Roger has been moved from the middle cell to the cell nearest the death chamber. All his possessions have been removed from the cell in which he lived for the past two weeks, and stacked together. The cell he now occupies is completely bare, except for a chair, a bare bunk and a toilet. Roger's head has been shaved down to the skin, and apparently whoever did it nicked him in several places, which are covered with little puffs of cotton or tissue. He is dressed in slippers and loose-fitting pants and shirt, fastened with Velcro. Plastic or metal will melt, and remain too hot to touch for too long.

By regulation, Roger's glasses and dental plate, apparently considered potential instruments of suicide, have been taken away—God forbid he should cheat the executioner—but Russ has succeeded in the negotiation Roger asked him to conduct with the head of the execution squad. Russ will be permitted to take the glasses and plate into the death chamber, and the captain of the death squad will give them to Roger when the time comes to read his last statement. That way he can see to read, and his words will be understandable. Without his glasses he can see almost nothing, and without the plate he has a bad lisp.

Sitting in his chair with his shaved head and robes, Roger looks to Jim like a little Buddha.

As the time approaches nine o'clock, with still no word from the Court, a guard finally motions to Kitty that she has a telephone call at the guards' station. Her arrangement with the death-penalty clerk is to contact her at the prison when a decision is reached. This is surely the call.

But it's not. It's Bruce Kovacs, Kitty's DNA expert. How he has gotten through to Kitty in the death house is difficult to explain, but he has, with an important message. The night before, Kovacs had dinner with a close friend of New York governor and death-penalty opponent Mario Cuomo. He told the friend about his involvement in the Coleman case and what he considered to be the gross misuse of the DNA evidence by the state. When he was done, the man insisted they call Governor Cuomo, who might in turn be able to talk to Governor Wilder. Apparently Cuomo had done so, because a few minutes earlier Kovacs had received a call from a political operative in Wilder's office, saying that the governor had asked that he call and inquire about Kovacs's view of the DNA evidence. Kovacs proceeded to explain why he questioned the legitimacy of Blake's conclusion that two of the three alleles he had detected in the sperm sample from Wanda McCoy could be paired to match Roger Coleman and only about 2 percent of the population. The National Academy of Science report, he said, supported his proposition that pairing alleles in a mixed sample is unreliable. When he was done, Kovacs said, the man expressed dismay, and asked Kovacs to explain it again, which he did, several times. Each time, the man again expressed dismay, and finally said, "Why didn't we know about this? Why is the governor just learning about it now?"

Bruce Kovacs said he didn't know. He had provided an affidavit for Coleman's lawyers which said the same thing he had just said, and he had seen and indeed helped draft a separate document explaining it that was submitted to the governor through Walter McFarlane. Either McFarlane had failed to pass it along, or the governor somehow missed it or failed to understand it. Finally, Kovacs reports, the man thanked him and asked where he would be the rest of the evening in case he needed to reach him again. Kovacs says he assured the man he would remain available throughout the evening.

"Did he say he would call back?" "No, but he implied he might." "What do you think it means?" Kovacs says he doesn't know. Now, Kitty thinks, there are two chances. In addition to an apparent fight in the Court, the governor must be reconsidering clemency, or else why would he have the man call Kovacs? She tells Roger about the call, but not about her reaction. Roger barely reacts at all. He seems unconcerned.

As eleven o'clock grows closer, with no call from the Court and no further call from Kovacs or the governor's office, the talk again grows more personal. Suddenly Roger stops talking and, looking as though something has just occurred to him, walks over to his bunk and begins writing on a piece of paper. When he is done, he walks back to the front of his cell and passes the paper through the bars. Jim and Kitty look at it. It is Roger's last words. He asks that one of them make a copy to read to the press when they leave so that they get it right. Jim copies the words into his notebook and hands the paper back through the bars to Roger, then turns away and walks down the corridor and back, composing himself.

Roger Coleman and Kitty talk about what they mean to each other.

> He was almost euphoric, like he was in another world. He was talking about how much his relationships with Sharon and Marie and me had made him realize how important human relationships are, and what it means to be loved. He had come into prison really not having any deep relationships—he had relationships that were

important to him, but now he felt they had been kind of casual, and he felt like he had matured, and understood more about how to care for someone and love them. And he said to me that it had all been worth it—that as much as he hated prison, being sent to prison was worth it, because he had been able to meet all these people, like me and Sharon and Marie, and Robert White and Jim and Russ, kinds of people he would never have met if he had just stayed in Grundy and been a coal miner all his life, which is probably what would have happened.

And then we also talked about what would happen afterwards— he hoped that his case would have some impact on the death penalty. He said that even when he came into prison he had been in favor of the death penalty, but now of course he saw how wrong it was, and he thought maybe he had done some good, had some impact. He said something like, "I bet these people never expected this poor kid from Grundy to be able to go on national television programs and defend himself." He thought he had done a good job, and of course he had, he had done a tremendous job, and I told him so, and that he'd made everybody who cared about him very proud of him. And I told him that it might take a while for it to be recognized, but that I thought his case, and the number of people who believed in his innocence, would have a tremendous impact. And that someday the fact that he was innocent would be proven, and that would have even more impact.

And then I was telling him how important he had become to me, how important his friendship was, and how proud I was to represent him. And he was telling me how much he appreciated the work I had done, how much he valued what I had done, what a good job, and that he was afraid I would think I had failed, but I hadn't, I had done my best and done everything possible.

And then I guess I just asked him if there was anything else I could do. And I told him that I loved him, and I would miss him. And then I just held his hand, through the bars, and we didn't talk anymore, except he did say, just once, "I'm scared."

And then the guard came up to me and said, "You've got to go." And I said, "I'm not going." I hadn't heard from the Court yet, and the call was supposed to come to me, and I told him I needed to stay here so I could consult with my client when it came.

But the guard said, "No, you have to go. You have to go!" And

Russ was looking at me, like, "Do you want to fight this or not?" And I decided I was about to cause a scene, and that was not going to be the right thing for Roger. And Russ was going to be there, so I just said, "Roger, I have to go." And I let go of his hand and stood up and said good-bye, and we just walked out the door.

As Kitty rides back to the administration building on the tram, she worries that the call may come in or something else important may happen while she is unavailable. The tram ride seems to last forever, but when they get back to the administration building someone says no call has come, so Kitty sits down in the entrance hall to wait. She realizes it is already past eleven. Would they go ahead and kill him without waiting for the Court to act? Without a stay, there is nothing legal to prevent it. She is frantic. No one tells her that the Court has in fact ordered a fifteen-minute stay to collect votes from several of the justices who are attending a dinner party somewhere. It is apparently an oversight, not a deliberate omission.

Finally, an assistant warden appears at a door leading into the entrance hall. There is a call for her. He leads her down a long corridor to a large room and gestures to a telephone, off its cradle, sitting on a desk.

The room is full of people. They are state people, here for the execution. As she approaches the room she hears them talking and laughing. It sounds like a cocktail party. But as she enters everyone falls silent. Everyone watches as she crosses the room:

> The phone was sitting on the desk. They were all watching the phone and watching me, and I picked up the phone and it was Chris, the Supreme Court clerk for death-penalty cases. Chris is really a nice guy. So he said to me, he just said, "It was denied." I said, "What was denied?" and he said, "Everything." I asked if there were any dissents, and he said, "Blackmun." Then he said he hadn't called the attorney general's office yet, he was calling them next, so I knew I was the first person to hear.
>
> I looked up, and everyone was just standing still, watching me, and suddenly I felt like I was in the middle of a bad story—"The Lottery," where they stone somebody. Everyone was standing around me in a circle, and it seemed like they were just drooling, licking their chops, because I was the person who had messed things up

for them, made them wait, and they wanted this thing to get over, and they were looking at me, and I said, "It was denied." And then I put the phone down and walked out. As soon as I got out the door I could hear them laughing and talking again.

So I knew he was going to be executed then, and I walked back to the waiting room. I didn't know what I was going to do. I just felt sick.

When Mark, Jim and Kitty left, the door to the outside world closing with its solid, uncompromising clunk, Roger Coleman knew he would hear that sound only once more in his life. When it opened again it would be to admit the warden and the members of the death squad who would escort him to the execution chamber.

Roger turned away from Russ Ford for a moment, and when he turned back there were tears in his eyes. Russ knew they were not for what was ahead, but for the loss of those Roger would never see again. For Sharon, whom he loved; and for Jim, who believed in him and discovered so much, and yet somehow not enough; and for Kitty, who had fought for him like a tiger, fought longer and harder than he thought anyone could fight, fought even at the end, when they said she had to leave and there was really nothing left to fight for, and then had the wisdom to stop fighting rather than destroy the peace that had settled around Roger.

Roger had seen the tears streaming down Kitty's face as she left, tears she held back until she turned away and thought he could no longer see her face, and he had seen her shoulders heave, but if she sobbed it was not until the door closed and blocked the sound. "Kitty will be all right," Roger said, tears now streaking his own face. "Yeah," said Russ Ford, "she's tough, she'll be fine."

Roger Coleman was calm, his tears dried, and he and Russ continued to talk quietly. Out of Roger's sight a guard signaled to Russ every several minutes, indicating how much time remained, and Russ Ford in turn told Roger. "We've got about fifteen minutes," he said, and then, "About ten minutes more." Russ could not see the clock, but he knew it was already past eleven. For some reason there was a delay, but the guard at the table said nothing, and Russ decided to say nothing unless Roger asked. There was still no word from the Supreme Court, and Russ assumed that the Court was the source of the delay, but that the authorities were still expecting a ruling at any minute. In the unlikely event the Court granted a stay beyond midnight, the execution would have to be postponed and they would surely be told at once.

"After I read my statement, they'll put on the death mask. What does it smell like?" Roger asked, with a tone of real curiosity. Russ Ford laughed. "I have no idea. You're the first person who ever asked me that." "It must have an odor," Roger mused. "I hear they've used the same mask for two hundred executions." He began to name some of the men he knew who had died wearing the mask, continuing to muse about its odor. "I guess it's like what you said about pain," Russ responded. "No one ever came back to tell me."

They were quiet for a moment, and Roger's face and voice turned deeply serious. "Are you sure I'll be able to see the witnesses," he asked again. "I'm sure," Russ said. "As you walk into the room, you'll see them through the window to your left." "What about when I'm sitting in the chair. Can I see them then?" "Sure, they're right in front of you. Why?" Roger Coleman looked straight at Russ Ford, and spoke very slowly: "I want to look at them when I read my last words. I want to look them in the eye so they will have to look me in the eye. I want them to see what an innocent man looks like when he dies." "You'll see them, and they'll see you," Russ said softly.

Now Roger closed his eyes, and again began to cry silently. His eyes opened, and he brushed away the tears with an angry motion. "I don't want to be like this. I don't want them to see me crying. They'll think I'm afraid." "You're not afraid," Russ said. "Those tears aren't for you. They're for the people you love, and the people who love you." "I know, but the people watching won't know that. They'll think I'm afraid. I don't want to be like this."

Roger Coleman appeared calm. There was no quiver in his voice, no shaking in his hands or shoulders, no weakness in his legs—but the unwanted tears continued to run down his cheeks. "I don't want to go out there like this, but I keep thinking of Sharon, and I can't stop." He closed his eyes again.

Russ Ford remembered a dream Roger had told him a few days earlier, a dream in which he and Sharon were walking in a forest together, through a soft rain. "You're walking in the rain with Sharon," Russ said.

His eyes still closed, Roger Coleman smiled. He wiped his eyes again, and the tears had stopped. "You can feel the warmth of her body," Russ said. Eyes closed, Roger stood silently and continued to smile. "You know," he said, opening his eyes and looking at Russ Ford for a moment, "nobody's going to believe this—but I want you to tell them. Tell them I spent my last minutes walking in the rain with Sharon." Roger Coleman closed his eyes again.

The guard signaled. "The warden's coming now," Russ said, and they could hear the outside door open. Warden Ellis Wright entered the death house, followed by the captain of the death squad and his five assistants. Marching straight to Roger Coleman's cell, the warden stopped and began to read the death warrant, as the law required. He was not a good reader.

Roger Coleman opened his eyes and stood motionless, staring at the warden. Russ reached his left hand through the bars into the cell and took Roger's hand in his, and then, fearing Roger might think it would seem like a sign of weakness, he let go, but Roger reached back to him, and the two men stood hand in hand as the warden continued to read.

When Warden Wright finished, the captain moved forward and unlocked the cell. The heavy door swung open and Roger stepped out. Russ reached out to him, and the two men embraced for a long moment. Eight steps away, a guard opened the door to the death chamber, and the warden moved toward it, followed by two members of the death squad. Russ nodded his head to Roger, and the two of them fell into the line. The captain and three more death squad guards moved in behind them.

Roger Coleman's eyes were half closed, and he was smiling again. "You can taste her breath," Russ Ford said, and Roger's smile broadened as they began to walk. "You're embracing her fragrance."

With Russ Ford on one side and Sharon Paul on the other, Roger Coleman walked through a gentle rain into the death chamber and sat down in the dark oak electric chair.

As soon as Roger sat down, heavy black leather belts were strapped around his chest, wrists and ankles, and across his lap. A thick ground wire was attached to one ankle, and a metal cap lined with a spongy material was placed over his head. The sponge was wet with brine, to ensure better conduction. Since the day Russ Ford was almost electrocuted two years earlier, the hookup of the wire that would deliver eighteen hundred volts of electricity through the cap and into Roger Coleman's body would wait until the last minute, after Russ had moved away. Thus restrained, the only parts of his body Roger could move were his hands, his mouth and his eyes.

Holding a telephone connected directly to the governor and the attorney general in Richmond, the director of the Department of Corrections nodded to the warden to proceed to the next step. The warden turned and addressed Roger Coleman. "Roger Keith Coleman, do you have any last words?" As the warden spoke, the captain of the death squad stepped between Coleman and the window where the witnesses watched, blocking their view. He carefully placed Coleman's glasses on his head, slipped the dental plate into his mouth and stepped aside.

"Yes, I do," Roger said in a clear voice. Russ Ford held up the paper on which Roger Coleman had written his last words an hour earlier. He held it between Roger and the witnesses, at a level that permitted Coleman to move his eyes between the paper and the witness window. Roger sat for a moment, looking at the witnesses, and then began to read. After each sentence he looked up, his eyes meeting the witnesses, and then resumed speaking:

> An innocent man is going to be murdered tonight.
> When my innocence is proven, I hope Americans will realize the injustice of the death penalty as all other civilized countries have.
>
> My last words are for the woman I love. Love is eternal. My love for you will last forever. I love you, Sharon.

When Coleman finished, Russ Ford leaned over and kissed him on the head. "God bless," he said. "God bless you, Russ," Roger responded. Ford turned around, took a step or two away from the electric chair and turned back. He sensed that something was wrong. Usually, the instant the condemned man completes his last words the death squad moves quickly, strapping the death mask around his face, attaching the wire to the metal cap and stepping back from the chair. If all goes smoothly, within seconds the necessary signals are given and the electrocution begins. But when Russ Ford turned around, there was no movement in the room.

Roger Coleman was still staring at the witnesses, eye-to-eye, and most of them were staring back. To Russ Ford, it seemed like fifteen seconds or more before anyone moved.

"I don't know for certain whether Roger Coleman was innocent or guilty," Russ Ford says today, "but I know for certain that Roger Coleman believed he was innocent as he sat in the electric chair that night, waiting to die. And the people in that chamber, and the witnesses who were looking back at him, saw how an innocent man dies."

Two members of the death squad strapped the death mask over Roger Coleman's face while a third attached the cap on his head to the wire that would carry the massive jolt of electric current into him, boiling his blood, fusing his joints and cooking his body from the inside out. On one telephone, an assistant warden watched and listened, dictating everything into the phone, which carried it to a recorder. On the other phone, the director of the Department of Corrections spoke to the governor: "We're ready." "Go ahead," said Governor Wilder. The director nodded to Warden Wright: "Proceed."

Russ Ford leaned toward Roger Coleman for the last time. "Go with the flow," he said quietly. Coleman moved his right hand in acknowledgment as Ford turned away and walked toward the door. Russ Ford no longer watches executions.

Across the death chamber the warden moved to a box attached to the wall and turned a key, lighting a green light on the wall above. Behind a one-way window on the other side, the executioner saw the light go on, and threw a switch. Roger Coleman's body lurched forward against the restraining belts as the roar of the electric current filled the room. After a pause, the process was repeated, and a faint odor of burning flesh rose from the now still figure slumped in the chair.

When the noise stopped one of the guards started a time clock to mark off the five minutes it would take for the body to cool off enough to touch. A doctor entered the chamber, and when the clock showed that the time was up, another guard, using some kind of pad to protect his hand against burning, pulled back the tunic from Roger Coleman's chest. The doctor moved forward, placed a stethoscope to the bare flesh and listened. After a moment he removed the stethoscope and stepped back. Looking at the warden, he announced in an official voice: "This man has expired."

And so he had. May God have mercy on our souls.

Chapter 43

A Circle of Light

When Kitty got back to the waiting room after talking to the clerk, Jim called Roger Lee Coleman and told him about the Supreme Court decision. Then a man entered the waiting room through the door leading to the death-house tram. As he walked across the room toward the administrative offices he said, as though talking to himself, "It's over."

Kitty, Jim and Mark gathered their things and walked out the door of the prison and into the night. Television crews flooded the scene with light and hundreds of flashbulbs began popping like a good batch of popcorn. Kitty and Jim moved up to a stand where a microphone had been set up facing the press area and Jim read Roger's last words. Kitty said something she can't remember exactly, but it had to do with Roger being innocent and how someday, when his innocence was proved, people would understand how outrageous the decisions were that had prevented him from getting a hearing, and the press people began shouting asinine questions like, "How do you feel right now?" and after a minute they fled to their cars.

As Kitty and Jim moved away, Wayne Brown, the prison operations officer, came out the door and up to the microphone to make the official announcement of the execution. The lights and cameras reacted again as he spoke.

Mark had agreed to drive his car back to Richmond alone so that Kitty could ride with Jim. As the two cars headed across the parking lot toward the long exit road, an ambulance came screeching around the corner of the prison buildings going fast, and pulled onto the exit road ahead of them. They followed it down the road.

I just thought, "There goes Roger. There goes my case." It was just weird to think of him in the back there, all burned up. There's this person in this ambulance, dead. He's been burned up intentionally by the state because of a series of decisions and words on paper that are so meaningless—that have nothing to do with justice but very much to do with expediting this whole process. And it was like, "Well, there's nothing more for me to do." He was going, and we were following, bringing up the rear.

It was completely dark and silent once you got away from the glare of the cameras and the ugly questions, and it was a funeral procession—the hearse and the mourners. And then, as we drove down this absolutely dark road, we came to this circle of light. It was a group of people standing in a circle holding candles. They were death-penalty opponents, protesting the execution. It looked like some kind of ancient ritual. I could imagine them starting to dance in a circle. It was very eerie and seemed full of symbolic meaning. I'm not a religious person, but it was very religious and moving to me.

Then we drove on to Richmond, and I was just in complete pain. When we got to the hotel Jim and Mark wanted to go to the bar and get a drink. They wanted to talk about what happened, that was their way of dealing with it, and I stayed with them for a few minutes, but I couldn't stand it, and I just left and went up to bed and went to sleep. I cried some, but not too much, until the next morning, and then all of a sudden it just came out. The flood gates opened and I cried and cried and cried, and then fell sound asleep for I don't know how long, and then Mark and I drove back to Washington.

At Marie Deans's house, after her last phone conversation with Roger, Sharon lay on the sofa, alternately crying and sleeping and telling Marie she was sure something would happen to prevent the execution. Even after it was over she thought in the back of her mind that he really wasn't dead. It was some kind of a trick, she thought, so they could say he was dead and satisfy the people who wanted him executed, and then let him out and give him a new identity or something. It was several days before she really, completely believed he was dead.

——

Chapter 44

Dave's Branch, May 23

On Saturday, May 23, a sizable group of residents of Grundy and the surrounding area gathered in the shade of a tent erected in the space between Roger Lee Coleman's trailer and the white frame house where Roger Keith Coleman was raised and which he had inherited from his grandmother after her death. They were joined by Sharon Paul, Kitty Behan and Russ Ford.

After a while, Russ Ford called the group together and delivered a short prayer. Then Kitty read a eulogy for Roger that had been written by Jim McCloskey, and added some words of her own.

The day before, Roger Lee had worked most of the day clearing a path through the underbrush and up the mountainside to an outcropping of rock that forms an overlook of the valley below. When the eulogies were completed, Roger Lee stepped forward and said that when Roger was a boy he had loved nothing more than roaming the hills and valleys surrounding them, and that his favorite place of all was the outcropping of rock above them, where he would often sit for hours looking out over the valley and the hills beyond. He said that Roger had asked that his ashes be given to Sharon, and that she take them to that place and scatter them to the wind while his favorite music played.

Solemnly, Roger Lee picked up the little container of ashes and handed it to Sharon, and then turned on a portable cassette player sitting on a table under the tent. As Sharon took the box and began walking up the path, the sound of a lone bagpipe playing "Amazing Grace" filled the tent and followed her up the mountain. When Sharon reached the top, she stood for a minute, listening to the music and looking out over the valley and the ranks of misty blue-green mountains beyond. Then she opened the container, and, taking out a handful of ashes, kissed her hand and tossed the ashes into the wind, which swept them away into the valley. She stopped a minute, and then, gathering herself, repeated the gesture until the box was empty. Sharon turned and walked back down the path to the tent, where she was hugged and kissed by Kitty and Russ and Roger Lee and some people she didn't know, including Roger's mother.

Everyone stood around under the tent for a while, talking quietly and drinking iced tea or soft drinks, and then slowly began drifting off. Finally, Sharon, Kitty and Russ said their good-byes, walked down the steep drive to where their rented car was parked by the side of the road and began the drive to the airport in Roanoke.

Chapter 45

Afterword

Brad McCoy and his brother Mike made the long trip to Greensville for Roger Coleman's execution. It seemed out of character for the mild, soft-spoken man to want to witness the execution, but he did. When prison officials told him it was not permitted, that the witnesses were drawn from a waiting list, and that in any event the victim's family was excluded, he came anyway, to stand outside and wait for the announcement of Coleman's death. He told reporters he had waited eleven years for justice for Wanda, and he wanted to be there.

No one from the Thompson family went to the execution, but according to Wanda's sister Peggy, their views were not much different from Brad's. As far as they were concerned, what was done to Roger was up to the courts. The important judgment would be passed by his Maker. But they thought the courts did the right thing—it just shouldn't have taken so long.

As certain as Brad McCoy, the Thompsons and the prosecutors were that Roger Coleman was guilty and that the state had done the right thing in executing him, Kitty Behan, Jim McCloskey and Roger's close friends and family remained certain that he was innocent, and that a terrible miscarriage of justice had occurred. They had told Roger they would continue to try to prove his innocence, and they intended to keep that promise, although they knew it would be even more difficult than before, now that Roger was dead. Not only would the media and the public quickly lose interest, making it harder to uncover new witnesses; there was no longer any forum in which conflicting evidence could be tested, no longer any judge or governor who could order the state to produce documents or compel the attendance of witnesses.

Any lingering doubt about how much harder the task had become was resolved when Kitty wrote to Walter McFarlane in the governor's office and asked for a copy of the results of Roger's polygraph test and any documents the governor had received in opposition to clemency.

McFarlane's reply was one sentence: "The Roger Coleman case is over and the further involvement of this office is concluded."

Compensating for McFarlane's abrupt dismissal was a letter Kitty received at about the same time from Justice Blackmun. Dissenting from the Supreme Court's denial of a stay of execution, Blackmun had sharply criticized the Court for allowing Coleman to be executed without a hearing on his serious claim of innocence. Kitty had written Justice Blackmun expressing her appreciation, and he responded with a gracious note praising her dedication and acknowledging the emotional toll exacted from lawyers who volunteer to represent the condemned, especially when there is reason to believe the client is innocent.

In July, Jim McCloskey returned to Grundy. He met and talked to Pat Daniels and concluded that her story of what Helen Ramey had told her about the night of the murder seemed credible. McCloskey also wanted to talk to a man who had called Roger Lee Coleman on the night of the execution and said he had heard Donnie Ramey confess to the crime, but the man would not talk to him. McCloskey did locate Jerry Vanover, Debbie Vanover's husband. Back in May he had offered to talk to Donnie Ramey about the murder while secretly tape recording the conversation. At the time, however, Vanover was confined to a court-ordered drug-rehabilitation program. Now he was out, and agreed to proceed with the plan. McCloskey gave him a miniature tape recorder. He never heard from Jerry Vanover again. The rumor came back that Vanover had pawned the tape recorder.

Two weeks later, on August 7, 1992, Donnie Ramey sued Kitty Behan, Marie Deans and Arnold & Porter for libel. The charge was based on press releases issued in the period before Coleman was executed. The releases had flatly stated that Donnie Ramey had killed Wanda McCoy. Jim McCloskey was spared, probably because, other than affidavits filed in court, his name did not appear on documents making that accusation. Besides, he was not a deep pocket.

The inclusion of Marie Deans at first puzzled everyone. Marie's name was on only a few documents that arguably accused Ramey of the murder, and she was certainly not a deep pocket. Then someone pointed out that by including Marie, a resident of Virginia, the plaintiffs avoided the chance that the case could be removed to a federal court. With Marie in the case, there was no "diversity of citizenship," so the case would remain in state court. The plaintiff's lawyers understandably wanted it heard in the circuit court of Buchanan County.

Typically, assertions that someone other than the accused is the "real" killer are made only in court filings, which are privileged and don't provide the basis for a libel claim. With the press releases, Arnold & Porter had gone further. Arguably, the releases were summaries of court documents, which should also be treated as privileged, but some went beyond the court documents, and the defendants' effort to have the case dismissed on the basis that the releases were privileged as a matter of law was rejected by the trial judge. The defendants also sought to transfer the case from Buchanan County. That motion was denied as well, although a judge from outside the region was appointed to hear the case.

Faced with the prospect of a trial before a jury in Grundy, Arnold & Porter had a serious problem. Ramey was represented by Roberts "Rabbit" Moore, a top trial lawyer and senior partner in a Roanoke law firm that was considered one of the best in southwest Virginia. Arnold & Porter hired William Poff, an equally well-regarded lawyer in the other major Roanoke firm. Marie Deans did not have the financial resources to hire a prominent lawyer, but her long years of working on Virginia death-penalty cases had made her many friends, and one of them agreed to represent her free of charge. He was David Kendall, who would later be chosen by President Clinton as his personal attorney in the Whitewater investigation.

If Donnie Ramey's lawsuit was an unhappy turn of events for Arnold & Porter, it was received with mixed emotions by those interested in proving Roger Coleman's innocence. On the one hand, that a

```````````

man like Donnie Ramey would file such a suit seemed outrageous to those who believed he was responsible for Wanda McCoy's murder. On the other hand, by filing the case, Ramey had supplied two of the things that were most needed if there was to be any chance of proving Coleman's innocence—a legal forum in which that question was at least indirectly an issue, and the investigative resources to pursue it.

In the meantime, my own decision to write a book about the case assured that at least one additional person had a continuing interest in any new information about the murder of Wanda McCoy.

While the libel case interrupted my access to information from Kitty Behan and the other lawyers and paralegals at Arnold & Porter, I was able to follow most of the investigation conducted by the parties to the libel case through court filings and independent sources I developed in the Grundy area.

Over the next several years old witnesses were reinterviewed, new witnesses discovered and new documents produced. Donnie Ramey and members of his family were required to appear and testify under oath at depositions in the libel case. And ultimately the Buchanan County Commonwealth's Attorney gave me access to his file on the McCoy murder after it had been subpoenaed and examined by Arnold & Porter's lawyers.

For a long time it appeared that Ramey's libel case would be tried, and while the results of such a trial would not resolve Coleman's guilt or innocence, at least Donnie Ramey would be required to testify, subject to cross-examination, as in all probability would the women who had accused him of attacking them and the people who had allegedly heard him confess involvement in the murder. Then, early in 1994, the case was settled. The parties agreed not to disclose the terms, but they were rumored to involve payment to Ramey of a sum that was approximately what Arnold & Porter and their attorneys thought it would cost in attorney's fees and expenses to try the case to a verdict. If so, it was a significant sum.

Kitty Behan and Marie Deans refused to participate in the settlement, and were said to be furious at the prospect of Ramey receiving any money at all, but for Arnold & Porter the risk was too great to stand on principle. Ramey had nothing to gain by continuing the case against the other defendants, so his lawyers voluntarily dismissed the case against Kitty and Marie with prejudice.
```````````

While termination of the libel case again closed the door on a legal forum in which at least some of the questions surrounding the McCoy murder might have been resolved, that case and my own investigation led to new information about several of those questions.

The issue that was most directly involved in the libel case, of course, was the claim that Donnie Ramey had been involved in the murder. That claim, or at least any chance of proving it, had been dealt a terrible blow by the death of Teresa Horn and by the evidence that Donnie Ramey had type A blood.

The effort to find proof that Ramey was involved in the murder continued during preparation for defense of the libel case, but without significant success. At one point, Harold Williamson, the friend of the Rameys whom Jim McCloskey had located only days before the execution, told a new story in which he claimed that Donnie had actually confessed the crime to him and even revealed how he had gained entrance to Wanda McCoy's house—but within a few days Williamson retracted the story and blamed everything he had said about the case on his own illness and pressure from Jim McCloskey. The tape recording of McCloskey's visits with Williamson showed that his claim that McCloskey had pressured him was not true, but, as indicated above, in light of Williamson's erratic behavior, not much credence could be given to any of his statements about the Rameys.

Despite the efforts of investigators hired by Arnold & Porter's lawyers, no other witness was located who claimed direct knowledge that Ramey was involved in the crime, or had admitted involvement.

In his deposition in the libel case, Donnie again denied any involvement in the murder, as did his brother Michael. Donnie also repeated his denial that he ever told Teresa Horn he had been involved in the murder. He admitted knowing all the women who said he had attacked them, and in some instances admitted being with them on the occasions they mentioned, but insisted he was innocent of any sexual assault.

He said Teresa Horn had stripped off her own clothes before he carried her into a bedroom, and he decided himself not to have sex with her. He was just joking around with Linda Mullins at the airstrip. All he did was "squeeze her titty." When she complained about it, he took her back to Grundy. He denied having threatened her with a knife.

He did put "two fingers up in" Jamie Sword Ross, but she had removed her tampon herself and invited him to do so to prove that her husband "had a dick on him exactly fourteen inches long." He denied doing anything at all to Deborah Vanover or the woman who had claimed she had been attacked but declined to give an affidavit. He characterized all the women as liars, but was not asked and did not explain why five separate women would have lied about his conduct.*

While the search for new witnesses was unsuccessful, the release of the Commonwealth Attorney's file provided new information to keep the question of Ramey's involvement in the murder alive. One document in the file was the letter Coleman wrote to Wanda's sister Peggy shortly before his trial, which showed that even then there had been rumors that Trouble Ramey was involved.

One other document in the Commonwealth Attorney's file mentioned the Rameys—and when it came to light, Roger Coleman's supporters were furious that it had not been revealed before his execution. The document was Jack Davidson's handwritten notes of his interview of Brad McCoy the night Wanda was murdered. For the most part the information in the notes were reflected in the typewritten interview report that Davidson prepared several days later and which was included in the packet of material McCloskey obtained on his first trip to Grundy. In the final paragraph of his notes, however, Jack Davidson had written down something Brad McCoy told him which he did not include in his typed report. The notation read: "Had problems w/Ramey."

Prior to Coleman's execution, no one on his defense team knew that Brad McCoy himself had mentioned Ramey on the night of the murder. When I obtained a copy of the notes from the Commonwealth Attorney's file and showed them to Davidson, he said he could not recall what "Had problems w/Ramey" meant, or why it had been left out of his typed report. He did complain bitterly that I should never have been given access to his handwritten notes.

Several days later, when I asked Brad McCoy about it, he seemed ready for the question. He first said Davidson must have asked him if he had any problem with Trouble Ramey. When I pointed out that the

---

* The depositions of the Rameys taken in the libel case were under oath, but the case was settled before they were signed and filed. Thus the deponent could have still corrected his answers if he thought they were wrong or erroneously reported.

note seemed to refer to something *he* had said about having problems *with* Ramey (there was, of course, no indication of *which* Ramey), Brad retreated and said he wasn't sure but it was probably just that the Rameys sometimes stood down by his house and shouted up the hill to their house. Nothing serious. It was the first and only time I thought Brad was being less than candid.

Of course, the revelation that Brad McCoy himself had mentioned having problems with Ramey when he was first questioned about the murder does not mean that any of the Rameys were involved in Wanda McCoy's murder. It does suggest, however, that the Ramey family is likely to have received more attention from the police at the time of the murder than the state wanted to disclose, either when they charged Roger Coleman with the crime or later, when Kitty Behan and Jim McCloskey zeroed in on Donnie Ramey as a result of Teresa Horn's accusations. And that in turn may explain one of the strangest mysteries in the case—the fact that the reports of the police interviews with the Rameys are apparently missing.

The prosecutor's file is full of typed reports and handwritten interview notes with the other McCoy neighbors whom the police interviewed, as well as other potential witnesses who were contacted during the investigation—but not the Rameys. This is so even though the Rameys were Wanda McCoy's closest neighbors, even though the Rameys say they were interviewed and even though the state filed affidavits claiming that such interviews were conducted and indicating that reports summarizing those interviews had later been reviewed both at the time of Coleman's trial and in 1991.

Not only is there no report of the Ramey interviews in the Commonwealth Attorney's file; despite repeated requests of Jack Davidson, Randy Jackson, Tom Scott, Mickey McGlothlin and two former Grundy policemen who participated in the interviews, no one admits to having such reports, or to knowing where they are. Even an effort by Judge Persin to assist the author in obtaining them failed. Of all the witness-interview notes and reports, these are the ones that were most important in the months before Roger Coleman's execution, given his lawyers' emphasis on the claim that Donnie was the real killer.

In the end, it must be said that even if it is true that on one or more occasions Donnie Ramey did say he was involved in Wanda McCoy's murder, it does not necessarily prove he was in fact involved.

According to Harold Smith, when Ramey suggested he "had a hand" in the crime, someone asked if he was telling the truth or "just blowin' again." It is quite possible that if Donnie Ramey said anything, he was "just blowin'."

Even if Donnie Ramey was not involved in the murder of Wanda McCoy, however, that does not mean Roger Coleman was guilty. The postexecution investigation revealed several new facts that add to the substantial doubts about Coleman's guilt raised by Kitty Behan and Jim McCloskey before his execution.

Sandra Stiltner, located by the author in West Virginia, conceded that she probably did not tell Davidson about the clock when he first interviewed her. She insisted, however, that there *was* a clock, and that it *did* say 10:20 when Coleman came to her trailer. However, she went on to say that after she told Davidson about the clock, and also about the fact that she remembered there was a commercial playing on television when Coleman arrived, Davidson returned and questioned her again about the time, saying he had checked the times when commercials were shown on the *Hart to Hart* show that night, and none had been on at 10:20. Sandra says she then told Davidson that the clock was battery-operated, and could have slowed down or stopped. That was also what she had told Jon Cooper—not that she was uncertain about what the clock said, but that it could have been off.

Jack Davidson says he has no recollection of either checking the times of the television commercials or of Sandra mentioning that the clock was battery-operated.

Could the Stiltners' battery-operated clock have stopped or slowed down enough to account for the discrepancy between Sandra Stiltner's testimony and that of Philip VanDyke? It seems unlikely, but more likely than that either she or Philip VanDyke deliberately lied to the police and under oath at Roger Coleman's trial.

Could the pry mark on the McCoys' front door reasonably be interpreted to suggest someone broke into the house, or at least tried to do so?

Jack Davidson vehemently denies it, citing the fact that the mark was made with very little pressure, and appeared only on the door frame, not on the door itself. However, a measurement of the door shows that the location of the mark, three feet two inches above the floor, places it right next to the door latch—just where it would be if someone used the common trick of slipping a knife blade between the frame and the door to trip the latch.

Of course, that does not mean anyone pried open Wanda McCoy's front door, or even tried to, on the night she was murdered. The mark Jack Davidson reported could have been made by anyone, and it could have been made years before. Moreover, Brad McCoy testified that there was a dead bolt on the door which his wife usually kept locked, although he had no way of knowing if it had been bolted that night. The location of the mark, however, does explain why Jack Davidson said in his report that it "appeared to be a pry mark," and why, when they searched the crime scene, the police thought it was relevant to their investigation. A jury might have thought so too, if they had known about it.

While nothing in the postexecution investigation significantly advanced the position of either side on the DNA issue, there were some interesting developments regarding Elmer Gist's blood and hair analysis. For one thing, the Commonwealth Attorney's file includes a piece of paper in Jack Davidson's handwriting that appears to be a copy of notes he made when Gist gave him the preliminary results of his blood-type analysis in late March 1981.

Among the notations on the document is one that suggests Gist reported to Davidson that he had found type A blood on some clothing taken from the McCoy house. In addition, Brad McCoy says Davidson told him back in 1981 that type A blood had been found on a white washcloth in the house.

Gist's official report fails to mention any finding of type A blood— and the result he did report on his test of several items of clothing and a "white cloth rag" from the murder house was "inconclusive." It is the same term he used in reporting the results of his test of the sperm on the anal swab.

Why *did* Gist report that his test of the anal sperm was inconclusive? Can we infer anything from the fact that Gist apparently reported a blood type to Davidson from other tests that he called inconclusive in the report provided to the defense? The answers may appear in the contemporaneous notes Elmer Gist made as he conducted his tests, but he refused to show them to Kitty Behan, and refused to show them to me as well.

Gist's notes were subpoenaed in the libel case, but the state responded with a letter from the Division of Forensic Science. The letter says that the notes were placed in the McCoy murder file, which was sent to the state archives after Coleman was executed, but that the file *is now missing*.

One other recent development bears on the strength of the forensic case against Roger Coleman, although the relationship is indirect. In Nelson County, Virginia, in 1985 a man named Edward Honaker was convicted and sentenced to life in prison plus thirty-seven years for rape and abduction. In 1993 Jim McCloskey's assistant, Kate Germond, began an effort to prove his innocence.

The most important evidence against Honaker, according to the trial judge, was a comparison of Honaker's hair with hairs found on the victim. The state's forensic expert said that they were comparable, and that it was unlikely the hairs found on the victim could have come from anyone other than Honaker.

With the cooperation of a conscientious prosecutor, Kate Germond had the hairs reexamined by one of the world's leading experts on hair analysis and DNA tests performed on sperm found on a vaginal swab taken from the victim at the time of the rape. The hair expert said that in his opinion the hairs were *not* comparable, and the DNA analysis proved beyond doubt that Honaker was not the rapist.

In October 1994, after nearly ten years in prison, Edward Honaker was released. The state forensic expert who had testified in 1985 that the hairs were comparable and unlikely to have come from anyone other than Honaker was Elmer Gist.

Perhaps the most interesting information to emerge after Coleman's execution involves the possibility that the murder was committed by a third person unidentified by either the police or the defense. On the morning after Wanda McCoy was murdered, Jack Davidson interviewed her neighbor Patton Johnson. Johnson said he had left home the previous night at about 9:40. When he left, Johnson noticed three vehicles parked in the area behind his house where the Ramey family parked their cars. He recognized two of them as belonging to the Rameys, but the third, which was the one closest to his house and directly across from the McCoys' house, was not familiar. Its parking lights were on, but he did not see anyone inside. He thought the vehicle's taillights were round.

Davidson's notes and report of his interview with Johnson were in

the Commonwealth Attorney's file and came to light when that file
was subpoenaed for the libel case. Also in the file was the report of an
interview with Johnson's wife, which confirmed his time of departure.
These reports were unknown to Kitty Behan and Jim McCloskey, and
when McCloskey finally succeeded in talking to Pat Johnson in April
1992, Johnson had apparently forgotten when he left for work on the
night of the murder. Nor did he mention the strange vehicle he had
seen.

Another interview report in the file revealed that at 10:15 on the
night of the murder, Ralph Glover, also a neighbor, had heard a vehicle go by his house traveling so fast that he jumped up and looked
out the window to try to see who it was, but it was already out of
sight.

According to what they originally told Jim McCloskey, at about the
same time Pat Johnson saw the unfamiliar vehicle parked in the
Rameys' parking area, Donnie, Michael and Helen Ramey saw a truck
parked in the same place. Donnie had said it was Roger Coleman's
truck, and his mother had supported him—but that was impossible. In
the sworn but not yet signed depositions they gave in Donnie's libel
case, Michael and Helen Ramey again placed a truck next to the
Johnsons' house between 9:00 and 9:30 P.M. on the night of the murder.
Donnie still said he saw Roger Coleman's truck that day, but now
placed the time much earlier, around 5:30. The consensus among the
Rameys was that they told the police about both the truck and the figure Michael thought he had seen lurking near their porch at about
9:45. (Jack Davidson and one of the town policemen have told the
author that while the Rameys certainly never said anything about seeing *Roger Coleman's* truck at the scene on the night of the murder, they
do vaguely recall the Rameys saying something about some truck
being in their parking area that evening.)

Could the vehicle Pat Johnson saw at 9:40 be the same one the
Rameys said they saw? Could it be the same one Ralph Glover heard
speed off at about 10:15? Could the driver of that vehicle be the figure
Michael Ramey thinks he saw lurking by his house?

Did the police simply fail to put these things together into a scenario pointing to the killer, or did they have some reason we don't
know about to reject that scenario? Or did they ignore it because the
timing did not fit the theory that the killer was Roger Coleman, who

all the independent witnesses placed elsewhere during this time period, and whose 1976 Chevrolet pickup truck had long, rectangular taillights? And, one must ask again, where are the Ramey interview reports—and what, if anything, do they say about a strange vehicle and a lurking figure near the McCoy house on the night Wanda McCoy was murdered?

In my office, surrounded by piles of documents, photographs, forensic reports and interview notes, the fruits of fifteen years of investigation of the murder of Wanda Fay McCoy by the police, by forensic experts, by lawyers, by defense investigators and even by writers, I am struck by the realization that much of the information in these files has never been tested in the crucible of a courtroom confrontation between skilled advocates—the foundation of our system of justice.

And I am struck by how curious it is that a civilized society would kill someone in the name of the people without exhausting every effort to be certain that the right person is executed, and especially that it should abandon that inquiry simply because a young lawyer arguably misinterpreted a time limit and filed a document one day late.

But then, as the Supreme Court told us, this was not a case about Wanda McCoy, or Roger Coleman, or justice. This was a case about federalism.

The Court, of course, was wrong. Even now, fifteen years after Wanda McCoy was murdered and four years after Roger Coleman was executed, to the men and women who loved them it is a case about flesh and blood—the flesh and blood of Wanda and Roger.

It is about a lovely and loving young woman who was brutally murdered in her own home. A woman whose husband, Brad McCoy, is happily remarried with two young children, but who still cannot erase from his mind the sight of his wife lying motionless on a bedroom floor, surrounded by a growing pool of blood. A woman whose parents have fifteen other children, but still think of her every day; whose brothers and sisters still mourn her and find it difficult to talk about what happened; and whose youngest sister and best friend, Patricia, was married to the man who was convicted of killing her, and cannot bear to talk about it at all.

And it is about a young man who was strapped into a chair and electrocuted by the Commonwealth of Virginia for a murder he always denied, and which many believe he did not commit. Sharon Paul, after years of mourning, has begun to forge a new life, but she still believes passionately in Roger Coleman's innocence, and in the qualities that made her love him. So does Robert White, who continues to speak of how deeply Roger enriched his life; and Marie Deans, whose anti–death penalty organization was bankrupted by the expenses incurred in fighting for him; and Kitty Behan, whose skills and reputation as a lawyer have flourished, but who still works on death-penalty cases, and still keeps Roger Coleman's photograph on her office wall. And so does Jim McCloskey, who has freed many innocent men and women from prison since Roger Coleman was executed, but who cannot accept his failure to save Coleman, and is still trying to find a way to use today's more sophisticated DNA technology to prove his innocence.

But even if McCloskey succeeds, he cannot bring Roger Coleman back to life from the ashes Sharon Paul spread over a green, hazy mountain valley in Grundy, Virginia, on a warm spring day in 1992. Nor could Wanda Fay McCoy be returned to life by the men who killed Roger Coleman in a bleak, concrete death chamber a few days earlier.

Acknowledgments

At one time or another I have spoken to almost everyone who played a major role in the foregoing events, and with few exceptions they have given freely of their time and recollections. In particular, Jim McCloskey and Kitty Behan spent scores of hours answering my questions and providing documents reflecting their investigation of the case on behalf of Roger Coleman. From the "other side," Jack Davidson, Randy Jackson and Tom Scott also cooperated in answering questions and providing information about their investigation of the murder and their perspective on Coleman's claims of innocence.

Despite the pain it caused them, Brad McCoy and several of Wanda McCoy's siblings agreed to talk to me and help me try to convey some sense of the loss they suffered and still live with. It is an impossible task, but I hope I have succeeded in some small measure, and I deeply appreciate their help.

Sharon Paul not only allowed me to intrude on the painful memories of her loss but provided me with invaluable letters, photographs and the right to use portions of Roger Coleman's diary. Most important, she opened her heart to me in a way that allowed me to understand Roger, and her feeling for him, far better than would otherwise have been possible.

The help of Marie Deans and Robert White was also essential to my understanding of the man Roger Coleman had become by the time he was executed, and without Russ Ford's description of the last minutes of Coleman's life this book would have been greatly diminished.

Roger Lee Coleman not only helped me describe his nephew and adopted brother's early years but also spent hours helping me find my way around Buchanan County and assisted in a dozen other ways.

The cooperation of Philip VanDyke and Sandra Stiltner (now Lane), the two most important fact witnesses at Coleman's trial, was invaluable in allowing me to conclude that despite the difference between them on the subject of time, both seemed to have testified in good faith—and to discover at least the possibility that their testimony could be reconciled.

Judge Nicholas Persin not only provided valuable insights into the trial but also went out of his way to try to help me in many ways, including my efforts to obtain the mysteriously missing police interviews with the Ramey family. Steve Arey also gave generously of his time.

Dozens of other men and women whose roles were smaller nevertheless tried to help me in any way possible, even though I was a complete stranger and even though they knew I was writing a book that some of them would have preferred not to see written.

Only four major "characters" in this story refused to cooperate with me—Elmer Gist, Donnie Ramey, Mickey McGlothlin and Terry Jordan.

Donnie Ramey's refusal to cooperate is understandable whether or not he participated in the murder of Wanda McCoy. Fortunately, access to the affidavits he filed and his desposition testimony in the libel case have enabled me to describe his responses to the charges against him in greater detail than to simply say he denies them.

Mickey McGlothlin talked to me briefly before Coleman was executed, when I was writing an article on the case for *The New Republic*, and promised on several occasions to talk to me again when he had time. Later, he asked me to put my questions in writing, which I did, but he still didn't answer them, even after Judge Persin interceded for me. I was especially anxious to see if McGlothlin had any recollection of the Ramey interviews, and to inquire about some of the other documents that were in the Commonwealth's Attorney's file. It is tempting to suggest a sinister motive for McGlothlin's refusal to cooperate, but in truth I suspect he simply believed the book would be unfair to the prosecution and saw no reason to assist with it. He may still think so.

Elmer Gist said he couldn't talk to me without permission from his boss, the head of the Division of Forensic Science. His boss said Elmer had told him he didn't want to talk. Why I do not know. His now "missing" notes are among the documents that are most likely to shed additional light on the question of Roger Coleman's guilt or innocence, and in my opinion it is a special outrage that Coleman was executed without their being examined by his counsel and an independent expert.

Terry Jordan's refusal to answer any questions despite my repeated efforts to persuade him to do so was both a puzzle and a great disappointment. Both he and Steve Arey were put in an extremely difficult position by their appointment in a case that was well beyond their level of experience, but I suspect that some of the deficiencies in their defense of Roger Coleman were the result of not having some of the information that has now been discovered. Why Mr. Jordan declined the opportunity to defend himself regarding those matters and to explain the circumstances that led to his providing an affidavit for the state I cannot say.

There are other people whose help and encouragement made this book possible. My agent, Judith Riven, not only sold the book, she taught me how to write a salable proposal. My editor, Starling Lawrence, insisted that I make the book readable to the general public—and provided the editorial suggestions that hopefully made that happen. My wife, Jayne Barnard, and my friends Rodney Smolla and Jim Beaman also provided essential editorial suggestions and much needed encouragement, as did my four children and several other friends who read all or parts of the manuscript. Della Harris not only typed much of the manuscript but kept me going with her frequent expressions of interest in the story. To all of them I am deeply grateful.

Index